4/00

The Emerald City
And Other Essays on the Architectural Imagination

The Emerald City

And Other Essays on the Architectural Imagination

Daniel Willis

Princeton Architectural Press, New York

Published by
Princeton Architectural Press
37 East 7th Street
New York, New York 10003
212.995.9620

For a free catalog of books, call 1.800.722.6657
visit our web site at www.papress.com

All drawings by Daniel Willis
Editing and design by Clare Jacobson

Special thanks to: Eugenia Bell, Jan Cigliano,
Bernd-Christian Döll, Jane Garvie, Caroline Green,
Therese Kelly, Leslie Ann Kent, Mark Lamster, and
Anne Nitschke of Princeton Architectural Press
Kevin C. Lippert, publisher

Cover: Sweeny Chapel, 1986
Photo: Balthazar Korab
Architect: Edward Larrabee Barnes
Glass design: James Carpenter Associates
Client: Christian Theological Seminary, Indianapolis, IN
Cover design: Sara E. Stemen

Library of Congress
Cataloging-in-Publication Data
Willis, Daniel, 1957–
    The emerald city and other essays on the
architectural imagination / Daniel Willis.
        p. cm.
    Includes bibliographical references.
    ISBN 1-56898-174-0 (alk. paper)
    1. Architecture and society. 2. Architecture—
Philosophy. I. Title.
NA2543.S6W525 1999
720'.1—dc21   98-48641
                                                  CIP

Table of Contents

For my mother
in loving memory

Acknowledgements

Twelve years ago I was a reasonably competent architect, but I had no particular insight into the nature of that which I practiced. To the extent that this situation has changed (and I, at least, believe that it has) I primarily owe to two faculty colleagues at Penn State. The first of these is my friend Donald Kunze, who, through the example of his teaching, his scholarly writings, and his delicious homemade pies, has shared with me his wisdom on art and architecture. His writings are referenced repeatedly in this volume, but my citations hardly begin to record the ideas I stole from him over lunches, by eavesdropping on his classes, or by attending the impromptu summer symposia he routinely organizes in his back yard. If my few scattered notes of attribution fail to do justice to Don, they are even less adequate to describe the debt I owe to Katsuhiko Muramoto. Katsu, over innumerable meals, during meetings, reviews, road trips, and parties, has offered me insights into architecture, philosophy, and automobiles. Each of these men read early portions of this book, but I am afraid they are much too loyal to have given me their honest opinions. May they forgive me for whatever muck I have made of their thoughts.

When I began teaching architecture I was amazed to discover what all teachers know—that we learn far more from our students than they from us. I have been privileged to associate with so many outstanding students that I cannot thank them all. However, I would like to call attention to those who were most directly influential to this book. They are James Radock, William Sharples, James O'Toole, Merilee Meacock, Michael Kaiser, Ellen Pannell, Richard Alderiso, Lynn Gaffney, Kenneth Roscioli, Edward Clark, Michael Drury, Jodi LaCoe, Victor Chapparo, James Mehaffey, and Todd Woodward. Todd, in his undergraduate honors thesis, explored the "conviviality" of architecture—an association that has become one of the main themes of this book. He also diligently read and reviewed my developing manuscript.

I have tried to solicit reviews from as many colleagues, both academic and professional, as time would allow. My sincere appreciation to Steven Temple, Daniel Conway, and James Willis; each of them read major portions of the manuscript, and offered detailed commentary. My other readers included Kelleann Foster, Thomas Purdy, Michael Fifield, James Oleg Kruhly, Anthony Lucarelli, Jennifer Lucchino, Lauren Horne, Douglas Hoffman, Robert Fedorchak, Shannon Duval, Romolo Martemucci, Gregory Merges, Mary Frecker, and William, Christopher, and Coren Sharples. Thanks also to the students in my current building materials course, and in several of my past studios, for their comments.

As with the students I have taught, I have learned a great deal simply working alongside my colleagues at Penn State University. One who has published extensively, Gideon Golany, shared with me some hints on manuscript preparation. A former colleague, Scott Wing, of the University of Arkansas was kind enough to invite me to present a portion of my research at that school. Jessica Hecht and Jodi LaCoe arranged for me to speak to their class in the History and Theory graduate program at McGill University. Thanks to Alberto Perez-Gomez and Torben Berns for their helpful comments during that presentation. My appreciation also to the office of Fay Jones and Maurice Jennings for consenting to my request for a tour and interview.

I have been privileged to work for and with some very fine architects. Thanks to Louis and Dennis Astorino, James Oleg Kruhly, William Sippel, Bruce Padolf, Gordon Ketterer, and the late Edward Horley for giving me the opportunity to practice for their firms. My appreciation, too, to all of the experienced architects in these firms who have been my mentors.

Much of this book has been inspired by those who make and fix things. I have been fortunate to know and learn from a number of convivial contractors. Some of my appreciation for construction can be traced back to a teacher at Carnegie Mellon University, the late Maxwell G. Mayo, a "damn near excellent" instructor on the subject of building. The rest is owed to a man who could fix anything, and explain to his kid how he did it—my father, Earl Willis.

Thanks to Clare Jacobson at Princeton Architectural Press for making the editing process relatively painless. Lastly, I would like to acknowledge that a portion of the travel and research for this book was supported by a faculty research grant from The College of Arts and Architecture, The Pennsylvania State University.

Preface
Robert Harbison

It is hard to suggest the qualities of this book quickly. That would probably not bother (or surprise) the author much. He has a lot to say about time in architecture and argues that the modern world, always speeding the pace, has corrupted our sense of time. Some of the most powerful pages here are part of a critique of efficiency that periodically resurfaces throughout the book. Dan Willis ends with the most refreshing piece on computers I have read, which starts from the time they save and the speed with which they produce "drawings" that it would have been very laborious to draw.

He mistrusts this speed first for assuming that the act of drawing that it replaces is meaningless, and that only the product counts, and then for all it overlooks and cannot include, so that the CAD product's resemblance to a drawing is in crucial ways a dangerous illusion. He compares the "choices" offered by computers, where you must say OK to something with which you don't really agree, to confessions extracted by oppressive regimes, and finds an architectural parallel in navigating a computer program to being trapped in a labyrinth. It is in this last analogy that Willis unexpectedly locates the true promise of computers in architecture.

Perhaps I have singled out only the vivid bits and left behind concentrated bouts of reasoning and in the process made Willis appear more whimsical than he is. But really it would be no good disguising that this book is a concerted attack on modernity. However, it is more than a lament. Willis is interested in discovering cracks and crevices in the conventions modern societies rarely question. In essays such as "Seven Strategies for Making Architecture in the Twenty-First Century," he finds niches beneath the apparent homogeneity of modern life, where the ground for architecture is as fertile as ever. Political conservatives as currently defined will not find comfort in this critique, which is radical in the style of Ruskin, the style that is of imprudently pursuing one's thoughts wherever they lead, regardless of received wisdom or convention. Sometimes Willis takes my breath away, he is so unashamedly romantic, as in the argument for the hearth and against central heating or in his appreciation for the gypsy way of life.

But who ever reached truly interesting conclusions who did not have a streak of unrealism? (This despite—or maybe because of—the fact that Willis is a "real" architect who builds, as well as a teacher and an artist.) Willis's goals and opinions are usually more than interesting, but even better is the kind of route he follows getting there. Any one of the essays is full of exhilarating indirection and a life-enhancing inclusiveness, but I will take my own favorite, "The Weight of Architecture," as an instance. It starts from Milan Kundera, followed by Greek myth, the Bible, deconstruction, the *I Ching* (a "vegetative" view of time), Galileo, Darwin, Bachelard, and Kant.

I must stop there, though I am only halfway through the essay. Kant is introduced not as a philosopher but as a general exemplar of human culture. When, near death, he was visited by his doctor, Kant stood to receive his guest and would not sit down again until the doctor was seated. This incident made a strong impression on the visitor who knew how weak his patient was and what this exercise of courtesy cost him. Willis pushes the episode further: his subject is gravity and architecture's struggle to defeat or rather to acknowledge it in the most meaningful way. I will not spoil the story by revealing the conclusion, but to me Willis's use of this anecdote exemplifies the subtlety and humanity of this book. He casts light on a wide range of topics so basic they are generally overlooked, like joints and roofs further on in the same essay. It is a pleasure to learn that someone is doing this kind of fearless thinking now. Somewhat paradoxically, given its sometimes dark sense of the future, Dan Willis's writing also gives one hope; it expresses the most positive view of the role of architecture that anyone has voiced for a long time.

Snow-Covered Statue from Frank Lloyd Wright's Oak Park Studio

This swift business I must uneasy make, lest too light the winning
Make the prize light.

> William Shakespeare
> *The Tempest*

The loosely connected essays in this volume do not comprise yet another text bemoaning the "death of architecture" or the crisis of the architecture profession. That argument has been thoroughly covered since Victor Hugo predicted, in *Notre-Dame de Paris*, that the book would "kill" the building. *Something* in Europe's buildings may indeed have begun petrifying in the fifteenth century, but I suspect that Hugo identified the corpse a bit hastily. Perhaps the form of architectural practice Hugo declared doomed is, at last, nearing the end of its half-millennium-long death throes, but architecture's spirit lives on in other, less recognizable forms.

Architecture has always been a "practice"—a word that both conveys a sense of action and also denotes an activity without a definite conclusion. Practices are by definition extremely adaptable enterprises; they are not so easily killed. I believe that architectural practices have always been very difficult to pursue. Just as only a small portion of all the sounds human beings make can be considered music, only very few of the constructions we make, or have ever made, deserve to be called "architecture." The world resists the creation of architecture, a fact that provides architectural practices with both their reason for being and their significance.

Architecture has forever come into being in response to something we lack. Premodern architectural "practitioners" most often lacked choice. Vernacular builders built in ways that promoted convivial relations with their neighbors, and sustainable interactions with their environments, primarily because they had so few alternatives. Architecture occurs most "naturally" among primitives and outcasts because architecture thrives most readily in the face of abjection.[1] In places and times when nearly anything is possible, architecture will be superfluous. This is why, according to philosopher Karsten Harries, no architecture would be found in paradise.[2] It is tempting to say that our present situation, where we possess nearly godlike powers to transform our world, has also rendered architecture (the ever-changing practice, not the profession) nearly impossible if not unnecessary. But it is also possible to look to what our lives, at the turn of the millennium, typically lack—fulfillment, significance, spirituality, a sense of belonging, *weight*—and to conclude that the ground for architecture has never been more fertile.

I believe that the practice of architecture in the late twentieth century has come to seem so difficult because we have been slow to adapt from dealing with abject conditions of one sort—the historically familiar problems of shelter, site, material constraints, and limited resources—to an entirely different set of hostile circumstances, stemming from our current cultural situation *itself*. As it has become ever easier to make buildings, it has become increasingly difficult to make architecture. This is due to what sociologist Richard Sennett has labeled the "terrible paradox" of human nature.[3] When things become for us too easy, too predictable, they also become insignificant. But we architects deserve at least some of the blame for the banality of our structures and environments. We have failed to recognize that the rules of architectural practice have changed substantially. We have been nostalgically praying for the resurrection of the corpse Hugo eulogized, which was but one way of building, while the potential for architecture has remained vital, though largely invisible.

Practices, unlike techniques, do not attempt to solve all of the problems they encounter. Consider the practice of sailing. It would make little sense for those who love to sail to treat traveling across the water as something to be minimized or eliminated. If sailing is made too easy or too quick, if it no longer requires skill and dedication to master, it ceases to be a rewarding experience. Once the technology became available to make traveling over water efficient, sailors had to *artificially* restrict the techniques they would apply to their practice in order to preserve its significance. So it is, or should be, with architecture. In the past, architectural practices needed to deal with material and climatic limitations. Like the early sailors, primitive architects could not overcome these obstacles directly. They could not alter the environmental circumstances they were forced to engage, could neither select among "alternative building technologies" nor create "climate-controlled spaces." They were forced to utilize a clever architectural form of tacking (such as fabricating roofs that were not waterproof, but that could shed water). Now, building techniques (such as impervious roof membranes) have eliminated the need for such ingenuity, have removed the connection between a building's form and what it is made of, or where it is built. We now have the ability to build far more efficiently than our ancestors. However, like a motorboat no longer dependent on the wind, the very efficiency with which we now build has had the corresponding effect of reducing the significance of our achievements.

It would be absurd, as well as self-defeating, to suggest that architectural practices retreat from advanced technology. The recommendations contained in these essays are both more subtle and more difficult to implement. These essays suggest that architects, like the sailors who race on hulls made of the latest high-tech resins, must find an appropriate level for the application of advanced building, designing, and drafting techniques to architectural practice. This proposed ethic is far more complex than either the naive rejection of, or blind faith in, technology.

Just as primitive architects could not directly overcome the material obstacles of yesterday, neither can we make architecture by engaging head-on the cultural obstacles of today. The paradox of architectural practices is that they depend on cleverness and imagination to transform their incapability into an advantage. Think of yet another "practical" example, the masonry arch. An arch is a cunning solution to one particular lack: the absence of tensile strength in un-reinforced masonry. In order to achieve a horizontal span, a masonry arch literally finds a way around the tensile forces it would be powerless to resist. If only we would devote attention to what we as builders still lack—to the things we can only do indirectly, with difficulty—instead of the things we accomplish easily, our impotence might lead us to where we wish to be. That, at least, is the contention common to the essays that follow.

There are, of course, many fine architects working today, and they continue to find ways to endow their creations with this metaphorical weight, this significance. The best works of architecture, whether or not they are produced by professional architects, result today from practices that create, artificially if necessary, areas where the commonly assumed ideal conditions for efficient building production are lacking. An architectural practice should be an on-going engagement with the world, involving a highly learned ignorance, a creative impotence that accepts the limitations, inconsistencies, and surprises living always brings. The essays that follow are, in varying degrees, tales describing the rich soil of limits, where all forms of abjection—rebellious materials, incomplete understanding, uncooperative builders, inadequate budgets, unappreciative clients, a disinterested public, hostile social and economic conditions—may give rise to the imaginative flowering of weighty architecture.

Architecture as Medicine

Two views of the Hospital of the Holy Cross and St. Paul
Barcelona

Life is at the start a chaos in which one is lost. The individual suspects this, but he is frightened at finding himself face to face with this terrible reality, and tries to cover it over with a curtain of fantasy, where everything is clear. It does not worry him that his "ideas" are not true, he uses them as trenches for the defense of his existence, as scarecrows to frighten away reality.

José Ortega y Gasset
The Revolt of the Masses

If we accept the argument that architecture's primary role is to imbue the structures and locations around us with meaning, it will only be a matter of time until the subject of the hospital will come to mind. When we consider a hospital, our first reaction is to wonder what interest a deathly ill patient would have in the meaning of the building that surrounds him. This immediate response can be attributed to our contemporary tendency to define building functions in a highly reductive way. In this case, we tend to see a hospital as a "machine for healing." However, we are presently witnessing a steady stream of "discoveries" in modern medicine indicating that the patient's attitude and beliefs have a significant impact on his ability to recover.

Medical researchers are finding that things such as family support, visits from friends, religious convictions, and even prayer play a positive role in the patient's well-being. The mechanistic image of the body that has been the accepted doctrine of modern medicine has been recently under assault as overly simplistic. The "divide and conquer" strategy so often favored by medical science appears to have reached the limits of its efficacy, so that scientists and physicians are becoming increasingly open to other possible methods of treatment. Human beings do not readily cooperate with efforts to model them upon far simpler machines, or to separate them into a mind and a body. Exercise physiologists are discovering strange phenomena such as when a test subject exercises her right arm alone, she gains measurable strength in the left arm as well. Our senses and bodily "systems" appear to be wired together in ways that defy any attempts to neatly isolate them. Everyone, except perhaps those who produce the meals served in our hospitals, now knows that the appearance of the food on the plate has an effect on its taste. Here is how the ethnologist Michael Taussig describes the intermingling of sense impressions, as exploited by Putumayo healers of the Upper Amazon region:

> Likewise, medicinally triggered visions . . . are surely effective not only
> because of visual imagery, but also on account of nonvisual imagery
> conveyed by nausea, sound, smell, and the changing cadence of chanting,
> not to mention the less tangible qualities of presence, atmosphere, and
> movement. Furthermore, the senses cross over and translate into each
> other. You feel redness. You see music. Thus nonvisual imagery may evoke
> visual means. The medicine creates nausea—one of the great untheorized
> territories of experience—and one which has an enormous effect on
> cognitive process and hermeneutic endeavor, no less on the medley of the
> senses bleeding into each other's zone of operations.[4]

All of this would suggest that instead of treating the patient as an inert
lump of tissue, a hospital should address her as a thinking, feeling, and
imagining whole being. Yet most of our hospitals, those built or
extensively modified in the latter half of the present century, still adhere
to the dominant conceptualization of architectural function—a
mechanized conceptualization every bit as suspect as the simple-minded
body-as-machine metaphor. Our understanding of function suffers from
the same proclivity towards reductive abstraction that has infected
medical science. We restrict our definition of function only to that which
readily fits our prejudice that the building is some kind of machine. The
functions of a machine are most easily described in the mathematical
language preferred by the "hard sciences," and so we apply statistics,
motion studies, and measures of travel distances to our designs for
hospitals. Those aspects of healing, caring, or dwelling that do not easily
submit to mathematical abstraction are abandoned—not because they
are irrelevant, but simply because they do not fit the conceptual schema
of "function" we have created. When we evaluate function, we do not
measure what is most important to know, we measure what is most
readily measurable.

Modern hospitals therefore share many of the attributes of other
highly mechanized building types. Their obsession with efficient
movement leads to wide corridors and abundant signage such as in
modern airports. The nurses' station becomes a point of surveillance
modeled on the well-established principles of panoptic control first found
in prisons. The concealed mechanical systems of the hospital are
disguised behind dropped ceilings, utility corridors, chases, and
bulkheads. These mechanical "guts" have progressively consumed an
ever larger portion of the hospital construction budget, yet they remain

invisible, without architectural expression. In this they resemble the hidden "backstage" spaces we find in the service corridors at the shopping mall, the baggage handling portions of the airport, or the immense archival and support spaces of the modern museum. As the volume devoted to this mechanized *poché* has grown, the area hospitals had traditionally devoted to grand lobbies, monumental stairs, vestibules, interior courts, and gardens has been eliminated. Nurses' stations seldom have direct access to natural light; operating rooms no longer have windows.

Hospitals, like airports, run on an abstract time of twenty-four-hour sameness. Thus they suppress awareness of daily temporal rhythms. For (supposedly) sanitary reasons they are hermetically sealed, isolated from the fragrant scents of the varying seasons. Using sophisticated environmental controls, they are generally held at a uniform temperature throughout. In hospital waiting rooms there are no fireplaces around which concerned families can huddle; attached to patient rooms, there are no balconies oriented towards the cooling evening breeze. Even hospital chapels are likely to be devoid of natural light. The chapel is now seldom placed in a location of great dignity, so that its presence might become evident in the spatial ordering of the hospital. Instead, the chapel occupies a "convenient" position, near the hospital's main entrance (if there is one), off the diminutive lobby. The ideal large urban hospital seems to aspire to a boring uniformity everywhere. Control is more important than comfort, and the imaginations of a hospital's workers and patients are never engaged by the architecture. These hospitals are conceived as efficient instruments of medicine, no different from x-ray machines. The "functions" of the hospital are objectified, just as are the bodies of the patients that enter them.

In contrast to this sort of hospital, we might compare its alternative. Such a hospital design exists in the form of the Hospital of the Holy Cross and Saint Paul in Barcelona, designed by Lluís Domènech i Montaner. If one were to measure a deceased architect's importance by the size of the role assigned to him by world history, Domènech must either be judged a nonentity, or the unluckiest fine architect ever to be denied deserved recognition. His misfortune was to practice at the identical time and place as an even more talented, or at least more audacious, man: Antonio Gaudí. The Hospital of Saint Paul, however, stands as proof that Domènech's obscurity is unwarranted. The gigantic complex sits on 360 acres to the northeast of Barcelona's Eixample—the expansive, gridded, portion of the city, where each block has a unique chamfered corner (as expressed by the shape of Gaudí's Casa Mila). Domènech began his design of the huge city hospital with the conviction that it would be neither monotonous nor recall a labyrinthine prison. He oriented the complex at forty-five degrees to the grid of the Eixample to face the southern sun. In so doing, he established a direct axial connection between the hospital and the other civic monument in the area, Gaudí's Expiatory Temple of the Sagrada Familia.

Domènech brilliantly combined the convenience of one large building with the openness of many small ones by creating a village of mostly houselike pavilions linked by underground service corridors. At numerous points between the pavilions, light wells illuminate and ventilate the tunnels, and at the same time allow access to and from grade. The separate buildings make isolating infectious patients simple, while they provide light and air to everyone. The great majority of patient rooms have trees and chirping birds outside their windows. Every pavilion features one large and several lesser domes, all uniquely decorated in brightly colored glazed tiles. The large dome caps a circular, semidetached, and generously glazed tower, which contains the day rooms for the patient floors. Each pavilion also has its own patron saint, portrayed in a statue enshrined under one of the small domes. According to Domènech's son Pere, who oversaw the completion of the hospital project after his father's death (the building was under construction from 1901 to 1910, and again in 1930), Domènech "thought that everything that could give a feeling of well-being to the sick was also a form of therapy."[5] Art critic Robert Hughes describes a portion of the hospital:

> To buoy up the spirits of the patients and their families, and banish at least some of their association of hospitals with death and suffering, Domènech lavished his ingenuity on the detailing and color of each building in the Hospital [of Saint Paul]. The note of care is struck as soon as you come up the double ramp into the reception block, whose facade glitters with mosaic murals depicting the history of the hospital from the Middle Ages. . . . Inside, octagonal columns with Domènech's signature floral capitals . . . bear up shallow domes sheathed, surprisingly, in dusky pink tiles; a broad space of this vestibule is bathed in golden light from a big stained-glass *claraboia*, or skylight, in the roof. The whole space is ceremonious, exciting, optimistic.[6]

The Barcelona hospital denies the "building as efficient instrument" conceptualization in favor of a more wide-ranging and imaginative understanding of function. It produces well-being *indirectly*. Through the actual creation of carefully executed buildings that are "exciting, optimistic," Domènech creates an invisible air of regeneration and recovery. This relationship between what has been built and what qualities it is believed to possess relies to some extent on the belief, common among premodern peoples, that a thing and its image always remain connected. Thus, by creating the image (and by this I do not mean merely the "look," but a full-bodied, imaginative construct possessing, in addition to form, weight and depth) of a healthy and full life, Domènech's architecture contributes to actually bringing this situation about. His hospital calls into question the reductive literal understanding of "functionality" as well as the naive belief that the boundary between truth and fiction can be precisely established. As Michael Taussig observes, "illusions thus serve the cause of belief, if not truth, thanks to the magical series of transfers between theater and reality." In Taussig's view, the mimetic imagination "sutures the real to the really made up."[7]

One reason that such secularly constructed truths are necessary for architecture today is that the historically common method of imbuing a place with meaning—the fictional "auras" once supplied by foundation myths—is now denied to us. In the past, an invisible presence could be maintained at a particular site by virtue of the fact that some supernatural event was believed to have occurred there. Consider the various hospitals that have, for over two thousand years, occupied the Tiber Island in Rome. Legend has it that when the ancient city was beset by plague, Roman sailors were sent to Greece to solicit advice from the famed healer Asclepius. Asclepius assured them he would help, but gave them little in the way of practical advice. Returning to Rome, the sailors observed a serpent leave their ship and swim to the Tiber Island. As the serpent wound around a pole that hung from the island into the water, the sailors recognized that the healing spirit of Asclepius was taking up residence on the island. Henceforth, all who came to be treated on the island were spared death by plague. A small hospital still stands on the island, and a carved image of a snake climbing a pole can be found on the northern side of the island's rocky base (the snake-wrapped staff is now the emblem of the medical profession). Who can say to what extent the success of the medical treatment dispensed on the Tiber Island owes some credit to the patients' belief that a spirit of healing occupies the island? The functional weight of an imaginative effect is a most difficult thing to establish.

Now that architecture can seldom count upon the imaginative presence once supplied by foundation myths, it must dedicate itself to creating a "sense of place" out of authentic constructions—those that pay suitable attention to both the real and the really made up—such as the Hospital of Saint Paul. In order to pursue this goal, we will have to reject the simple-minded "building as machine" conceptualization that has been with us implicitly since the Enlightenment, and explicitly since the Modern Movement. Or we could go about this another way, by recalling that before the sixteenth century, a machine, with the exception of those devoted to warfare, was as likely to serve as an object of amusement as it was to satisfy practical needs. Pre-electronic machines have generally relied upon some variation of a powered wheel, so at least unconsciously their rotating mechanisms recreated our conception of the circular movements of the cosmos. In many early mechanical clocks, such as the magnificent celestial clock at the Strasbourg Cathedral, it is this symbolic aspect that attracts our attention most, while the indication of the correct time is relegated to a trivial side-effect. To paraphrase Alfred W. Crosby, to say that the cathedral clock "tells the time" and to say no more would be like saying its exquisite rose and stained-glass windows "admitted light," saying no more.[8] A similar proportion of qualities are left unsaid in the behaviorists' once-popular mechanistic definition of architecture as "environmental problem solving." Whether we expand the understanding of "function" or of "machine," something must be done to preserve a place for the usefulness of imagination in architecture.

The association between machines and warfare is not accidental. The thinking, which is often called "instrumental," that defines hospitals as machines and objectifies beings into bodies to be cured or lives to be saved, is at its heart aggressive and dominating. What it strives to dominate is, of course, "nature." However, since we too are part of nature, we end up dominating ourselves within the artificial constructs of our own reason, often in unintended ways. Thus, Ivan Illich writes that "'a life' is amenable to management, to improvement and to evaluation in terms of available resources in a way that is unthinkable when we think of 'a person.'"[9] In the 1985 address from which I quote, Illich's

mention of "evaluation in terms of available resources" predicted the
ethical debates we are now witnessing in the face of the cost-benefit
analyses applied to human lives by the health-care industry. Imagine the
magnitude of objectification that must occur before we can submit the
care of our loved ones to cost-benefit analyses. (Such an enterprise
highlights our contemporary terror of death through the desire to
preserve a life—although not necessarily a whole person—at all costs,
while at the same time it forces us to justify this reaction in terms of
"available resources.") Now consider what the similar objectification of
architecture into "functional building" removes. In either instance we are
asked to put a price on what is priceless, and to quantify what is not
amenable to instrumental representation.

Alternative-medicine advocate Dr. Andrew Weil has written
critically on the instrumental aggression of conventional medicine. Weil
notes that the language of Western medicine is rife with talk of weapons,
"magic bullets," and "victories" over disease. But he cautions that
weapons are inherently dangerous, that they "may backfire, causing
injury to the user, and they may also stimulate greater aggression on the
part of the enemy."[10] Weil goes on to describe other characteristics of
modern medicine:

> If you look at the names of the most popular categories of drugs in use
> today, you will find that most of them begin with the prefix "anti." We use
> antispasmodics and antihypertensives, antiarrhythmics, antitussives,
> antipyretics, and anti-inflammatories, as well as beta blockers and
> H^2-receptor antagonists. This is truly antimedicine—medicine that is, in
> essence, counteractive and suppressive.[11]

Weil questions many of the institutionalized practices that have become
accepted features of the "biomedical model." Most of these—over-
specialization, lack of appreciation for mind-body interconnectedness,
aggressive invasive treatment, as opposed to promoting healing—have
corollaries within the contemporary practice of architecture. Our
"mechanical model," with its tendency to overvalue aspects that are easy
to represent mathematically—the quantifiable aspects of size, function,
and (especially) cost, as well as, through the use of descriptive
geometries, building shapes—and to undervalue all else, constitutes a
kind of antiarchitecture.

An architectural analog to medicine's mind-body dilemma is
our discipline's function-aesthetics problem. Both dichotomies are

comprised of abstract concepts—artificial creations of our own, with their own histories and peculiar origins. We usually think of "our body" as something simply given by the fact of our existence. However, as Illich and others have shown, "the body" is an artificial construct, with its own "historicity." So also are the seemingly ubiquitous architectural terms "form" and "function." Dalibor Vesely writes that what we now understand as "form" has only existed in this sense since the late eighteenth century. "Until then a whole spectrum of terms such as paradigma, typos, symbol, allegory, emblem, impresa, schema, figura were used to grasp the meaning that was later given to . . . 'form' itself."[12] Aesthetics, which we often assume to be an area of inquiry or of artistic production, independent of scientific objectivity or "mere function," is, on the contrary, simply another territory on the same conceptual map drawn during the Enlightenment. Architectural aesthetics, seen as either those considerations opposed to function or as those dependent on it (as the ideology of modern architecture would have it), must rely entirely on the scientific "machine model" of architecture. It is this manner of abstract instrumental thinking that allows us to remove "form" from the realm of construction, materials, and workmanship, or to reductively speak of a building's functions as unrelated to history or culture. Vesely describes this situation:

> Science, technology, and aesthetics belong together. The development of scientific objectivity depends . . . on the role of the subject responsible for the project of science. In other words, the more objective reality becomes, the more subjective must be the position of man, because in modern science he encounters by definition, as it were, only his own projection of reality.[13]

Our projection of reality, and therefore of function, cannot escape the limitations of our chosen representational system. Thus, it becomes very difficult to say if the elimination of windows in operating rooms is truly a matter of economy and efficiency, or if we simply cannot represent the desire to have the windows in the same apparently rational language, bolstered by statistics and analyses, used to argue against their inclusion. When a surgeon writes that visual access to the stars is useful to "deflate the surgeon's ego," and requests the return of this "celestial connection" because it "did the patient no disservice to have heaven looking over his doctor's shoulder,"[14] he does so without recourse to a conceptual model that will allow him to produce experimental evidence, statistics, and cost-saving projections. The situation the surgeon describes, like most architectural situations, is too complex to readily submit to the reductive logic of the experiment. Even if experiments were arranged utilizing existing hospital operatories with and without windows, how would we control for the variables of different locations, multiple solar orientations and climates, assorted hospital staffs, disparate patients (with dissimilar ailments, inconsistent family support, or even diverse religious beliefs), and different surgeons?

The apparent rationality of function is also undermined when we consider that any analysis of function is always from a particular point of view. We have no access to a godlike perspective of the world. Functional assessments are always made by somebody, and they cannot be made independent of that somebody's individual interests. For the obstetrician it may make functional sense to maximize his own view and therefore control and comfort during a childbirth. However, from the mother's point of view, the position in which she is placed for the sake of her doctor's comfort and control denies her the assistance of gravity during labor—it in fact requires the contractions of her muscles to overcome the slight gravitational resistance caused by her "unnatural" birthing position, and therefore could easily be judged dysfunctional.

If Weil and Taussig are correct in their presentations of the work of tribal healers and witch doctors, including their belief in the well-documented phenomena of the power of suggestion (as evidenced in the "placebo effect"), then this type of dysfunction from the patients' perspective serves to undermine their faith in the treatment they receive. Poorly designed hospitals, those that pay insufficient attention to the patients' point of view, might then be said to promote what Weil calls a "negative placebo response." The intimidating institutional character, the gratuitous and often frightening imagery of high technology, and the lack of variety that characterize most large contemporary hospitals would then be judged as impediments to the function of healing. In such hospitals, we are faced with functionality taken to the point of diminishing returns, a situation Theodor Adorno called "the impracticality of the mercilessly practical."[15] This must also apply not only to the physical characteristics of the hospital, but also to its administrative policies—the forced donning of the humiliating hospital gowns, the lack of privacy, the illegible jargon recorded on the patient's chart. According to Illich,

> The patient in the grip of contemporary medicine is but one instance of
> mankind in the grip of its pernicious techniques. This *cultural iatrogenesis*
> [Illich's term for dysfunctions originating within the practice of medicine
> itself] . . . is the ultimate backlash of hygienic progress and consists in the
> paralysis of healthy response to suffering, impairment, and death. It occurs
> when people accept health management designed on the engineering
> model, when they conspire in an attempt to produce, as if it were a
> commodity, something called "better health."[16]

The point I wish to draw from this is that it has, since the Renaissance,
traditionally fallen to the architect to interpret, assess, and provide for the
needs of the client. Because of the architect's broad learning—which
Vitruvius counseled should include not only drawing and geometry, but
also history, philosophy, music, medicine, law, and astronomy—the
architect was ideally qualified to critically assess the less sophisticated
understanding of the building's intended purpose presented by the
client. In this professional role, the architect could speak for those
"users" of the building who lacked a voice of their own. I do not mean to
overplay the charitable nature of this advocacy. The self-interest of
architects has always required them to be highly deferential to the wishes
of their clients, and only a rare architect would compromise these wishes
in favor of those of the weak or downtrodden. What I am trying to
describe is not a humanitarian impulse so much as the architect's
tendency to always see the building as a "difficult whole" that defied
precise conceptualization.

Architects were trained to look at the world in many different
ways. Following Vitruvius, those serving in the capacity we now identify
as the architect employed the eyes of a craftsman, a geometer's eyes, the
eyes of a jurist and a scientist; these were philosophical and literate eyes,
eyes able to discern subtle distinctions. However, beginning in 1435 with
Alberti's treatise on linear perspective, the architect's eyes increasingly
fell under the spell of mathematics. During the Enlightenment,
architectural theories focused the formerly many-faceted gaze of the
architect through either of only two possible lenses—the lens of form or
that of function. Architects gradually came to subscribe to the dominance
of the Cartesian gaze, the single technological eye that sees only
mechanisms. This monocular perspectival vision would both literally and
figuratively result in a loss of depth in the worldview of the architect. And
it is this shift in architecture, but even more so in the conceptual beliefs

of the clients who pay for it, that has removed the windows from our operating rooms, and the wonder from our buildings.

It is important to add here that I am not questioning the usefulness of science. What is at issue is the aggressive zeal to apply scientific principles to all areas of lived experience, such as architecture, without regard for the demonstrable limitations of the scientific "picture." Genuine scientists are often very cautious and circumspect regarding the application of their discoveries. It is generally the technocrats and administrators one step removed from the "pure" science of the laboratory, but who very likely support it financially, who disregard the prudent caution of the true scientist. This is not science but scientism, the belief that anything may be objectively conceptualized without distortion, that the scientific world picture is infallible and complete, and that the only alternative to objective knowledge is the "descent" into relativism. This is science driven by the technological will to power, by the desire to bring everything and everyone into the grip of its "pernicious techniques."

A quick look, with both eyes, at a general example of scientism in action is in order before I return to the architects and architecture of hospitals. Around 1905, Alfred Binet produced the first scientifically plausible test of human reasoning. Until that time, most "scientific" attempts to measure human intelligence had actually depended upon measuring aspects of the body—like cranial capacity or slope of forehead. Binet's test, which involved an interview wherein the subject was asked to solve numerous problems, was designed to allow him to establish a "mental age" that would serve as a measure of the subject's reasoning capacity irrespective of learned abilities. (It was a German psychologist named Stern who proposed dividing Binet's subjects' mental ages by their chronological ages, in order to produce an "intelligence quotient.") A prudent scientist, Binet was skeptical of his own creation from the start. He believed that intelligence was too complex to be represented by a single number, that it could not "be measured as linear surfaces are measured." He considered the test only effective for identifying persons of abnormally low intelligence, whom he hoped to help through a program of "mental orthopedics." He cautioned that "for *the sake of simplicity of statement*," we might "speak of a child of 8 years having the intelligence of a child of 7 or 9 years; these expressions, if accepted arbitrarily, may give place to illusions."[17] Binet's cautions fell on deaf ears as American psychologists and educators rushed to make use of this measure of the newly invented objective quality—intelligence. Amazingly enough, people still tend to believe that a numerical I.Q. provides an accurate measure of mental capacity, even though we simultaneously recognize that it takes not one, but at least two, numerical measures to satisfactorily represent something as comparatively simple as thermal comfort. (In cold weather we need to know the temperature plus the wind speed, which gives us the wind chill factor; in hot weather we need at least temperature and relative humidity readings, if not wind speed as well.)

The I.Q. test reinforces my earlier statement regarding our pseudo-scientific tendency to measure not what is most important, but what is most readily measured. I.Q. tests do not measure creativity, diligence, curiosity, imagination, and artistic or musical aptitudes. Hospital design guidelines do not weigh the injuries inflicted on the patient's dignity, or the degree to which the building engenders in the patient a sense of well-being. The price of a building does not adequately measure the social or environmental costs of constructing it, nor its benefits in terms of forming social bonds between those who build it and those who use it, nor its ability to embody cultural memories, to put the sick and worried at ease, or to contribute to human happiness. When I mention these qualities in the case of the intelligence test, as well as in the design and cost of hospitals, I assume the reader is likely to acknowledge their significance. Yet in actuality these qualities are relegated to secondary status, not because we deny their value, but simply because they are difficult to quantify.

In his fascinating book *The Mismeasure of Man*, Stephen Jay Gould characterizes the reductionist enthusiasm that many psychologists and social scientists exhibit as a kind of "physics envy." He observes that they strive "to practice their science according to their clouded vision of physics—to search for simplifying laws and basic particles."[18] In referring to a "clouded vision of physics," Gould alludes to the many destabilizing discoveries that have influenced physicists in the quantum era to adopt a more circumspect understanding of their discipline, particularly when compared to the blustering confidence of their Newtonian predecessors. By indiscriminately applying a research methodology applicable to discrete phenomena, along with the unstated metaphysical assumptions of Newtonian physics, to highly complex indiscreet phenomena, such as architecture, a distorted and overly simplistic model results. There are two reasons for the dominance of this model of architecture, and neither of them is related to its "truth." The first is that it produces reassuringly simple abstractions that may be contemplated, measured, and manipulated with objective certainty— Ortega's "curtain of fantasy where everything is clear." Just like a person reduced to "a body" or "a life," architecture reduced to either "functional building" and/or "formal composition" is more "amenable to management, to improvement, and to evaluation in terms of available resources." The second reason, which is more applicable to those who commission architectural services than to architects themselves, is that by casting architecture in the reduced role of an instrument, it loses its claim to be anything other than a pure economic factor.

The main objection that would today be raised against constructing a hospital like Saint Paul would be its initial cost. Under the ever-shorter planning horizons required by competitive capitalist development, we would be told that it is simply too expensive. Of course, if Saint Paul really were effective as architectural medicine, in a way that was measurable, and we could also measure the pleasure it brought to those who visited it, the suffering it helped to ease, the tourists it brought to the neighborhood, the jobs it created, and all the other intangible benefits of it, would it *still* cost too much? I am not suggesting that a thorough cost-benefit analysis would eventually justify expending capital to produce architecture (although it might help). Architecture, like all matters of real consequence—health, justice, love, virtue, beauty, friendship, happiness, wisdom—is not susceptible to the kind of transitive measurement we apply to linear surfaces. Architecture will *always* remain underappreciated in a society that values only what can be represented in unambiguous terms, using uniformly segmented units of measure. Because of this, advocating for architecture to an audience of bureaucrats is nearly an impossible task. The very language these individuals speak excludes the possibility that such "immeasurables" as I have listed can be adequately addressed.[19] Due to what Illich has termed "the industrial corruption of language"[20] hospital administrators are already predisposed to making certain kinds of investments, which are no more "rational" than the money that might be spent on architecture, but are more readily made to seem rational because the certainty of their measurement contributes to the self-justification of the status quo. Here sociologist Richard Sennett describes such an investment strategy:

> Technological innovation has a curious relationship to bureaucratic
> expansion. For instance, a study of computerization of hospital record-
> keeping in an American city reveals that the advent of the computer steadily
> decreased the efficiency of the bills rendered and paid in the hospital. The
> computer cost so much to install and activate, however, that it forced the
> hospital to create a whole new staff for its care and feeding, which in turn
> stimulated the hospital to engage in a major fund-raising campaign, which
> in turn produced a large amount of new contributions, which were then
> diverted to the building of a new hospital wing. The deficits for the
> bureaucracy as a whole piled up, but the expansion and subdivision of
> white-collar labor convinced those in charge that the hospital was
> "modernizing."[21]

Notice, in Sennett's (admittedly dated) example that the expansion of the
hospital building—of the part of the institution that actually provides for
the care of patients—was an afterthought, occasioned only by the
existence of excess funds. We can be certain, when the hospital building
is seen in a subservient role to the hospital's computerized billing
system, that there would be little chance for its architect to advocate for
an architecture that goes beyond quantifiable function and marketable
imagery. Yet this is exactly what must happen if we wish our hospitals to
be more than additional pieces of bureaucratic equipment. In the design
of our hospitals, it is left to the wisdom of architects to speak in favor of
what cannot be readily objectified and commodified. This leads to two
questions. Do contemporary architects possess the wisdom that will
allow them to provide this counsel, or are they too preoccupied with the
"meaningless certainties" of form and function? And, assuming the
architect has the requisite binocular global view to question the myopia
of the technocratic eye, would anyone listen?

These questions might lead to another: what sort of man was
Lluís Domènech i Montaner, whose wisdom and talent produced the
humane Hospital of Saint Paul? We know that by the time Domènech
designed his hospital he had, like so many of his European *fin de siècle*
contemporaries, fallen under the spell of the Wagnerian ideal of the
"total work of art." Such a work required, in the words of Ignasi de Solà-
Morales, a "return to origins, a descent into hell, in which the myths of
blood, love, nature, and death figure as the sources of a collective dawn."
Domènech, born two years before Gaudí, seventeen years the senior of

Puig i Caldafalch, and nearly thirty years older than Jujol i Gilbert, was the elder statesman of the most influential Barcelona architects, and an enthusiastic advocate of the Wagnerian utopia. As Solà-Morales describes it,

> The Wagnerian utopia is an urban utopia, composed for the anxious populace of the industrial city, no longer secured by roots, identity, or nation. The Wagnerian total work of art is the harbinger of a society saved by art, by means of the exercise of that art, of the bright flame of sacrifice, of truth, of the power and the life announced by Ruskin, forming part of a programme in which the fancies of Romanticism replace the pain and fatigue of the prosaic urban life of the industrial city.[22]

In 1877, Domènech authored an article entitled "In Search of a National Architecture." In it, he advocated a brand of pragmatic and critical eclecticism, advising his colleagues that they should be willing to appropriate from the past anything that might be useful in their present circumstances. "If engagement in this selective and contradictory operation of rescuing what was of value in the past was to be eclectic, then, Domènech i Montaner affirmed, 'we declare ourselves dedicated to eclecticism.'"[23] He seemed to feel that there was nothing intrinsically sacred about any of the previous historical styles; his buildings became collages made of historical references, local traditions, and his own inventions.

From works such as the Hospital of Saint Paul, and the equally sumptuous Palace of Catalonian Music, it appears that Domènech was foremost a lover of ornament, color, and the effects of daylight. However, what I find most interesting about Domènech, beyond his ideas about architecture, are the activities Solà-Morales believes "clearly reflect [his] capacity to approach and understand the creation of the new architecture on a number of different fronts."[24] He was a well-educated intellectual and an active politician, elected to the Madrid parliament in 1901; he was an architectural and political historian, and an author, not only of theoretical and technical articles, but of complete monographs, including the *Historia General del Arte y la Arquitectura* (co-edited with Josep Puig i Caldafalch); he was an expert on the archeology of ancient buildings, on the metal arts, on ceramics, and on heraldry; he was an influential teacher, and from 1900 until 1920 the director of the Barcelona School of Architecture; he also helped found the weekly political newspaper *El Poble Català*. In short, he was a nearly "encyclopedic personality" in whose projects

> as much attention is given to the technological problems raised by the use
> of new materials as to technical innovations in the typologies of urban
> buildings; to attention to decorative detail, to the integration of the various
> crafts and techniques in a conception of architecture which, as with his
> friend and contemporary Anselm Clave's conception of choral mass, the
> different elements united together in the task to be accomplished each
> seeks to bring its own creative voice to bear, in pursuit of the totality which
> has the same significance in architecture as does the idea of the total work
> of art in the Wagnerian aesthetic project.[25]

While we may be suspicious, ultimately, of Domènech's Wagnerian
Romanticism, we can see by his architecture that he was able to
transcend any of the weaknesses in that ideological scheme. On the other
hand, a "total work of art" is a reasonably apt description of the best of his
projects. His ability to produce inventive yet "contextual" solutions at
both the urban and detail scales has seldom been equaled. His
organizational and persuasive skills—enabling him to recruit the finest
artisans, to maintain control of them yet encourage their expressive
freedom, while simultaneously coordinating the efforts of so many
different building specialists—were extraordinary. And yet what
fascinates me most about him is how, as much as any architect in this
century, he fits the Vitruvian ideal of the well-rounded architect. Without
intending to advocate an educational (or extracurricular) determinism, I
cannot help but ask if Domènech's wide range of interests and learning
did not contribute greatly to his ability "to approach and understand . . .
architecture on a number of different fronts." It is perfectly in keeping
with both his own "encyclopaedic personality" and the Catalan
modernisme quality of "uniting a communal cause with a widely accepted,
dynamic mode of expression,"[26] that he rejected the overly simplistic
building-as-machine concept that was soon to overtake the rest of
European modernism.

      If we permit that the wisdom that allowed Domènech not only to
design the holistic architectural medicine that is Saint Paul, but to
advocate for it and convince his banker patron, Pau Gil, to pay for it is in
some limited way attributable to the broad scope of his activities, is it not
reasonable to ask if there is a lesson here for the structure of architectural
practices? Domènech's career, during which he produced excellent
buildings for all conceivable uses, might lead us to question the sort of
specialization by function toward which architects' offices have recently

tended. Does not practice based on this engineering model only exacerbate clients' tendency to objectify architecture into a pure commodity and to underscore that function, narrowly defined, is the be-all and end-all of the profession? One might also consider modeling the education and internship of our professional architects, to whatever extent possible, on the lives of well-rounded architects such as Domènech. Our intent would be to avoid producing the sort of "technical professionals whose wonderful creativity is often accompanied by appalling narrow-mindedness."[27] If this emphasis on liberal education and broad life-experience proved to be impractical, could we at least, following from what we have learned of the pitfalls of functionalism and the limitations of objectivism, not base our professional licensing examinations on the dubious model of the i.q. test?

With this in mind, we turn to what in the United States is known as the Architectural Registration Exam (A.R.E.). What we find is that in its conceptual makeup, and even more so in the various recent "improvements" that have been made to it, it tends to evaluate not what is most important to the practice of architecture, but *what is most easily measured*. The initial characteristic about the A.R.E. we notice is that, like the i.q., Scholastic Aptitude, and other standardized tests, it first and foremost objectively measures the subject's ability to take standardized tests.[28] From the multiple-choice format of most of its sections, to the multitiered questions that attempt to lose the test subject in their labyrinth of confusing choices, the A.R.E. challenges the abstract reasoning of the candidate. But no one has ever conclusively demonstrated that the ability to reason through the complex structure of multiple-choice questions makes one a better, or even minimally qualified, architect. This recalls Roslyn Lindheim's observation, with regard to hospitals, that "no one has ever demonstrated that reduction of walking distance for staff has any measurable influence on better patient care; actually, it is merely something we could easily record in standardized tables."[29] The use of questions that intentionally obscure the selection of the correct answer, even to a test candidate who has completely mastered the subject material ostensibly being tested, also suggests a connection with Binet's admission that, in his intelligence tests, it mattered little what the questions were, "as long as they were numerous." In the section of the A.R.E. exam known as "Pre-Design," the candidate is typically asked simplistic questions on the subjects of

programming and function; the questions are all based on the mechanistic and now highly suspect building-as-problem-solving ideology.
Domènech would most likely have failed this section.

　　The portion of the A.R.E. that most closely resembles the work
architects actually do has always been the so-called "Design Exam." This
is where historically the test candidates produced, in an uninterrupted
twelve-hour period, drawings of their graphic solutions to a particular
"design problem." In the mid-1980s, the comprehensive design problem
that addressed both building and site issues simultaneously was replaced
by separate "Building Design" and "Site Design" graphic problems. The
Site Design Exam was soon given in the form of several individual
problems, known as "vignettes," while the Building Design Exam
remained a single comprehensive problem. Then, in the mid-1990s, the
Building Design problem was also changed to a series of vignettes. It is
telling that these modifications to the Design Exam(s) were intended not
to more effectively test the candidate's skills, but to make the A.R.E. easier
to grade. Part of the motive behind the National Council of Architectural
Registration Board's (or NCARB, the administering body for the A.R.E.)
changes was its admirable desire to increase grading fairness and
uniformity across the nation. In order to make the A.R.E. evaluation more
objective, it was necessary to make it less like designing the sort of
"difficult whole" situations architects actually face in practice.
Throughout all of these various versions of the Design Exam, the method
of grading it remained constant; a panel of judges, all licensed architects,
would evaluate each candidate's drawings. Now, in the late 1990s, NCARB
has adopted a computerized Design Exam, with the intention that it be
entirely computer graded. The type of reductionism necessary to make
this last shift, which must certainly rely upon measuring travel distances
and other aspects that can be readily recorded in tables, is truly
frightening to contemplate.

　　I have no desire to ridicule the well-intentioned people who work
for organizations such as NCARB. Obviously, the vehicles available to
them for determining a candidate's fitness for professional licensing are
severely limited by economic and time constraints. However, we should
note that like all bureaucratic organizations, NCARB constantly seeks to
widen its sphere of influence. Thus, it has persuaded most states to make
its rationally structured apprenticeship plan, the Intern Development
Program, a requirement for architectural licensing.[30] Presently it is (or

was) engaged in "investigating the designation of advanced credentialing requirements" for such specialties as "life-safety design systems" and "project management systems."[31] It is now providing courses to fulfill the dubious continuing education requirements (in which an architect can receive credit for reading a magazine article about designing a building, but not for actually designing a building) required by the American Institute of Architects and some states.[32] It has also recently taken to promoting the use of its initials as a kind of title to be placed after the architect's name, apparently hoping, as Binet might say, "to give place to illusions"; never mind that its initials merely attest that the architect is licensed in some state and is willing to pay NCARB an annual fee to monitor his or her good standing in the profession.

The greater issue is that the expansionist tendencies of NCARB as an organization, and the reductionist thinking encouraged by the examinations it creates, are but small manifestations of the extent to which the discipline of architecture has become hijacked by the aggressively myopic technological eye. While it is certainly necessary that any architecture licensing examination emphasize life-safety issues, to reduce these to simply following codes or measuring distances is to eliminate what most distinguishes architects from engineers, thereby bolstering the latter profession's claim that the design of buildings should be permitted to them. To balance the reductive sense of architecture that prevails in the A.R.E., we should add another section to the test: one that requires the candidate to create a foundation myth, and to design a ceremony around it. Perhaps we might cheaply obtain the services of struggling novelists and poets to serve as our exam graders.

If the architecture profession hopes to escape the destiny Manfredo Tafuri foretold—that it must become a "pure economic factor"[33]— it will have to reject the overly simple-minded monocular vision of itself that currently prevails. We must take a closer look at our professional organizations and our schools to ascertain that they have not followed the path Illich finds nearly inevitable for "major institutional endeavors"—that they must eventually become counter-productive. We should not promote single-mindedness as a virtue among architects, or make adherence to it a prerequisite for obtaining professional licensing. Instead, we should follow the advice of the never professionally licensed Carlo Scarpa, who said an architect needed to have a double or triple mind, a cunning mind like that of a man planning a bank heist, and an architect required wit, "an attentive tension toward understanding all that is happening."[34] Now more than ever, there is a great need for the type of holistic or alternative thinking of architects such as Lluís Domènech i Montaner. Just as the medical profession has begun to move beyond the crude oversimplification of the body-as-mechanism, we must move beyond the building-as-machine. In what the philosopher David Michael Levin describes as the "postmodern situation"—where the gods have fled, our temples stand in ruins, and we are "disheartened, homeless"— there is a great need for places of healing. According to Levin, "without a home, the heart grows weary. Our age is not only the epoch of nihilism; it is also a time of chronic depressions."[35] Levin's chronic depressions cannot be treated with the snake oil of functional efficiency or the elixir of novel building shapes. They will require the type of medicine advocated by our friend Dr. Selzer, who asked that the windows be returned to his operating room.

> So what has all of this to do with the architecture of a hospital? Fountains and wind chimes, the sacredness of brick, the vitality of wood, the house spirits—these are the fantasies of a mere scribbler who cannot even read blue prints. And in turn I ask, where is the architect who, without sacrificing function and practicality, will think of the hospital as a pregnant woman who suffers the occupancy of a human being who enters, dwells for a time, and then passes forth? Where is the architect who, from the very moment he or she begins his or her design, will be aware that in each room of his or her finished hospital someone will die? Where is the architect who, while seated at the drawing board, will pause to feel upon his or her naked forearms the chill wind of his or her mortality? One day he or she, too, will enter this building; not as its architect but as a supplicant in dire need of care.[36]

The Valor of Iron:
An Introduction to the Material Imagination

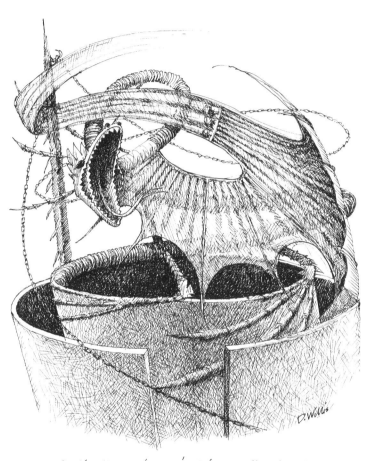

Gaudi's Dragon & Serra's Ellipses: Haunted by
the "Primitive Dreams of Iron"

With strokes that ring clear and metallic, the hour
to touch me bends way:
my senses are quivering. I feel I've the power—
and I seize on the pliable day.

Rainer Maria Rilke

In *The Nature of Art and Workmanship* David Pye discusses the relative merits of wrought and cast iron railings. He mentions that although the range of forms that can be readily created in wrought iron is quite small, "in the hands of a good smith [the work] is remarkably free and diverse within its limits.[37] Cast iron railings, Pye observes, are most often absent of this free and diverse quality, due to the higher degree of regulation inherent in the casting process. Thus, the argument for the superiority of one material over another hinges on the perception of less regulated, and therefore superior, forms that result from the use of wrought iron.

While I am generally sympathetic to Pye's point of view, I believe that a dependence on the formal limitations of a material or fabrication process to determine the relative merits of substances will ultimately result in a discussion of the suitability of *technique*. That is, the argument Pye makes in favor of wrought iron railings could be dismissed once a casting technique is devised that produces a cast iron railing with enough formal diversity to convincingly simulate wrought iron. The formal distinction will always lead us to the conclusion that one material is as good as any other, provided we are sophisticated enough to utilize it properly.

Unless, of course, one takes what I identify (in the following essay) as the "purist" position—claiming that such a procedure would result in a "dishonest" material. John Ruskin, and many since him, would maintain that it is immoral to produce a simulation of wrought iron. While again this ideology is one with which I might sympathize, it does not appear to rest on any firm theoretical ground. Still, it is difficult to totally abandon the notion of authenticity, such as Ruskin addressed in his "Lamp of Truth" essay. How can I proceed in a discussion of the suitable uses of materials, given that I am dissatisfied with the technologist's notion that one material is as good as any other, unless I rely, as did Ruskin, on the belief that the imitation of one material by another constitutes a fraud? My hope is to divert the argument from either strictly technical or moralistic grounds into the arena of the poetic imagination.

To begin, it would be helpful to examine the qualities of the materials in question. In so doing, we will be looking not just at objectively measurable properties, such as one might find in a physics text or engineering handbook, but also at historical and mythical associations. To fully understand substances, we must acknowledge what Ivan Illich has called "the historicity of stuff."[38] Wrought iron has been historically created by heating iron ore in a hearth or forge, often between layers of coal or charcoal. The metal thus obtained is continually reheated and reworked into a usable shape, often some variation of a rod. The continuous reheating and beating with a hammer gives wrought iron a characteristic longitudinal "grain," which means that its strength and elasticity will vary depending on the direction from which force is applied. When the smith's forge has been brought to about 1800°F, the iron bar will be soft enough to bend or cut. Using a variety of tongs, various hammers, and an anvil, the smith can manipulate the rod into some usable shape. Heating separate pieces to about 2400°F allows the smith to weld them together. If the iron is suddenly cooled while still hot, it will become incredibly stiff, almost brittle, and quite hard.

Cast iron also begins with the smelting of iron ore. Once a sufficient quantity of pure iron has been obtained, it will be heated until liquid, and poured into a mold of some kind. Historically, the molds have most often been made of sand. In order for the operation to succeed, sufficient quantities of the molten metal are required, because it is not possible to cast a shape in stages. Because the metal is poured at a uniform consistency and cools at a uniform rate, cast iron has a granular, non-directional, almost crystalline structure.

Compared to the wrought iron method, casting is a fairly dull procedure. It imposes a distance between the craftsperson and the substance; the immediacy of contact between the smith and the iron is lost. The significance of this closeness is evident from the accounts accomplished smiths give of their work, as documented in the book *Ornamental Ironwork*.

> Svetozar Radokovich: "The almost primitive molding together of fire and iron and force is fascinating. But this primitive force can be brought to a peak of elegant power and delicacy. . . . Even the simplest forms take on a

richness and strength they wouldn't have in another medium. . . . The pleasure is as much in the process as the result."

James Hubbell: "The simplicity and directness of the method is like being able to draw into the air."

Stanley Lechtzin: "It is the immediate response of the hot iron under the hammer that I find so exhilarating. I am attempting to capture the feeling of a fluid arrested in motion which is typical yet so elusive, in the best wrought iron of the past."[39]

Wrought ironwork is "direct," "primitive," and "simple." It requires a high degree of skill and runs an appreciable risk of error. The limitations imposed by the size of the smith's forge, the variety of anvils and dies at his disposal, as well as by the limits of his own size and strength leave their characteristic trace on the shape of any wrought iron work. Even the modern smith would acknowledge that his control of the metal is never total; there are things that the metal simply will not do, and others toward which it must be coerced. In primitive societies particularly important works would require a sacrifice to the furnace in order to assure the metal's cooperation.[40] The premodern smith, like the alchemist, was apt to anthropomorphicize the iron in acknowledgment of his incomplete understanding. This sort of thinking, the philosopher Giambattista Vico tells us, was a highly imaginative ignorance:

When men are ignorant of the natural causes producing things, and cannot even explain them by analogy with similar things, they attribute their own nature to them. The vulgar, for example, say the magnet loves the iron.[41]

The childish wonder that the very young, or the very primitive, demonstrate towards all things is a key to understanding why we prefer the wrought iron railing to its imitation. As Vico went on to note, the "imagination is more robust in proportion as reasoning power is weak." Even though our reasoning may lead us to believe that one metal, or one way of making a railing, is as good as any other, to what remains of our "robust" imaginations one method is likely to be more fascinating, and therefore superior to all others. It is this method and material that carries the greatest imaginative weight.

As the most powerful of metals, iron and steel are also among the most difficult to work. Their shaping requires a struggle, pitting human muscle and heat against the "will" of the metal. The blacksmith at his forge, working wrought iron, presents us with a heroic image of this battle of wills. In order to cast, we enlist the aid of great quantities of heat, literally "softening up" the metal before we begin shaping it. This makes for an unfair contest, and for most of the casting operation we are but spectators. The most skillfully demanding part of casting is the creation of the original form out of which future molds are made, and this does not involve iron. The actual shaping of cast iron fails to engage the imagination due to the speed of the process, as well as its relative invisibility. Once the metal is poured into the mold, there is little visual evidence that any work is going on. Casting occurs all at once, so there is insufficient time to size up the opponent, develop a narrative, to strategize and choreograph our interaction. Casting does not readily admit us into the true "cosmos of iron," because, as Gaston Bachelard has commented, this "is not an immediately accessible universe." On the contrary, to gain entrance, "one must love fire, hardness, and strength." The ferrous cosmos is "recognizable only through creative acts nurtured with courage."[42]

Through these thoughts the true cause of the superiority of wrought iron railing can be discovered. The shape limitations imposed by the wrought iron process are inherent to that method of making things. Because these cannot be avoided, the most creative smiths must learn to both master the metal as far as is possible, and to turn its lack of cooperation to their advantage when necessary. This ability to turn, twist, or trope unavoidable limits into poetic triumphs is an ability that is at the heart of all authentic making. The poetic methods and shapes that are native to wrought iron are foreign to the entirely different process that is casting. It may not be immoral to imitate the look of wrought iron in a casting, but it is uninteresting and unheroic. Casting possesses its own set of limits, and casters will be unable to discover ways of turning these to their advantage if they are preoccupied with the imitation of wrought iron. In this case, the material will cease to inspire them, and they will derive their forms from aspects entirely outside of their chosen material.

Without the robust mode of imagination that projects itself *into* substances (or draws the qualities of substances into itself), we lose the ability to give weight—the weight that comes from an intimate connection with tangible matter—to our works. In attributing human qualities to the work, a union between craftsperson and material occurs. Adolf Loos characterized this development with his story of the stonemason who developed an "eye of stone."

> Just think of it. The man had worked in the mason's hut twelve hours a day since he was fourteen. No wonder he saw the world differently from the

> painter. When one has worked in stone for his entire lifetime, he begins to
> think stones and see stones. The man had an eye of stone that turned all
> things into stone. He developed a hand of stone, and this hand of itself
> transformed all things into stone.[43]

Any material—stone, iron, or even plastic—will force accommodations from the person who would fabricate from it. The ability to foresee these accommodations as shape tendencies is to develop "the eye" of a particular material. In Loos's story the stonemason is ridiculed by a painter for grossly distorting a salamander he had carved. We can imagine that the stone would not allow the mason to, for instance, portray the salamander with a long slender tail. Instead of an objectively correct salamander, the stonemason would see, and therefore make, not a salamander but a *stone* salamander. The salamander would be re-presented[44] as a creature of stone, not amphibious flesh. This would necessarily involve distortions and displacements that a painter might be likely to interpret as errors on the part of the mason. It would also require that the successful stonemason continually exercise artistic judgment while crafting a piece. The objectively correct salamander proportions could not simply be projected onto a block of stone. The mason would not merely execute a shape that had been dictated to him (by an architect perhaps), but would modify any preconceived shape to fit the particular circumstances of a specific block of stone.

Craftwork involves continually making such choices. Unlike the designer who yearns for perfect materials and objects that are, as Octavio Paz describes them, "mute and intangible servants" like the genies of Arabic myths, the craftsperson allows the idiosyncrasies of materials to enter her body and imagination "by way of the senses." In craftwork "the principle of maximum utility is continually violated in favor of tradition, imagination, and even sheer caprice."[45] Bachelard designated the precon-ceptual awareness that an artist or craftsperson has of his materials "the dreaming hand."[46] Henri Focillon, in the same spirit, noted,

> Whatever the receptive and inventive powers of the mind may be, they
> produce only internal chaos if deprived of the hand's assistance. The
> dreamer may entertain visions of unimaginable landscapes and of ideally
> beautiful faces, but he has no means for fixing fast these tenuous,
> insubstantial visions. . . . What distinguishes dream from reality is that the
> dreamer cannot engender art, for his hands are asleep.[47]

As I have stated, the weight of the creations of the dreaming hand is owed to the fact that they respond imaginatively to verifiable and tangible limits. The imaginative depth we associate with a finely crafted article stems from our understanding that neither the object itself, nor the meanings it engenders, will be consumed by its use or contemplation. The well-crafted work is mysterious in that it cannot be fully known; we cannot codify what it means to us. The undeniable particularity and imperfect materiality of the work does not, however, indicate that in it the tangible nature of things has unequivocally triumphed over the idealizations of the human spirit. The ideal has merely been set aside, displaced, as it were, so that it can only be recognized indirectly. The imperfections of matter have been troped into imaginative demonstrations that transcend our fallibility and mortality. In such creations, the human spirit and the forces of nature have entered into a paradoxical struggle resulting in their mutual reaffirmation. Georg Simmel describes this symbiotic, but still antagonistic, state as it played out in the life of an object (his specific subject was a building aging into a ruin).

> Neither by the most decisive victory of one of these two parties [the building and the forces of nature] nor by their compromise does it ever arrive at a definitive state. For not only does the restless rhythm of the soul not tolerate such a state, but, more important, behind every single event, every single impulse that comes from one or the other of these two directions, there is something that lives on, and there are claims which the decision just made has not put to rest. This gives the antagonism between the two principles something unfinishable and formless, which breaks every frame.[48]

Well-made articles therefore invite our continual reinterpretation. They are profaned neither by use nor even disuse; Paz notes that we can "divert the object from its usual function and shift its meaning: it is no longer a vessel used for containing liquid but one for displaying a carnation."[49] The authenticity of something that has been made stems from a suitable mix of the ideal and the real, so that the materials used do not become "mute and intangible servants," but must remain enticements to our dreaming hands. If one material is to be called upon to imitate another— if stone is to become flesh, or a twisted iron bar a serpent—then it should not simply disappear into the illusion of the imitation, but remain present in an ambiguous state that can never be decisively "put to rest." As a material cannot be treated as a slave, neither can the will of the artisan accede to all the demands of the material. Eyes of stone or iron should not force the artisan into creating distortions simply for the sake of conserving effort or avoiding the possibility of errors.

It was for this reason that Pye designated craftwork "the workmanship of risk," and opposed it to industrialized fabrication, "the workmanship of certainty."[50] Because implements made of iron and steel have granted us mastery over most other natural substances, our imaginations find it inappropriate that this mastery be gained too easily, or made "certain." The daring act of Prometheus did not give humankind license to apply fire capriciously, or wastefully. It is through respect, sacrifice, and the resounding clangs of countless blows that we earn the right to command the power of iron. Our cast-iron-imitating-wrought-iron railing has erred by assuming that we can drastically change the difficulty of making something, replacing chance with certainty, and so eliminating all "creative acts nurtured with courage," without altering the meaning of what we have made. We are misled if we believe an identical cast reproduction of a wrought iron railing would retain the same imaginative weight and depth, simply because their forms were identical. The superiority of the wrought iron railing will elude us if we insist on judging "purely in terms of form works which are dedicated to the glory of matter."

◇   ◇   ◇

Iron is power. The twin qualities of hardness and elastic strength are the most useful and most inspiring properties of iron. Iron and steel allow us to form chisels that can split or carve the hardest stone. As Bachelard puts it, "At the limits of the *dream of hardness,* iron stands supreme." It is the great strength of iron and steel that have allowed us to construct the skyscrapers of our modern cities. "Iron is nothing but muscle. Iron is straight, sure, essential strength. You can build a world using iron for every part."[51]

Our earliest contact with this element of power probably occurred when ferrous meteorites fell to earth. From the outset the material was unique, having fallen flaming from the heavens. The discovery of magnetism, an invisible force affecting only iron, no doubt added to the material's reputation as celestially "charged" and sacred. The actual strength of iron was reinforced by the spiritual power it derived from its other-worldly origins. The rare circumstances and valuable properties of the metal begged that a suitable use for it be found. The development of all metallurgy has been spurred by our quest to produce

ever better means for slicing and carving nature, or our fellow man. Even
the sober prose of an elementary metallurgy text laments this truth:

> Generally speaking, metals and alloys were developed primarily for military
> purposes, after which their value as material for other implements and as
> ornamental material came into being. From the philosophical point of view
> this seems a rather sad commentary on the history of mankind, for first and
> foremost in man's mind has been . . . the development of implements in-
> tended at least for his self-protection, if not for the subjugation of others.[52]

That iron and steel are synonymous with strength is evident from their
frequent use as metaphors. Metal's ability to resist human will engenders
our respect, and sometimes fear. In *The Forge and the Crucible* Mircea
Eliade describes the frightened misgivings that have historically
accompanied works made of iron—suspicion generated by the smith's
seemingly demonic activities.[53] These fears, that our own creations might
escape our control, were perhaps unmatched until the advent of nuclear
power. Paradoxically, it is just this incomplete control of the material that
guarantees the diversity in wrought ironwork that Pye and the smiths
quoted earlier praise so highly.

Obviously the power of iron is not most conspicuously displayed
in its use as a railing. Artifacts and implements with a longer (and
bloodier) history—tools and weapons primarily—are closer to the
fundamental nature of iron. Eliade writes that "the Iron Age was
characterized by an uninterrupted succession of wars and massacres, by
mass slavery, and by almost universal impoverishment."[54] Thus the
sword is the true embodiment of the will of iron (and its derivative, steel).
Furthermore, the most heroic battles between men can only be fought
with swords. Authentic valor can only exist in the real presence of death.
In unarmed combat, the threat of death is remote, unless the combatants
are unevenly matched, which in itself precludes that the conflict be
considered heroic. In modern warfare, battle has been reduced to
pushing buttons—hardly a poetic expression of fortitude. The sword
however, despite its functional obsolescence on the battlefield, remains
potent as an image of courage.

It is for this reason that the dress regalia of many modern
military uniforms still incorporate swords. If this were only a matter of
convention, the swords might be made only to *appear* real. But a
declaration of war made while pointing one's imitation sword at the
enemy would be absurd. The general, like the material, would seem to

lack conviction. Indeed, the hopelessly brittle sword, or the sword that bends like rubber, are frequently devices used to inspire ridicule, particularly in slapstick comedies or animated cartoons. The heroism of the sword is at its essence not representational. The sword does not so much signify heroic deeds as facilitate them. Its ability to signify is inextricably linked to its potency as a weapon. It demonstrates bravery by allowing its user to be brave. In this sense a man with a sword is not the same person as he is without it. How quickly even the bravest knight turns and flees when his sword has broken! Because the sword makes the soldier "a new man," the sword is often attributed a personality and a life. It is "no longer an abstraction but a Personage, endowed with human as well as superhuman qualities."[55]

The power of the sword's steel originates in the union between the fruits of the earth and stars—the iron ore and fire—as orchestrated by the will of the smith. Alloys, such as steel, are complex unions, mixed marriages if you will, for which the smith's skill might at times prove insufficient to promote. Chinese myths tell of a smith unable to alloy the steel necessary for a pair of swords until—in various versions—either the smith's wife threw herself into the furnace, or they were both sacrificed, or only their hair and fingernails were added to the flames.[56] Some physical trace of the married couple was necessary to consummate the sacred bond between the materials that would produce another couple— a pair of swords. The sword always has two natures; it can be put to good or evil uses, just as its masculine parent, fire, can both purify and destroy. Those whom Vico described as being "ignorant of natural causes" believe the mystical fire that gives birth to steel remains trapped within the sword. The trapped heat is what gives the sword its cutting edge, as well as its hardness or *temper*. The act of tempering the steel is another sexual encounter—the enflamed desire of the heated metal being too suddenly quenched by cool water.

In primitive societies, it was thought that whoever possessed the most powerful sword was destined to command all others. Through the magical power of Excalibur, King Arthur gained his throne. Only the human weakness of Arthur's will, his vanity and jealousy, diminished the authority of his sword. According to sword historian Richard F. Burton,

> [The sword] was a sentient being who spoke, and sang, and grieved. Identified with the wearer he was the object of affection, and was pompously named as a well-beloved son and heir. To surrender the Sword was

> submission; to break the Sword was degradation. To kiss the Sword was, and in many places still is, the highest form of oath and homage. . . . The Sword killed and cured; the hero when hopeless fell upon his Sword; and the heroine, like Lucretia and Calphurnia, used the blade standing.[57]

Only recently has the human imagination developed an image of courage in action equal to that of the steel sword—the "light sabers" found in the *Star Wars* motion picture trilogy. This invention has freed the fire within the sword, so that the combatants may do battle with the pure power of light. Despite the array of futuristic weapons shown throughout these movies, all of the truly heroic battles are fought with the light swords. And while earthly metal has been removed from the sword, it should be noted that it was necessary to add sound effects to the light saber duels to achieve an acceptably real struggle. In place of the swish of metal cleaving air, the films substitute an electronic hum of changing pitch. Instead of the metallic clang of meeting swords, we hear the crackling of an electrical short circuit.

In recent years recruiting advertisements for the United States Marine Corps have also used the sword image to advantage. One television commercial depicted a beam of light honing the edge of a sword. In another a raised sword held by a king is energized by lightening. In a third advertisement a conflict is played out on a chess board, with the opposing chess men battling with light swords. All are very melodramatic, but the images are undeniably effective. The commercials customarily end with the image of a modern-day marine in dress uniform, with sword in hand.

While both the *Star Wars* movies and the Marine Corps advertisements are certainly examples of the mass-media tendency to exploit romantic nostalgia, this does not contradict the imaginative power of the images they employ. Even in obsolete associations and customs we may still recognize images that have retained their resonance. When Bachelard authored one of his last books, *The Flame of a Candle*, he anticipated the objection that his subject was no longer relevant. Maintaining that his text was not merely a catalog of long-dead poetic images, Bachelard explained:

> There is an easy answer to these objections: dreams and reveries are not modernized as rapidly as our actions. Our reveries are true, deeply rooted *psychic habits*. Active life does not disturb them in the least. The psychologist has an interest in finding all paths to the most ancient familiar things.[58]

Like the candle, wrought iron and steel swords have long been surpassed by more technologically advanced means. Yet, as Bachelard shows, they have not been superseded as fundamental materials of the imagination. There is an analogy here between, on the one hand, the myths of the forge and similar deeply ingrained "psychic habits" of our species, manifesting themselves most notably in the robust imaginations of primitive peoples not yet dominated by reason, and, on the other, the fascination our children continue to exhibit toward tales of knights' chivalry, of monsters, and of other extraordinary creatures, particularly dinosaurs. For those who retain imaginations unencumbered by petrifying concepts, the universe remains an inexhaustible dynamic force, and is therefore devoid of the solidity of finished forms. Children prefer to daydream *actively*, of monsters that must be defeated, of castles to be stormed, of "black knights" that must be overthrown.

This variety of imagination, an imagination of forces, is appropriate to our discussion of iron because iron and steel are the most forceful, most muscular, of substances. The childish delight in dinosaurs is owed to the great power we attribute to these extinct creatures, and also to their grotesqueness. But it is also due to our tendency, when we create in our daydreams the most powerful creatures imaginable, to invent beings whose nature cannot be precisely known, especially those that combine the attributes of several others or that have the ability to assume many forms. Unlike simple beings, with readily understood single natures, these monsters possess the additional power of mysteriousness. We regard them with awe and fear because they thwart our understanding. As Marco Frascari informs us, the grotesque body of our imagination is "a body in continuous metamorphosis." It is not "the unique and finite image of the metaphorical body but rather it is a body that transforms itself continuously."[59] The body images of which Frascari speaks would not include the *literal* descriptions of dinosaurs, but what we in our childish imaginations find dinosaurs most closely resemble: dragons. Bachelard explains:

> Let the imagination devote itself in all sincerity to metamorphoses and we find it making monsters, monsters which are reserves of strength, inexhaustible sources of aggressiveness. . . . The painter would perhaps hesitate before fixing such daring shapes, but since this is the time of metamorphosis, the embryonic moment of a work of art, the man who enjoys the demiurgic power of modeling goes all the way in exploring forces that are born in the substance of earth.[60]

In the active universe of our robust imaginations it is the transformative powers of things that engage us most. Here again we note that a painter, lacking the "eye" of a "substance of earth," must invent forms without benefit of the suggestions (or taunts) of a willful material. Without these provocations the painter is likely to "hesitate before fixing these daring shapes"—these monsters—of an animalizing imagination. It should come as no surprise then that the most powerful image of a dragon exists not in a painting, but in wrought iron. If the sword is the most human embodiment of the will of iron, we must acknowledge its nemesis, its other, which is the dragon. And no greater dragon has ever been fabricated through human imagination and skill than the wrought iron beast who guards the entrance to the former Güell estate in Barcelona.

This terrible creature was created between 1884 and 1888, the result of a collaboration between Antonio Gaudí and a number of skillful artisans. The dragon image has particular relevance in Barcelona, for Catalonia long ago adopted Saint George—the dragon slayer—as its patron. (I speculate that dragons were invented to give the brave bearers of steel blades and lances a suitably formidable foe about which to dream.) Gaudí was fascinated with the dragon motif, particularly as it might be realized in iron. In an earlier work, the Casa Vicens, Gaudí surrounded the mansion with an iron fence upon which numerous baby dragons cling. It is as if the dragon image matured in Gaudí's dreams for several years (Casa Vicens was designed by Gaudí in 1878, and under construction from 1883 to 1885) before reaching its maturation in the Güell Pavilion gate.

Several features of Gaudí's gate are striking. While the iron dragon is a more-or-less two-dimensional construction, and it is confined to a space at the top half of the gate, this only contributes to the dynamism of the image. As a visitor approaches the gate, the dragon appears to have been roused from its rest; it seems ready to uncoil itself, to swell beyond its frame. Much of this effect is owed to the coiled and convoluted spine that connects the various parts of the dragon's body. This element—as a neck, a backbone, and a tail—must be able to, indeed must long to, stretch to its full length. This reading is enhanced in that the "spine" is also an iron spring, whose compression implies additional potential energy. The actual flatness of the dragon is further belied by its intricate layering. The overlapping of the translucent wings, of the claws, spikes, and spine creates a virtual depth that again exceeds its physical frame. The dragon's iron scales and spikes aggressively penetrate the space surrounding it, as does its terrible iron tongue, as it voraciously reaches towards the approaching guest.

Dragons and serpents have always been among the most popular wrought iron motifs, undoubtedly because of the formal similarities between a pliable heated iron bar and a snake, but also because of the muscular suppleness both possess. (Ruskin found the snake to be the embodiment of "the grasp and sting of death."[61]) The kind of imitation, the mimesis, that turns an iron bar into a serpent, or a spring into a spine, does not rely on formal similarities alone. There are many analogous relationships between these animals or animal parts and wrought iron constructions, such as the relationship both dragon and iron share with fire, and the inherent aggressiveness connecting the most dynamic of imaginary creatures to the most powerful of metals.

Dragons are usually attributed the ability to fly, and we can see that Gaudí's dragon emphasizes this with its predominant batlike wing. This leads to another aspect of wrought ironwork—the spatial freedom that may be realized in its open three-dimensionality. Two of the smiths quoted in *Ornamental Ironwork* remarked on this ability of wrought iron to "draw in the air," with a "fluid arrested in motion." Pye also praised wrought iron for its "free and diverse" qualities. In 1956, Bachelard wrote an essay on the Spanish sculptor-smith Chillida. Here Bachelard cites Chillida's ability to express the dynamics of iron in air.

> Dreaming more grandly still, Chillida decided he wanted iron to reveal the realities of air. On a rock facing the sea in the Basque coast village where he lives, he erected an iron antenna designed to vibrate to every movement of the wind. This tree of iron, which he made grow out of the rock, he called Wind Comb. The rock itself with its isolated peak only gives a massive response to the vagaries of the storm. The iron, wrought into a mass of branches by the dreaming hammer, does full justice to the streaming tresses of the wind.[62]

The archetypal dream Bachelard praises in the works of Chillida is the "dream of iron set free." In 1980, Octavio Paz described this aspect of the same artist's work, introducing an exhibit in Pittsburgh.

> At one extreme these works verge on a cruel sexuality, and at the other to a winged elegance. The sharp, the pointed, the penetrating and perforating, that which pierces, nails, punctures and, at the same time flies, waves, flutters, glides, sways, slithers: beak and wing, claws and feathers.

> Birds but also darts, arrows, javelins, the zig-zag of the electric
> current. . . . The undulation of lances and feathers, a black and blue
> undulation: iron and wind.[63]

For the craftsman who develops an eye of iron, who dreams the vigorous dreams of hammer and forge, these images—the sword, the serpent, the dragon, the darts, arrows, and claws that pierce the air—come closest to what Bachelard called "the great dreams of primitive humanity."[64] It is true that vegetative forms have also been popular in wrought iron; stems and stalks, too, have similarities to bent bars of iron. However, there is a slowness about vegetative growth that is out of step with the ferrous substance. Iron grill works of interwoven floral patterns tend to be too stable, too geometric, lacking the essential dynamism of animal images. Only occasionally has the smith allowed a portion of the metal plant life its freedom. If a vine starts to wrap around other bars too aggressively, if a root or stem begins to stray beyond its frame, if barbs and thorns begin to bristle dangerously—then we may begin to sense the oneiric possibilities of tenacious, uncontrollable plant growth, and the powerful image of iron set free will emerge again.[65]

There are, to be sure, less belligerent uses of iron and steel than those upon which I have dwelt. If the hammer is the father of the sword, the sickle is its domesticated brother. Yet these tools too, although less obviously, display the old family traits. The Norse god Thor harnessed the power of lightning in his hammer, and only a foolish man would turn his back to an enemy armed with a sickle. All ferrous implements—saws, knives, chisels, shovels, picks, scissors—perform their tasks amid an undercurrent of suppressed violence. In the former Soviet Union, the heroic image of workers—sweating harvesters of grain, butchers, carpenters, and mechanics—that once graced the walls of public places clearly displayed this concealed nature, as did the hammer and sickle emblem of the Soviet flag. Wrenches and pickaxes when hoisted overhead become the weapons of class struggle.

That the power of ferrous materials cannot be reduced to a matter of form is further underscored by works such as Richard Serra's *Torqued Ellipses*. This installation-sculpture, which occupied the warehouse-gallery of the Dia Foundation in New York, consists of three concentric groups of curved steel plates. The plates are approximately sixteen feet high, and the steel itself about two inches thick. While the shapes of the bent plates and the groupings they form are undeniably

amazing (the top and bottom edges of the bent plates are defined by
ellipses that have been rotated in relation to one another), there is
another, more visceral, effect to the sculpture. One wanders through the
maze of these giants, gingerly touching their disarmingly sensual
surfaces, realizing that any of the plates, should it fall, could easily crush
a human—or an elephant, for that matter. The sublime fascination this
work engenders is similar to what we might imagine walking around the
feet of an inattentive giant to be.

The plates are bent to just such a degree, in proportion to the
size and thickness of the steel, that they have lost none of their strength.
They create tension between our awe that they could be bent at all, and
the uncomfortable feeling that they would not have tolerated much more,
or that they might at any moment (like the spine of Gaudí's dragon)
spring back to their original shape. As Serra says, "there is a stress put on
the steel that you register."[66] The shapes of Serra's plates are inseparable
from the fact that they are made of steel that has been bent. As Serra
rightly asserts, neither their weight nor shape alone would be enough.
For example, "built in concrete, these pieces would totally lose the
tension of the torqued steel, which affects your experience of their
space."[67] To the aggressive images of claw and sword, Serra has given us
an image of steel that is both agitated and in repose, at once graceful and
lumbering, mighty and gentle.

The strength of iron presents us with an extreme case where the
violence of fabrication is often exaggerated. However, if we look closely,
we will find this connection with violence to be present in the manufacture of all artifacts (recall that *manu*facturing originally meant
"making by hand"). In order to perform their tasks repeatedly tools must
be durable, and they must be capable of violence. The attitude of all
human makers is to some extent aggressive, for the maker proposes to
change the world, to create new worlds, and this cannot be accomplished
passively. Hannah Arendt observes that material is "already a product of
human hands" as soon as it has been forcibly removed from its natural
setting. In the case of wood, the felling of a tree constitutes the killing of
a living specimen, and even iron ore has to be "torn out of the womb of
the earth."[68] All poetic making involves battles with materials; all
finished works are incomplete victories.

❖　　　❖　　　❖

Recall the railings with which I began this essay—two nearly indistinguishable iron railings that are most different in the ways they are made, and therefore in the dreams they inspire. On the one hand, the wrought iron process is essentially heating, beating, and bending. On the other, casting iron necessitates creating a mold, and pouring molten iron into it. In terms of production efficiency, the latter is a technical improvement over the former. While both employ techniques—or could themselves be rightfully called techniques—for producing railings, the casting method is far more a part of the "logic" of technique (that is, it originates in a manner of thinking that places the efficient cause above all others).

To a society that has adopted this logic, such as our own, there can be no argument for the superiority of one thing over another that does not rely primarily on evaluations of efficiency. This is why, to the technologist, all materials or methods are "equal" until one evidences superior efficiency in performing its task. It is also, partially, why Ruskin and other moralists have been so unsuccessful in their crusade for "truth." Most advocates of "truth to materials" are caught in an ideological double bind. They reject the technologist's notion that efficiency is the only defensible criterion by which to evaluate the use of a substance, and yet they accept the scientific standard of "objective truth." However, the objective properties of something can tell us whether it is performing efficiently, but cannot tell us whether its use is "true to its nature," or fascinating. Thus the moralists are left with no basis upon which to argue against using one material to imitate another, or upon which to distinguish acceptable imitation (wrought iron serpents) from *unacceptable* imitation (cast iron serpents imitating wrought iron serpents). What is needed is another understanding of truth—"poetic lies," "authentic fabrications," or some other term that conveys the sense of being true to the imagination.

The objective standard of truth relegates all concerns not readily quantified into unambiguous measures to the realm of the subjective, where they may be dismissed as mere caprice or personal preference. Bachelard's great contribution to our understanding of the uses, both practical and poetic, of substances was his persuasive demonstration that some uses are imaginatively superior to others. Bachelard's philosophy creates a new zone of "truth" where our dreaming bodies provide the proofs; the discoveries of the material imagination are therefore not merely subjective, but "trans-subjective," or, to use Hans-Georg Gadamer's term, they are "substantial."[69]

In industrially produced duplicates, the material imagination will find little to engage it. The cast iron process is aimed at making numerous duplicate sections of iron railing that are practically identical. This lack of variation is intentional, despite Pye's protests in favor of diversity, because the risk of failure inherent in the wrought iron process will have been deemed "inefficient."[70] The efficient production technique will tend to exclude the imaginative ignorance that anthropomorphicizes substances, because to the technical mind all materials are equally meaningless. In the never-ending search for the quickest, most economical and dependable method to make a product, the technologist cannot afford to hold an allegiance to any particular material or method. Thus, in a technological society, all materiality is destined to "melt into air."

When Bachelard wrote that the universe of iron was not "immediately accessible," he could have been describing any operation of meaningful fabrication. Contrary to Bachelard, the technologist would prefer the relationship between raw material and finished artifact to be one of pure projection: stone salamanders that are exact proportional replicas of actual salamanders, cast iron serpents that faithfully reproduce the shapes of wrought iron serpents. In these "perfect" translations from one material and process to another, the technological conceit is that material processes can be made transparent, and all universes rendered immediately accessible. A process such as that of wrought iron foils this assumed projective relationship, because our incomplete control of the material, its willfulness, prevents us from seeing straight through it in a projective manner. The preconceived ideal product is always distorted by the partially opaque lens of the substance or process; the "eye" of any material will always disrupt the projective focus. And it is for this reason that the products of the material imagination will be more varied, more dynamic, more monstrous, than those of an imagination that concerns itself strictly with forms.

Conversely, as a society becomes more technological, the imaginative opportunities opened within it will become increasingly formal. Once the process of making anything has been deemed irrelevant to the meanings attached to it, issues of shape, style, and visual appearance must gain in importance. One defining characteristic of modernity has been our cultural de-emphasis on the material imagination. This tendency has been further exacerbated by the problem of "mechanical reproduction," with which Walter Benjamin struggled in his widely read essay, "The Work of Art in the Age of Mechanical Reproduction,"[71] and by the invention of synthetic materials no longer pulled from the "womb of the earth." There are no myths associated with the creation of plastic.

Because of the importance he places on their historicity, Ivan Illich considers modern materials to be fundamentally different from their premodern predecessors. They are less enchanted substances, to which we attribute human characteristics, than they are inseparable components of supposedly transparent production techniques. Thus, a contemporary substance cannot be thought of, or dreamt about, in the way its chemically identical predecessor was centuries ago. Illich cites the example of water, which "the twentieth century has transmogrified . . . into a fluid with which the archetypal waters cannot be mixed." Illich distinguishes this new substance from "archetypal waters" by designating it "H_2O."[72]

Bachelard, perhaps because he wrote on the poetics of substances some thirty years earlier than Illich, typically remained more positive regarding the tenacious durability of our "deeply rooted psychic habits." Bachelard would maintain that the vigorous dreams of premodern iron, deeply buried though they be, could still be unearthed in the heart of the element our modern Periodic Table labels "Fe." In this spirit we would be mistaken to assume that cast iron must always be, in all uses, imaginatively inferior to wrought iron. It is indeed possible that an alternative poetic—an eye—of cast iron might be discovered. This discovery will not, however, be found if we look to imitate wrought iron. Direct imitation in substances implies an inferiority about the material actually at hand; in order to love casting iron, to dream of pouring molten metal shapes, an artisan cannot accept making do with a mere substitute.

To discover a poetic of cast iron, we would have to once again separate the substance from the technique. We might, for example, dwell upon the weight of iron during the casting process. While heat deprives iron about to be cast of its strength, its mass remains unaffected. A use that accentuates the heaviness of cast iron, an eye that sees in terms of temporary liquidity combined with persistent gravity, could perhaps engage our imaginations to the same extent that the willfulness of wrought iron does. Contrary to the dynamic wrought iron, cast iron products are mostly characterized by their substantial inertia, by their resistance to movement. The "weights" that are lifted by weight lifters are almost always made of cast iron. The phrase "pumping iron" metaphorically captures the nature of these repetitive movements. Manhole covers and tree grates form the mainstay products of today's larger cast iron foundries. All of these objects are usually imprinted with decorative designs. In this respect cast iron has more in common with other cast and molded materials—concrete for instance—than it does with its blood relative, wrought iron.

The passive nature of cast iron suggests an alternative image to the more aggressive iron derivatives that are wrought or forged. The cast iron artifact's strength lies in its ability to resist, rather than do. The stationary anvils and dies around which other metal works are formed are usually made of cast iron, as, until very recently, have been the blocks (the unmoving parts) of most automobile engines. These observations square with Bachelard's contention that every material is of a dual nature; for every hammer there is anvil, and every sword must have its shield. Our reveries upon any substance can proceed in one of two possible directions: "deepening" or "elevating." They are either, Bachelard tells us, "reveries of will" or "reveries of repose."[73] Cast iron dreams, those visions that can only be seen through cast iron eyes, tend toward resistant, defensive postures; the absurdity—the oneiric *inauthenticity*—of imitating wrought iron shapes in cast iron is further underscored.

The ambiguous duality that is the nature of all materials is, of course, a mirror of our own double nature. We, too, are torn between the desires for freedom and rootedness. We must be cautious not to interpret the substantial dreams of the material imagination as reductive rules, just as our own vacillating preferences for dynamic lightness or the weight of repose can never lead us to a definitive state. To access the universe of iron, a smith must be true to his or her own nature, in addition to that of the material. For an imagination as dedicated to freedom as Chillida's, even an anvil will begin to float away on dreams of lightness. This is demonstrated in a series of works Chillida executed under the title *Yunque de sueños* (Anvil of Dreams). In the words of Octavio Paz, describing one of these pieces, "The anvil acquires the properties of the dream and . . . denies itself, is transformed into its opposite, and so becomes again empty space."[74]

There are no unambiguous rules regarding what is true to a material. Even Louis Kahn's infamous conversation with a brick, where the brick expressed its preference to be part of an arch, could have turned out much differently had Kahn consulted a less passive, less constructive, brick. Should Kahn have asked the brick, once prominently featured in George Herriman's comic strip *Krazy Kat*, what it wished to be, he might have been shocked by its reply: "a projectile." Implausible as it might seem, a bonk on the head with Herriman's cartoon brick was often interpreted as a sign of love. In a similar counterintuitive yet convincing manner Chillida made iron anvils dissolve into dreams, and Edgar Allan Poe wrote of waters as heavy and dark as blood; Franz Kafka transformed young Gregor Samsa into an enormous insect, and then slowly petrified him, while Gian Lorenzo Bernini reversed the process, making stone into voluptuous flesh, where Pluto's hand pressed into the yielding substance of Persephone's thigh. All of these are true, if counterintuitive, poetic lies and authentic fictions. They reveal that every substance has within it something quite unlike itself.[75]

Unlimited power, or for that matter any "pure" condition, naturally leads to stasis. Such static conditions are unlikely to excite the always dynamic material imagination. Our robust imaginations demand that even the most powerful being or substance—like the mythical hero Achilles or the monstrous Martians who attacked the earth in H. G. Wells's *The War of the Worlds*—possess a potentially fatal flaw. The presence of this "tragic" flaw immediately sets innumerable narratives in motion. It would take a corrosive imagination like Poe's to give us an authentic image of steel weakness. Had Poe chosen such a literary task, he might have written of steel brought to its knees by something so disgustingly banal as to be beneath our notice, such as the way a number of our urban steel bridges have, in this century, succumbed to decades of acidic pigeon droppings.

Still, it is better left to the exceptional poet or craftsperson to fabricate a substance into an image of its recessive nature. The corruption or inversion of a substance must always remain a poetic counterpoint to its more dominant tendencies. The discovery of a weakness can only be heroic if the flaw has been well-hidden. There is also a difference between a poetic image of a material's weakness and a technique that makes our control of a production process *certain*. Therefore, we must acknowledge again the usual imaginative imbalance between works made of wrought and cast iron. As we have seen, the pouring of molten iron is not without its own excitements. Yet the chances of discovering poetic images of materials are progressively reduced as the manner of their creation subscribes more fully to the logic of technique. Give a bar of iron to any human being on this planet, and eventually he or she will try striking it against other things. This outcome is inevitable, both because of what iron is, and what we are. Our relationship to the material may be ambiguous (will we use it for good or evil? will it add to our freedoms or our burdens? make us heroes or villains?), but is also simple and direct. To conceive the casting process requires a sophistication that only members of a technically proficient society possess. The more we move to the highly, although quickly and less visibly, processed material, the more uncertain our relationship with it becomes. As the products we make and substances we use become evermore predetermined and predictable, so must our dreams of them. No longer guided in our making by primitive myths or divine truths, we will have to fabricate our truths for ourselves, in the authentic constructions of our own imaginations, if we are to dream deeply once again.

These artifacts will be increasingly difficult to produce as our society converts imaginative work to efficient labor, heroic risk into mind-numbing certainty, valorous iron to the predictable element "Fe." At the end of the millennium, we find ourselves members of a society whose hands are asleep. However, I would hold with Bachelard that there remains some life to the great iron "dreams of primitive humanity." The iron of our childish dreams is still the element of power. Produced and used in ways that respect this might, iron inspires us with reveries of glorious deeds. These are not the only proper uses of iron, but they are the most noble, and the most fascinating.

The Weight of Architecture

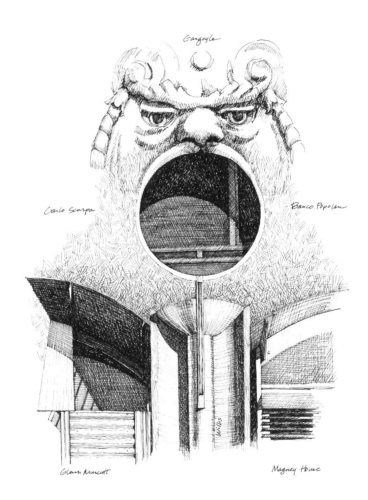

Gargoyle

Carlo Scarpa

Banco Popolare

Glenn Murcutt

Magney House

What then shall we choose? Weight or lightness?. . . That is the question. The only certainty is: the lightness/weight opposition is the most mysterious, most ambiguous of all.

Milan Kundera
The Unbearable Lightness of Being

What is it that gives weight to architecture? The "weight" to which I refer is not only measurable physical mass. Milan Kundera formulated his poetic opposition between lightness and weight in terms of the body's contradictory desires for fulfillment and freedom, and this involved literal weight only indirectly. However, I cannot dismiss the familiar physical dimension to his metaphorical question, for this would empty it of all meaning, and suggest that the noted author chooses his words arbitrarily. Thus, the question I pose must consider the literal weight of bodies and substances, just as Kundera does in his delightful novel.

If you read almost anything that has been published in the past two hundred years on the topic of "design," particularly in the specific subject area called "architectural theory," you would be led to believe that buildings and landscapes and cities weighed nothing at all. It is not that these authors prefer light constructions—neither do they write about fabrics or membranes, tents or temporary structures. Of course, in making these observations I use "weight" in a very literal sense, which is clearly not what Kundera had in mind. His contradictory opposition was intended, in part, to undermine such all-too-facile "plain readings." If we examine architectural treatises with this in mind, what do we find? Amazingly, we find that the question Kundera claims is the most mysterious, most ambiguous of all, has rather easily and definitively been answered! The case is closed, the problem solved. The lightness of freedom has unequivocally been declared superior to the weight of fulfillment.

Before going further with this point, I want to bring up a related phenomenon I have observed in architectural professionals, educators, and, particularly, students. It concerns their (our) attitudes towards technology. What I most often find is a curious combination of the fear of technology's effects (manifested, for example, in a preference for traditional workmanship and "natural" materials, or in political support of various environmental causes) and the fear of knowing too much about the specific technologies upon which the practice of architecture to some degree depends (students despise structures courses, not merely because they are difficult, but out of a principled distrust, while practitioners do not want to be bothered with concerns about construction—"let the engineer figure it out"). Simultaneously this group has a great fascination with the products of technology (with computers, the Internet, and virtual reality, or with building methods that produce "slick," "high-tech," or mechanistic-looking designs) and the faith that all difficulties must eventually succumb to technological solutions. One way to characterize this combination of seemingly contradictory attitudes is to say that we tend to both believe in the limitless possibility of the future, while longing for the simplicity of the past, and at the same time we harbor nagging doubts about each. Obviously these attitudes extend far beyond the disciplinary boundaries of architecture. The contemporary societal struggle between technological positivism and nostalgia appears, at first, to be one way we have chosen to frame the old freedom/fulfillment debate.

I say "at first" because this particular framing is a mirage. It is not a version of the mysterious enigma out of which Kundera spins his novel. Our vacillations between technological positivism and nostalgia are actually manifestations of the identical desire—the desire for what Kundera calls "lightness." As they are played out in architecture, each of these apparently contradictory values produce the identical effect: they withdraw weight from architecture by ignoring the question of materiality. The attitudes observed in architects and students therefore reinforce the opinions found in theoretical writings about architecture. Kundera's supposedly difficult question has been answered without so much as a healthy debate. In order to see how both positivism and nostalgia end up playing on the same side, let us return to Kundera's original question. Noting that modernity has chosen in favor of "splendid lightness," Kundera continues,

> But is heaviness truly deplorable and lightness splendid?
>
> The heaviest of burdens crushes us, we sink beneath it, it pins us to the ground. But in the love poetry of every age, the woman longs to be weighed down by the man's body. The heaviest of burdens is therefore simultaneously an image of life's most intense fulfillment. The heavier the burden, the closer our lives come to the earth, the more real and truthful they become.

> Conversely, the absolute absence of burden causes man to be lighter than air, to soar into the heights, take leave of the earth and his earthly being, and become only half real, his movements as free as they are insignificant.[76]

Notice that Kundera defines lightness as the "absence of burden." Think of it another way: lightness is the refusal to accept, to be weighed down by, limits. You can see that faith in the omnipotence of human reason, which we believe will allow us to "take leave of the earth," falls squarely under this definition. Conversely, everything in Kundera's paragraph on heaviness is some kind of burden, some limit to freedom. In order for a woman to experience the fulfillment of erotic love she must accept the burden of a man. His presence, as her lover, must necessarily constrain her movements: he may want to stick around, get married, or introduce her to his family. In Kundera's novel it is the leading male character, Tomas, who is first identified with the tendency towards lightness-freedom. Tomas, who is married to Tereza, wishes to have it both ways: to enjoy the fulfillment that is marriage, and yet still preserve the freedom to sleep with whomever he wishes. His existence does not become "real and truthful" because he never fully accepts the "burden" of marriage to Tereza.

And so it is with nostalgia. While nostalgia may originate in our wish for an authentic return to a simpler state where burdens are more accepted and freedoms are limited, our modern desire for autonomy is so strong that we cannot accept the limits in order to enjoy the rewards. What we end up with is lightness disguised as heaviness, the wish for freedom from the present dressed in the superficial look of the past. We appropriate those aspects of the past that can most readily be detached from their material circumstances—usually the appearances of things—and discard everything else.

The architectural choice in favor of lightness began in the Western European Renaissance, picked up speed to the point of no return during the Enlightenment, and continued through the nineteenth and twentieth centuries. It owes much to the advancements in science and technology that occurred during this same historical period, for faith in progress and reason, and therefore freedom, would not be possible without them. One of the fundamental postulates of science has been that the universe is basically a mechanism, and therefore follows mechanical laws. Because mechanical laws were most clearly expressed mathematically, by the end of the seventeenth century there was a widespread belief that "the true order of reality was mathematical and that mathematical forms were the most adequate representations of the universe."[77]

There are several aspects of architecture's weight loss that may be directly attributed to these ideas, but for now we need consider only one stream of events. The unquestioned existence of universal scientific laws expressed mathematically instigated a search for similar laws that could be applied to architecture. This had the effect of removing the "essence" of architecture from its material existence and placing it in an abstract, ideal realm where theory, through its uncovering of universal laws, could dictate proper practice. The aspect of architecture that could most easily be represented mathematically was the shape of buildings. Mistaking their own preference in method for a basic truth, Enlightenment theorists could then reductively claim that the composition of building shapes, or visual "form," was *the* fundamental quality of architecture. The weight of tradition, materiality, regional characteristics, local craft, etc. was abandoned in favor of a set of universal abstract principles.[78]

As would be expected, outbreaks of nostalgia simultaneously occurred with this "progress." These were expressed in the neoclassicism that dominated much of this period, in the various historical revivals of the nineteenth century, the Arts and Crafts movement of the early twentieth, in the search for origins (such as the primitive hut), and in our more recent interest in vernacular architecture. None of these historical trends was a monolith. There were always pockets of resistance and individuals that fought the prevailing current. There have also been many architects who vacillated between acceptance and resistance. The polemic writings of Le Corbusier, with their advocacy of elementary geometric forms, a mechanical conceptualization of architecture, and utopian urban visions, enthusiastically promote the positivism of the age, while much of Le Corbusier's mature work could just as readily serve as a critique of the same principles his writings espouse. The dominant ideology of architectural modernism could only with great difficulty account for works such as Le Corbusier's Chapel of Notre-Dame du Haut at Ronchamp and La Tourette monastery. The decisive victory in favor of the idealization of architecture has never quelled our doubts that something valuable may have been lost or overlooked.

I should mention that the physical effects of this victory, speaking once again of the literal loss of weight measured in units of mass, have not been nearly so pronounced as the effects on how we *think* about architecture. It is true that curtain walls and steel frames have largely replaced heavy masonry bearing walls, and that we no longer build castles and fortifications. Buildings today are physically lighter than they have been at most other times in human history, but there have been and still exist cultures that traditionally produce constructions far lighter than we "moderns," and yet these somehow maintain their imaginative weight, their substance.[79] Architecture's loss of physical mass is only a symptom of a far more significant shift in attitude. Neither physical lightness nor impermanence need be an absolute impediment to the production of the kind of weight Kundera describes.

Early in his novel, Kundera introduces the debate between lightness and heaviness in the myth of the eternal return. This is the belief that time is cyclical and each second of existence repeats itself eternally; it is the idea, he tells us, that Friedrich Nietzsche thought to be the heaviest of burdens. If a mere idea can possess such weight, then the relationship between imaginative weight and physical mass, while not arbitrary, does not conform to the sort of mechanistic causal relationships with which we moderns are most comfortable. Kundera sees a relationship between burdens, which can be other people, our mortal bodies, or even ideas, and significance—that is, meaning.[80] His novel presents a question that he never finally answers: does the meaning in our lives originate more in the realm of what we cannot do than in the realm of our greatest freedoms? This is the question, in slightly modified form, that I wish to pose to architecture. Rather than retrace the path of Kundera's example, either once or eternally, I shall now explore a few mythical examples of my own, in the hope that I may find in them additional insights into this vexing question of architecture's weight.

◇   ◇   ◇

When the great is excessive, the ridgepole bends.

I Ching, Hexagram 28
"Excess of the Great"

It is probable that some vestige of both of the contradictory desires I have been calling "lightness" and "heaviness"—the desire for separation or autonomy, versus the desire for association or immersion—have always been a part of human nature. Long before René Descartes proposed that thinking (or logical doubt) was the fundamental essence of being— thereby reducing growing, aging, loving, making, and playing to secondary status—human beings dreamed of escaping from the "prison" of the mortal human body. This wish is explicitly addressed in the dialogs of Plato, and it is dealt with extensively by Christian theologians and philosophers. Early in human history similar desires were expressed in an embodied manner: through architecture (in the dream of the Tower of Babel, a construction so tall that it would give humans access to heaven) or through the fantasy of human flight (as in the fable of Daedalus and Icarus, who flew with miraculous wings designed by Daedalus, the prototypical architect-inventor). Escape *from* the body was, at this time, either inconceivable or too unbelievable to be seriously entertained. Escape from earthly squalor or persecution meant escape *with* the body. Even the belief in reincarnation involved abandoning a particular body to resume existence in a new one.

In religious teachings, and in ancient mythology, the dream of escape is always entertained at great risk. By succumbing to the temptation of knowledge, Adam and Eve were cast out of paradise. Prometheus, who rescued humanity from the fate of darkness and ignorance, was chained to a rock, where he was daily tortured. In all of these tales, any form of escapism is cautioned against in the harshest possible terms. Icarus fell victim to youthful exuberance and excessive pride. He refused to accept limits to his behavior, even the prudent instructions of Daedalus not to fly too close to the sun. In the Biblical story of the Tower of Babel, God observed another instance of humans' arrogance in their refusal to accept limits. If the tower had been completed, humans would have ascended to equal footing with God, and "nothing [would] be restrained from them." God's sabotage of the Tower of Babel proceeded in an ingenious way:

> Go to, let us go down, and there confound their language, that they may not understand one another's speech.

> So the Lord scattered them abroad from thence upon the face of the earth: and they left off to build the city.
>
> Therefore is the name of it called Babel; because the Lord did there confound the language of all the earth: and from thence did the Lord scatter them abroad upon the face of the earth.[81]

The fact that the builders' inability to communicate ended the project underlines the necessary social aspect of all large-scale construction—a subject worthy of close consideration in its own right.[82] More important for now, however, is the possible interpretation that not only the tower but the language of humanity had become too advanced for God to tolerate. From the Biblical account, we might infer that the tower, as an architectural expression of hubris, was a natural outgrowth of the condition whereby a people spoke with a single language: "the people is one, and they have all one language; and this they begin to do."[83] Does this suggest that there is a connection between the total dedication to the dream of transcending all human limits and a particular form of speech? Could it be that the existence of a single language, of a universal means of representation and its attendant modes of thought, is still a useful indicator that significant human limits are about to be exceeded? If we imagine what the single language of the tower's builders might have tended towards, given that it would have to serve as the vehicle for the efficient organization of humanity's most massive collective project, is it reasonable to suspect it would have developed in the direction of the system of universal signs we know as mathematics? For, to move in the direction of absolute universality, it would have to abandon all regional dialects and all vernacular patterns, along with all potential ambiguities and traces of subjectivity. It would have to seek to be a language not bound to a particular point of view—a language appropriate to the God's-eye view of the universe, which the builders assumed the completed tower would grant them.

However, given that the tower fell short of its mark, both the view from its uppermost incomplete portion and the increasingly abstract language that the builders would use to describe it were paradoxically condemned to a single limited perspective. Intoxicated as they were with the power of this "commanding view," the builders remained unaware of what it concealed. The price for the universality of their language would be that "such a system would express only a small part of what can be thought, it would serve only to designate such concepts as are formed by purely rational construction."[84] Such a system of conceptual thought, lacking, as it must, any recognition of a distinction between the sacred and profane, might naturally spur its users to ever more audacious actions aimed at overcoming limits, including the invasion of the forbidden territory of heaven. Perhaps the greatest affront to God was not the tower itself, but the fact that humanity had become too single-minded—that the human race had abandoned its promise of richness and diversity to pursue godlike power while still in its infancy.

This interpretation, whether or not any Biblical scholar would endorse it, allows us to see God's method of thwarting the tower's construction as more than merely a clever method of demolition. The confounding of the one language into many allowed the human race to start anew, reconstituting itself so that the widest range of things that could be thought might once again be realized. Had He merely destroyed the tower, this additional aim would not have been achieved. Yes, the single language must be judged a greater sin than the physical building because it did finally presuppose the possibility of completely abandoning the body. When those men and women that God scattered across the earth should encounter one another and seek to communicate, is it not likely that they would resort to gestures and pantomime, where meanings were acted out through movements of their bodies? Perhaps one moral of the Tower of Babel tale is that the excesses of the human desire to escape material circumstance must be periodically corrected through a return to a more immediate appreciation of the body. Or, to put it another way, the ideal and the universal must always be infused with some measure of the real and the particular.

One goal of this essay is to engender a renewed appreciation for the architectural body as a necessary condition of weight. I will argue both that architecture has fallen victim to a universal attitude toward signification, and that the way to correct this is to revive those qualities that define what is real and particular about the architectural body: its corporeality/materiality, processes of building, maintenance, decay, and renewal, as well its unavoidable conditions of imperfection and mortality. Simply put, buildings must be made by fallible human beings, of imperfect materials, and they do not last forever. Far from being irrelevant, these "burdens" are architecture's richest source of significance. To make these arguments, I will refer to qualities of language, including figures of speech, word etymologies, and word relationships. This is not to reprise the worn-out metaphor "architecture is a language," but to conscript to my cause those aspects of language and myth that are illustrative for architecture.

The architecture-language connection has been frequently abused by those who wish to deflect attention from the corporeal aspects of architecture. For example, the practice of referring to anything meaningful as a "text"—so that a novel, a symphony, a building, and the instructions for operating a household appliance are made in this sense equivalent constructions—while it may produce useful insights, is finally unacceptably reductive. I am not thinking here of the various hermeneutic approaches to the interpretation of works of art, but to formulations that proceed, in typical Enlightenment fashion, to use their own methodological choices in self-justifying ways. To equate anything meaningful with a text is a reasonable enterprise; to then disregard all aspects of the phenomena you are studying that confound the equation is not. Structuralism and deconstruction, in the bastardized forms they have taken on when reshaped as the bases for architectural theories, betray their common Enlightenment ancestry by their disinterest for the material aspects of architecture. Their emphasis on the immaterial and immutable aspects of written texts obscures the value of architectural processes, leaving the inherently unfinished nature of all material constructions unaddressed. In order to mask this poverty, the advocates of such theories frequently attribute to visual form powers that it simply does not possess.[85]

Architecture is not so much like a language as it is like the poetic use of a language. (At least since the Renaissance, this poetry is *not* written by the architect. The architect is commissioned to tell someone else how to write it—a situation that obviously has a profound effect on the end result.) The poetic use of a language requires that attention be paid to sounds, to accidental similarities of words, to the rhythms and cadences of speech. Poetry, in other words, makes use of the materiality of language. It is language in its least abstract, least convention-bound form, language that proceeds in the opposite direction from the universal aim of mathematics.[86] This is not to say that poetry may not be used to express very abstract ideas, or that it does not utilize abstractions. Poetry expresses the universal through the most particular means, through the medium of a specific language. It forces the abstract to appear indirectly, to construct itself out of the "stuff" of language; it confounds the reduction of language to a communication code by burdening phrases with multiple meanings. No separate content can be extracted from a poem without doing harm to its meaning. Sometimes poetic meaning even moves in a direction that is at odds with the factual understanding of what a poem explicitly "says." This is why poetry is virtually untranslatable. Should the translator strive to reproduce the meaning of the poem, or its patterns of sounds? Obviously, the most successful poetic translations, which are original poetic creations in their own right, must adequately recreate both aspects.

Poetry and myth possess the ability to maintain contradictory opposites in a single image. This is not the same thing as reconciling two opposing forces, or seeking a compromise. Neither does it follow the preferred schema of Enlightenment thought, which is to pair ideas "in opposition to each other," so that later "a higher order of ideas can be formed out of the synthesis of such pairs."[87] This higher-order third idea contains the original pair only in a vague or reductive sense. Poetry and myth operate differently, joining ideas in an unstable but secure union that may actually make their differences more, not less, apparent. There are innumerable mythical beings that embody contradictory natures or forces, combining them while never obscuring their essential opposition. Many of these are monsters; others are gods or demigods. The mythical figure of Janus, the Roman deity with two identical faces, each looking in opposite directions, is perhaps the most useful such image for architecture. Janus was the god and guardian of all gates and doors by virtue of his ability to see both inside and out simultaneously. Hermes/Mercury embodied other contradictions. He was a charming thief and a shrewd negotiator. Manifestly unreliable, he was paradoxically the trusted messenger of the gods. Assuming that the reader accepts these examples as proof of the possibility of productive opposition-contamination, I can offer a tentative answer to my question regarding the weight of architecture: architecture, at the present time, would do itself great service by becoming both more real ("heavy") and more imaginative ("light").

◇   ◇   ◇

Great power is beneficial when correct.

I Ching, Hexagram 34
"Great Power"

Architecture itself will see no contradiction in striving at once for the real and the imaginary, as we can see in all the instances of architecture that we have historically admired. These structures have possessed without exception both qualities. It is primarily Enlightenment-based theories of architecture, with their single-minded proclivity toward abstraction, that have created the supposed conflict between the real and the imaginary. In addressing this point, Marco Frascari cites the ideas of the anti-Enlightenment philosopher Giambattista Vico.

> In his questioning of the aridity of the "rationality" of Cartesian thinking, Vico sets a contrast between intelligible universals *(universali intellegibili)* and imaginative universals *(universali fantastici)*. The search for intelligible universals is described by the Neapolitan philosopher as the product of a rational, but soporific mind (the French: *esprit*), whereas the search for imaginative universals is seen as an outcome of a productive poetic mind (the Italian: *ingegno*). The present "official" research in architecture is a result of the search for intelligible universals, based on a research agenda monopolized by a trivial theory of abstraction. This is a theory that is able to produce an understanding of architecture through a system of generalized notions; it creates catalogs, codes, guidelines, or normative prescriptions. These are anthological data, which contribute to making buildings safe and durable, but do not prevent a production of trivial designs.[88]

Intelligible universals are necessarily reductive; their reliance on distinct objective "concepts" must require that they express only the purely rational, only a "small part of what can be thought." Imaginative universals, characteristic of mythic and poetic thought, deal in images, such as the figure of Janus, that are synthetic and constituent. "Image" in this sense does not respect our contemporary practice of reducing the meaning of the term to "visual appearance," a quality detached from the materiality of things. Rather, the poetic image is a "sudden salience"[89] of the psyche, an ecstatic condition of mental reverberation, that produces imaginative weight and depth. The reductive modern connotation to the word "image" is mirrored in the naive contemporary prejudice that *anything* can be adequately represented in abstract conceptual form. It is obvious, if any thought is given to the matter, that this is not so. Instead, we soon realize that, particularly in the area of lived experiences, conceptualization kills all emotion and urgency. A purely conceptual language is a language eternally doomed to the passive voice—nothing happens, and no one is responsible. Thus, we may certainly fear death, but no one fears the concept of death; we may dread the prospects of unemployment, but only economists care about the concept of unemployment.

Architecture that restricts itself to the purely conceptual is architecture devoid of life. A wholly conceptual architecture would be as static as a wholly conceptual language. This is why the advocates of an architecture of pure form often rely on what architectural theorist Robin Evans referred to as a kind of "ventriloquism." In order to imbue static creations with the illusion of life, they use verbs in their adjectival form—"'punctured volume,' 'compressed planes,' . . . 'interpenetrating spaces.'" "Always," Evans writes, "it is words that help us believe that static things move." In reviewing an exhibit of the work of Peter Eisenman, Evans commented:

> The pulling of one cube through another is typical of a host of morpho-logical fictions that have grown up around contemporary architecture, not least through the influence of Eisenman himself. Integrated in the language of criticism, they are, for this very reason, in constant danger of becoming explanations rather than perceptions; of becoming justifications of the thing with which you happen to end up rather than properties engendered by the imagination confronted with the thing with which you happen to end up.[90]

The danger in this is not that "morphological fictions" have no place in architecture. It is that this one particular mode of imagination, relying as it does on intelligible concepts that may express only a small fraction of what can be thought, comes to be accepted as the only type of creative activity open to the architect. The counterpart to the late-twentieth-century avant garde's pretensions to movement is, of course, the neoclassical tendency to extol timelessness. In order for pure forms to move (without their creators pulling the strings) or a material building to be timeless, "actual physical properties—spatial, material, temporal—have to be mentally dissolved," as Evans might say, and "the imagination has to work in a region outside the recognized limits of the world we occupy."[91] But is it not true that, by so willfully taking leave of the earth and the earthly being of architecture, these illusory movements, these flights from the terror of death, these freedoms lose their significance?

Architectural designs may proceed from a premise, an interest in developing certain themes, or in a preference for particular motifs. Seldom do any of these points of beginning actually rise to levels of clarity necessary to justify calling them "concepts." Nor, I would argue, should they. A too rigid adherence to a design concept that is by nature immutable prevents the architect from being open to other inspirations as they come, from remaining flexible, agile, light on her feet. The preoccupation with fixed conceptual categories, which has led to the mistaken assumption that "timelessness" is something for which architecture should strive, is called into question by Vico's philosophy. Similarly, the Taoist system of wisdom, contained in the *I Ching* (Book of Changes), suggests that dynamism, not fixity, is the fundamental character of life. In the book *Understanding the I Ching*, the authors note, "It is only abstract thinking that takes [things] out of their dynamic continuity and isolates them as static units." To the Chinese

the opposite of change is neither rest nor standstill, for these are aspects of change. The idea that the opposite of change is regression, and not cessation of movement, brings out clearly the contrast with our category of time. The opposite of change in Chinese thought is growth of what ought to decrease, the downfall of what ought to rule. Change then, is not simply movement as such, for its opposite is also movement. *The state of absolute immobility is such an abstraction that the Chinese, or at least the Chinese of the period which produced this book, could not conceive it.* Change is natural movement rather, development that can only reverse itself by going against nature.[92]

While there are some parallels between this worldview and Heraclitus's belief in the flux of all things, the *I Ching* is founded on a uniquely vegetative view of time, which sees human wisdom as growing at the slow and contented pace of plantlife. It is instructive to note that even the authors of the quotation I have used, full of appreciation for the distinctive nature of the system of thought they are studying, slip into their old Western habits by calling the lecture from which this passage was taken "The Concept of Change."

Such alternative modes of thought are useful for calling into question our overdependence on abstract conceptualization. But by using these examples I do not mean to suggest that we must look far outside of Enlightenment practices to recognize their self-contradictory nature. Initially, many of the very scientists and philosophers who helped erect this system also sensed its necessary limits, as well as the irrational desires from which it sprang. For example, Galileo wrote,

> As for those who so exalt incorruptibility, inalterability, I believe they are
> brought to say these things through their great desire to live a long time and
> through the terror they have of death. And not considering that, if men were
> immortal, these men would not have had the opportunity to come into the
> world. . . . And there is not the slightest doubt that the Earth is far more
> perfect, being, as it is, alterable, changeable, than if it were a mass of stone,
> even if it were a whole diamond, hard and impenetrable.[93]

And what of the "rational and soporific mind" that becomes too inflexible
in its imaginings, succumbing out of habit, as Vico had predicted, to the
"barbarism of the intellect?" In his autobiography, Charles Darwin
reflected upon the gradual impoverishment of his ability to imagine.

> Now for many years I cannot endure to read a line of poetry: I have tried
> lately to read Shakespeare, and found it so intolerably dull that it nauseated
> me. I have also lost almost any taste for pictures or music.—Music generally
> sets me thinking too energetically on what I have been at work on, instead
> of giving me pleasure. I retain some taste for fine scenery, but it does not
> cause me the exquisite delight which it formerly did. . . . My mind seems to
> have become a kind of machine for grinding general laws out of large
> collections of facts, but why this should have caused the atrophy of that part
> of the brain alone, on which the higher tastes depend, I cannot conceive. . . .
> The loss of these tastes is a loss of happiness, and may possibly be injurious
> to the intellect, and more probably to the moral character, by enfeebling the
> emotional part of our nature.[94]

It says something about the audience that presently exists for architecture that many supposedly educated men and women regularly leave our
universities as similar fact-grinding machines. Echoing Darwin's
worries, the French philosopher Gaston Bachelard observed, "a person
deprived of the *function of the unreal* is just as neurotic as the person
deprived of the *reality function*." Bachelard went on to counsel, "We must
find, then, a regular filiation between the real and the imaginary."[95]
Bachelard (whose "subversive humanist" philosophy may, I suspect,
eventually prove as significant an anti-Enlightenment force as Vico's
"new science") devoted much of his life to illuminating the circumstances for this "regular filiation." Seeing, as Galileo did, a kind of
perfection in the changeable, Bachelard argued for a renewed dynamic
awareness. "Consciousness," he claimed "is in itself an act. It is a lively,
full act. Even if the action which follows, which ought to have followed or
should have followed, remains in suspense, the consciousness-as-act is

still completely positive or kinetic."[96] Why then, does the static concept predominate, even in psychological studies of the imagination? Bachelard explains,

> A psychology of the imagination that is concerned only with the *structure of images* ignores an essential and obvious characteristic that everyone recognizes: the *mobility of images*. Structure and mobility are opposites—in the realm of imagination as in so many others. It is easier to describe forms than motion, which is why psychology has begun with forms. Motion, however, is the more important. In a truly complete psychology, imagination is primarily a kind of spiritual mobility of the greatest, liveliest, and most exhilarating kind. To study a particular image, then, we must also investigate its mobility, productivity, and life.[97]

The observation that it is easier to describe—that is, conceptualize—forms than motions recalls Frank Lloyd Wright's statement that formal composition in architecture, although "dead" since the Renaissance, still wore "the look of life"; "as method" it is taught only "because it is something that can be taught." Foreshadowing Frascari's assertion that conceptual rules stemming from the search for intelligible universals cannot prevent trivial designs, Wright wrote, "Composition is a tidy means to makeshift but is no true means to a great end."[98]

These thoughts return us to the present state of theoretical research in architecture, monopolized as it is by "trivial theories of abstraction." In order to respond to the hegemony of the dominant theoretical current, I have produced the preceding polemic against abstraction. However, I am neither unilaterally advocating heaviness as an antidote to the dominance of conceptual lightness, nor by referencing myths am I advocating mysticism or irrationality. This would be to fall victim of single-mindedness in the opposite direction, and it would produce a too simplistic response to the question Kundera correctly identifies as the most ambiguous of all.

◇   ◇   ◇

Contention: There is a blockage of the truth. Caution and moderation lead to good results, finality leads to bad results. It is beneficial to see a great person, not beneficial to cross a great river.

I Ching, Hexagram 6
"Contention"

Immanuel Kant is well-known as a philosopher who struggled with questions of weight. In *The Critique of Pure Reason* he strove to reconcile the existence of the empirically real with the transcendentally ideal. However, it is a story of Kant's life rather than his philosophy that is most relevant to my discussion of heaviness. The celebrated art historian Erwin Panofsky begins his book *Meaning in the Visual Arts* with a recount of a visit to the great philosopher.

> Nine days before his death . . . Kant was visited by his physician. Old, ill, and nearly blind, he rose from his chair and stood trembling with weakness and muttering unintelligible words. Finally his faithful companion realized that he would not sit down again until the visitor had taken a seat. This he did, and Kant then permitted himself to be helped to his chair and, after having regained some of his strength, said "Das Gefühl für Humanität hat mich noch nicht verlassen"—"The sense of humanity has not yet left me."[99]

As Panofsky interprets the event, he sees "a man's proud and tragic consciousness of self-approved and self-imposed principles, contrasting with his utter subjection to illness, decay, and all that is implied in the word 'mortality.'" I am fascinated by the image of a decrepit old man struggling to stand in honor of a guest who Kant must have realized, even then, would be judged by history to be his inferior. In light of the way I have framed the present essay, it is fitting that Kant's proud struggle is most immediately a battle with gravity. His effort to overcome the weight of his own feeble body is less impetuous, less arrogant, than the effort that was expended to defeat gravity in the Tower of Babel, and is therefore all the more tragic. His gesture to rise was an expression of proud autonomy but also a gesture to connect with a fellow man. Thus, his action simultaneously demonstrates a desire for lightness and heaviness. Panofsky tells us that both Kant and his visitor were moved to tears by the poignant combination of Kant's words and deed. How does a simple act of politeness, no matter what difficulties it involves, attain such significance?

It is possible to define all sources of meaning as language, as Walter Benjamin prefers to do when he writes, "all communication of mental meanings is language, communication in words being only a particular case."[100] However, this definition tells us nothing of the relationship between an old man's struggle to stand and the words he weakly utters; neither does it tell us much of the varying qualities that would have distinguished human communication before and after Babel. To arrive at some understanding of these things (as they pertain to the meaning of works of architecture, certainly not as the basis for a comprehensive theory of language) let us first look at the movements of Kant's frail body. We could understand his having risen in the presence of a guest as an effort dictated by his willing adherence to conventional social rules of politeness. Kant may have consciously self-approved these rules, but he could not by himself have constructed the social convention of rising until a guest has taken his seat. This practice is undoubtedly a convention of polite behavior in European society, but this does not tell us why it is meaningful. For this we must look to the aspects of the convention that are not arbitrarily based on social agreement alone— those aspects that originate in the material circumstances of the body.

In his article "The Sitting Position—A Question of Method," Joseph Rykwert tells us "everybody's first action is to get up."[101] Rykwert recounts how this vertical stretching reenacts the circumstances of our birth. To sit is not only to surrender to gravity and fatigue; it is also a return to the "mother," to bring "our lives closer to the earth," both literally and in the sense in which Kundera writes. To sit on the earth is to claim a portion of it ("squatters' rights"). Rykwert notes that it is a common practice for thrones to include a fragment of stone in or below the seat, as a symbol of the land that is "ruled over." To sit while others remain standing is to assume a right and also to maintain closer contact with the earth. For these twin reasons the privilege to sit while others stand is a nearly universal sign of superior authority. In the *I Ching* the father's place is to be seated while the son bows before him. The one who remains sitting is a chief, a king, or a judge who, by virtue of his or her proximity to the ground, maintains control over a portion of the earth. For the seated and honored person to rise and receive a visitor, the privileged position must be voluntarily abandoned, signifying that the two are meeting respectfully as equals. At the same time, rising contains traces of the desire to leave the earth and approach heaven. Kant's simple act of standing up touched off this network of potential interpretations, and thus differentiates his actions from those of the misguided builders at Babel. His movement is ambiguous; it is one thing but it says something else. In denying his superiority he affirms it, through a demonstration of heroic weakness. The term for such instances of the simultaneous existence of multiple meanings is "polysemy."

We can see now that physical movements, contrary to any assumptions that they must always and only be literal in what they "say," are capable of sophisticated multiple meanings, such as we find in poetry. Kant's showing-by-refusing-to-show and being-by-not-being represent schemas that are actually typical of the polysemous gesture. According to Ernst Cassirer, an expressive movement such as Kant's,

> instead of proceeding directly towards its object, instead of satisfying itself and losing itself in the object, encounters a kind of inhibition and reversal, in which a new *consciousness* of this same drive is born. In this sense the reaction contained in the expressive movement prepares the way for a higher stage of action. In withdrawing, as it were, from the immediate form of activity, action gains a new scope and a new freedom; it is already in transition from the merely "pragmatic" to the "theoretical," from physical to ideal activity.[102]

Maurice Merleau-Ponty referred to this same reversal, where an otherwise utilitarian bodily movement deviates from its preordained direction, as a "sort of *leakage*" that reveals "the genius for ambiguity which might serve to define man."[103] That a language based on physical need not be condemned only to literal meanings suggests that the gestural "speech" used in the chance encounters of the scattered citizens of Babel need not have been vulgar or vague. It also indicates that while the physicality of the architectural "body" may circumscribe its expressiveness, it in no way reduces it. (This unfounded fear is what I suspect energizes many advocates of a purely formal "language" of architecture.)

In *Six Memos for the Next Millennium* Italo Calvino wrote of this value of the indirect path to meaning. In retelling the myth of Perseus and Medusa, Calvino noted that the hero slays the monster by observing her in the reflection upon his shield, and then continues to carry her severed head concealed in a sack with him. Calvino attributes Perseus's battle successes to his refusal "to look directly, but not in a refusal of the reality in which he is fated to live; he carries the reality with him and accepts it as his particular burden."[104] This passage appears in Calvino's book of under the theme "lightness." At the point in his discussion where the story of Perseus appears, Calvino is most interested in evading the weight that comes from the too literal interpretation of language. Just as physical lightness need not preclude an imaginative weight in architecture, the physicality of bodies should not impede an imaginary lightness.

In reading Calvino's tribute to literary lightness, I am struck by a sense of ever-deepening mystery. For I notice that Calvino has pulled a clever inversion. What he is calling "lightness" at this point in his essay has nothing to do with abandoning the body! To the contrary, he reserves his greatest enthusiasm for a tale where the poet Guido Calvalcanti escapes a group of tormentors who believe they have him cornered in a cemetery by nimbly leaping over a tomb.

> Were I to choose an auspicious image for the new millennium, I would
> choose that one: the sudden agile leap of the poet-philosopher who raises
> himself above the weight of the world, showing that with all his gravity he
> has the secret of lightness, and that what many consider to be the vitality of
> the times—noisy, aggressive, revving, and roaring—belongs to the realm of
> death, like a cemetery for rusty old cars.[105]

What is intriguing is that where Kundera sees the denial of limits as leading to an existence "only half real" and therefore "light," Calvino sees in the same situations an ironic lack of freedom where single-mindedness itself becomes a burden. In the true spirit of poetic lightness Calvino cannot accept fixity of any kind. Whenever a mode of thought becomes oppressive he must leap away to another plane of imagination. We see this in his most popular book (among architects), *Invisible Cities*, where the single and simple-minded abstractions of Kublai Kahn are continually inverted by Marco Polo's more subtle logic, and rendered banal by the irreducibly radiant images of the cities themselves.[106] Calvino refuses to commit to a single way of thinking. His only commitment is to his own light-hearted and quick-witted imagination.

For Calvino any purported reality, any self-serious claim of fixity, must be treated merely as a jumping-off point for the nimble poetic mind. He is fascinated that "crushing images" of "iron machines" now follow the commands of "weightless bits" of computer software.[107] He is amused to know that science postulates that the entire universe is made of the same empty atoms, because this means even the heaviest things are made of the nearly weightless, and that everything could potentially transform into anything else. In everything Calvino sees its opposite, and nothing is ever simply what it appears to be. It is no surprise then, that he begins his essay on lightness by acknowledging that he does not find "the virtues of weight any less compelling, but simply that I have more to say about lightness."[108] Calvino sees ambiguity as the remedy for all single-mindedness, whether heavy or light.[109] All of his favored literary themes are freedoms wrested from the weight of language by the creative use of polysemy. It is only this possibility of language that allows him to champion both "exactitude" and "multiplicity," as he does in the later chapters of *Six Memos*.

As you will recall, Merleau-Ponty thought to define "man" by his "genius for ambiguity." He, like Calvino, found something petrifying in a purely conventional mode of expression.

> If there is such a thing as universal thought, it is achieved by taking up the effort towards expression and communication in *one* single language, and accepting all its ambiguities, all the suggestions and overtones of meaning of which a linguistic tradition is made up, and which are the exact measure of its power of expression. A conventional algorithm—which moreover is meaningful only in relation to language—will never express anything but nature without man. Strictly speaking, therefore, there are no conventional signs, standing as the simple notation of a thought pure and clear in itself, there are only words into which the history of a whole language is compressed, and which affect communication with no absolute guarantee, dogged as they are by incredible linguistic hazards.[110]

Merleau-Ponty argues here that there are no purely conventional languages and, later, that there are no strictly natural signs. Either extreme, he seems to think, will produce the condition Calvino fears most—words and phrases will be turned to stone. But words are not stone. I could offer no better proof than to admit that I began this essay intending to argue in favor of weight and now Calvino has convinced me that I prefer lightness, *and yet I really have not changed my point of view*. Such is the nature, the linguistic hazard, of language. Yet what if words had to be stone, literally stone—not made of sounds or letters but rock, steel, concrete paths, or planting beds? How would architects coax language out of these things? How would they teach stones to talk?

❖   ❖   ❖

It is difficult to undo our own damage, and to recall to our presence that which we have asked to leave. It is hard to desecrate a grove and change your mind. The very holy mountains are keeping mum. We doused the burning bush and cannot rekindle it; we are lighting matches in vain under every green tree. Did the wind used to cry, and the hills shout forth praise? Now speech has perished from among the lifeless things on earth, and living things say very little to very few.

Annie Dillard

Teaching A Stone to Talk

When we left Kant, wheezing in his chair, I was beginning to explain the apparent meaningfulness of his words and actions. I intended to move from this to a hypothesis of how architecture may be meaningful. In so doing I want to preserve a prominent place for the physical aspects of architecture and bodies, and at the same time I do not wish to limit what architecture can "say" to the merely literal. As absurd as it may seem to use a great philosopher primarily for his body, the story of Kant that Panofsky describes presents an unusually vivid store of gestures and situations that are analogously architectural. We have already seen some of the possible interpretations that may be applied to the act of rising from a seated position. To these I could add the associations between an aged body and the architectural condition of ruin. Or, as Joseph Rykwert has done in his book *The Dancing Column*,[111] I could compare the human capacity to stand erect with the verticality and corporeality of the column; I could then proceed to discuss what Bachelard called the "ascensional psyche" of a tower or skyscraper. Any of these associations would tell us that it is necessary to look deeper into the modes of thinking and imagining that allow us to interpret bodily positions and movements.

In *The Philosophy of Symbolic Forms*, Ernst Cassirer notes that psychological studies of sign language usually discriminate between gestures of imitation and those of indication. Imitative gestures reproduce through bodily movements some aspect of a thing—the fluttering of a bird's wings in flight or the rolling motion of ocean waves—so that this reenacted motion serves as the "word" for the thing. Indicative gestures involve some manner of pointing to things. In humans the first appearance of indicative gestures is traced back to a child's "clutching at a distance," to the effort to grasp objects that are out of reach. This otherwise futile grasping is soon recognized by the human child, as it is by no other species, as an intelligible (to itself and others) sign.

> [Grasping-pointing] is one of the first steps by which the perceiving and
> desiring I removes a perceived and desired content from himself and so
> forms it into an "object," and an "objective" content.... All progress in
> conceptual knowledge and pure "theory" consists precisely in surpassing
> this first sensory immediacy. The object of knowledge recedes more and
> more into the distance, so that for knowledge critically reflecting upon itself,
> it comes to appear as an "infinitely remote point," an endless task; and yet,
> in this apparent distance, it achieves its ideal specification. In the logical
> concept, in judgment and inference develops that mediate grasp which
> characterizes "reason." Thus both genetically and actually, there seems to be
> a continuous transition from physical to conceptual grasping.[112]

The trajectory of this development, the progression from merely doing to
indicating, from the concrete situation to the abstract awareness of all
that is beyond that situation, immediately suggests two possible
interpretations. One, in concert with the dominant philosophical outlook
of the Enlightenment, would be to take this as evidence that reason
obtains its freedom and power by leaving the concrete, as well as
imitation, further and further behind. The other, typical of philosophical
thought suspicious of abstract conceptualization, finds in the indicative
gesture the seed that will finally lead to the domination of the intelligible
universal. Vico scholar Donald Verene describes pointing and imitating
as the beginnings of the "two polar activities of mind." Following from
Vico's speculation that the first primitive peoples interpreted thunder as
the voice of Jove, he writes that "Jove can be apprehended as nature,
pointed at and affixed in the sky," while he can also be "imitated in a
ritual of fearful shaking." This duality of mind cannot be unified. "Jove is
not an internal principle of unity for mind because his appearance always
has two aspects." According to Verene, "He is not one sign any more
than pointing is imitating."[113] Here again we might consider the image of
Janus, embodying this doubling of the mind.

Vico proposed, Verene tells us, that we associate the "poetic arts"
(including logic, morals, economics, and politics) with the tendency to
imitate, and the natural or "poetic sciences" (physics, cosmography,
astronomy, chronology, and geography) with the tendency to indicate.
The first make use of our faculty for creating images, the second our
ability to form concepts. While the latter serve to structure human
knowledge, they never become fully intelligible because their objects of
study are not made by us—they cannot be known according to Vico's

verum ipsum factum principle. If we proceed along these lines it seems that we will either be forced to place architecture on the side of imitating or face the possibility that we are denied access to architecture's truths. However, I am not certain that architecture need make such an irrevocable choice. I wonder what occurs at the intersection of the two faces of Janus. Does the joint dividing the two polar activities of mind form an absolute barrier? Cassirer seemed to think it did not; that "neither 'imitation' nor 'indication'—neither the 'mimetic' nor the 'deitic' function—represents a simple uniform operation of consciousness, but that elements of diverse origin and significance are intermingled in both of them."[114] Even if "intermingled" is not quite the right word, there is still the possibility of a specular reversal in the Janusian gaze, or the agile leap from one pole to the other. And might not "grasping at a distance" be considered exactly the place where pointing is still imitating?

If we return to that spot, the place where pointing and imitating begin to diverge, could this be the joint between the minds of Janus? As with the earlier discussion of the Janus image, this need not suggest a compromise that would unite the duality Verene claims cannot be unified. A joint is a boundary condition that paradoxically unifies and divides at once. In architecture we call this sort of thing a "detail." Instead of pointing, which is always "the same gesture repeated on different objects,"[115] might this not allow for an infinite number of ways to point? Cassirer mentions the connection existing in many languages between the "terms for speaking and saying and those for showing and indicating."[116] We usually think of showing as simple indicating: "there is your room." But there is another form of showing that is demonstrative, as when a father shows to his son how to cast a fishing lure. In a sense the father is imitating himself. He is pointing out the correct method, not by simply casting, but by imitating someone properly casting, often by slowing down or exaggerating a particular aspect of the motion. He makes what would be invisible in a normal cast visible by pointing through imitating. From this we might say that a language based solely on convention would always point the same way, while a language that included traces of imitation could allow both saying and showing. Representation becomes re-presentation.

When Kant struggled to his feet to honor his guest, he may have first begun this motion out of habit. As he began his slow and shaky ascent, he must have realized that there was no longer any reason for either he or his guest to expect that he would conform to a convention intended to negate the privilege of the seated. When the seated person was near death the illusion of privilege was naturally dissolved. Any chance of the guest envying his "position" was out of the question. By rising anyway, Kant was imitating the movements appropriate to a younger man from whom politely standing up would have been expected. Kant was attempting to re-present himself as he once was. By adhering to a convention that the circumstances should have emptied of meaning, Kant restored it to profound significance. An act of humility became one of defiance and something invisible was made visible. Kant's words merely confirmed that his actions were both willful and understood.

Kant's motions were artificial—the deliberate work of a human being. In this regard they can be considered as something that was made. Therefore, we can link them with Marco Frascari's notion of the architectural joint as the demonstrative intersection of "construction" with "construing."[117] Following from Vico's phrase *verum ipsum factum*, Kant made a truth appear by virtue of his demonstration. I am not asserting that bodily gestures are necessarily more meaningful than speech; in another situation Kant's words may have carried more weight than his deeds. The crucial point is that neither speech nor gesture can be reduced to simpler, less material form without sapping it of meaning. As Merleau-Ponty said, meaning is not some added layer "on the phrase like the butter on the bread."[118] The joint between the construction and the construing is the line between the visible and invisible, what Merleau-Ponty called "the chiasm." It is the ambiguous line where imitating is indirectly pointing, as in the example of a mime who shows us a door that is not there.[119] The mime does not imitate a door; he imitates a man opening a door, often in an exaggerated manner. Through a hesitation, an inhibition, a reversal, or a single agile leap—by looking and acting indirectly—it is conceivable that a mime or an architect could make stones talk.

This then is how we might bestow the capacity for speech to the "lifeless things on earth." To explain further I will downplay some of the most obvious ways architecture "communicates," such as a classical pediment on a bank indicating institutional stability, or instances of direct imitation, such as a hot dog stand in the shape of a hot dog. Neither of these methods of saying things, when found alone, is very mysterious, and neither is particularly native to architecture. But architecture can generate meanings that are not so literal or so clear. I wish to explain how architecture could produce the invisible out of the merely visible; how a particular place comes to mean "home," or becomes sacred; or how the Vietnam Veterans Memorial in Washington can make us believe that the dead are present behind a simple retaining wall. In these instances, it is obvious that architecture cannot produce the hoped-for situation directly. However, is this not usually the case? Architecture is charged with the task to create spaces and imbue them with qualities, and yet it can never touch—never directly address—space itself. Perhaps architecture, like Perseus, is at its best when it refuses to look or act directly.

But let me retreat a bit in order to address this thorny issue of imitation as it applies to architectural meanings. I find it obvious that the mimetic faculty we possess, one of our "polar activities of mind," plays a role in our understanding, and making of, meaningful architecture. Yet I can see how, in the minds of many, the "hot dog building" approach would discredit all imitative aspects of architecture. Much of the thorniness of the question of imitation's role in architecture stems from the uncertainty of what, precisely, we mean by "imitation." There seem to be several possible roles for imitation in architecture. In an effort to clarify things, I will begin with what I see as the most basic, most general way that architecture makes use of imitation.

In their book *Metaphors We Live By*, George Lakoff and Mark Johnson convincingly argue that metaphors, far from being infrequently applied poetic devices, actually play a very large role in determining our "conceptual system." As they put it, "If we are right in suggesting that our conceptual system is largely metaphorical, then the way we think, what we experience, and what we do every day is very much a matter of metaphor."[120] In a later book, *The Body in the Mind*, written by Johnson alone, he attempts to describe how "forms of imagination that grow out of bodily experience" produce what he calls "schemata" (such as our understanding of verticality) and metaphors, which in turn serve "to organize our more abstract understanding." This metaphorically organized understanding is "not merely a matter of arbitrary fanciful projection from anything to anything with no constraints." The constraints are provided by concrete bodily experience. Johnson offers the example of the metaphor "more is up." How does the "verticality schema" become involved in our understanding of quantity?

> There is good reason why this metaphorical projection from UP to MORE is
> natural, and why MORE is not oriented DOWN. The explanation has to do
> with our most common everyday bodily experiences and the image
> schemata they involve. If you add more liquid to the container, the level
> goes up. If you add more objects to the pile, the level goes up. MORE and UP
> are therefore correlated in our experience in a way that provides a *physical*
> basis for our *abstract* understanding of quantity.[121]

Metaphors, which show one thing by pointing to another, therefore contain a hidden basis that is the imitation of concrete phenomena. As the metaphoric statement becomes conventionalized, as is the case with "more is up," it loses its force and immediacy as a poetic event so that eventually some sense of increased quantity is simply added to possible definitions of "up" in the dictionary. This progression from a live to a dead or conventionalized metaphor illustrates that a shift from imitating to indicating is indeed possible.[122]

What is most important, however, is Johnson's contention that metaphor and its cousin metonymy (where some salient feature or part is used to indicate the whole)[123] originate in embodied experience. The most dominant metaphors are those with the clearest and most familiar physical basis. Buildings, which have always been regarded, in varying degrees, as metaphorical bodies, thereby cease to be mere objects, and instead become exemplary determining features of our conceptual system. This accounts for the innumerable architectural metaphors that we commonly use, such as "your theory is without foundation," and it begins to explain the value the memory arts (that is, premodern mnemonic methods) have always placed upon architectural images. The omnipresence and concreteness, as well as artifice, of buildings has made them the most applicable metaphorical/metonymical models by which we structure our perceptions of the world. In this sense we exist in the world *as though we were buildings*. We, as they, struggle to stand vertically against gravity and to withstand what Edgar Allan Poe called "the corrosive Hours of Fate."[124] As my colleague Donald Kunze puts it, "We possess architecture by becoming possessed by it."[125] Any attempt to understand the way architecture is meaningful is complicated because of its tendency to both point and imitate, and because it imitates us, and we it.

Theories that have foundations, and buildings that have "feet," are examples of fairly straightforward architectural metaphors where we observe, based on concrete experience, that one thing is like, or imitates, another. One could object that this is not really imitation, but merely the recognition of similarities that are endemic to different things. This is a sensible objection, and one I do not entirely dismiss; however in architecture, we are seldom content to rely on the endemic qualities of things as we find them. This is where we begin to move to another, less direct, sense of imitation. Architectural structures frequently assume shapes that loosely imitate natural structures, as a pyramid resembles a mountain. But this imitation is never direct. No society that has built pyramids has ever bothered to exactly reproduce the geologic formations of an actual mountain. The pyramid is a re-presentation of a mountain— not a direct copy of a mountain, but a demonstration of how human beings can build stone, brick, or mud mountains. This architectural chiasm presents us simultaneously with a very particular construction, this pyramid, that also points to something universal—the nature of our understanding of mountains.

The pyramid-mountain comparison is not simply like any metaphor we might make between two objects found in nature, because we make pyramids, and we make them to resemble mountains. We decide which aspects of a mountain we wish to imitate, and which we will disregard. We might be tempted to say that the pyramid is an abstraction of a mountain, and this would be very close to the truth. However, it would be more accurate to describe the pyramid as a metonymical construction of a mountain. In other words, as we move to a more selective form of imitation, or a constructed similarity, we shift from a metaphoric to a metonymical trope.

Let me provide another example. Earlier, I mentioned the associations that might be drawn between a weakened old man and an architectural ruin. There are enough similarities between the aging of a human body and the aging of a building to lead us to a Johnsonian schema: "buildings are bodies that age." We might observe that the weathering of a building and the weather-beating of human skin are analogous operations. Given that these characteristics are endemic to most building materials and to skin, the metaphor offers little chance for the architect to show or say anything beyond what is already apparent. The first architectural mention of any such natural similarities may engender a degree of fascination due to its novelty. Soon though, it must become accepted as something conventionally held to be true, and the metaphor will have lost its life.[126] Here, merely comparing similarities from one thing to another, we are faced with the "truth" of materials in their naked, unadorned state. However, what if the architect were not simply content to "let nature take its course"? Could an architect re-present the activity of weathering so that it demonstrated more than simply the corrosive effects of the elements?

This is precisely what Carlo Scarpa did in his design for the drip channels that collect the rainwater from the circular window apertures of the Banco Popolare in Verona. Scarpa inserted a channel, projecting downward from the lowest point of the circular openings, to prevent a vertical stain from forming on the wall beneath the window. The bottom of the channel projects outward, away from the surface of the wall, in order to send the collected water away from the building (as gargoyles once did). This is a much more curious situation than it first appears. To prevent a vertical stain, Scarpa added a channel to the wall—a channel more obvious than the stain would have been. And as moving water erodes substances, the accelerated movement of the water caused by the channel must be judged a counterintuitive solution to the protection of the wall. In their book *On Weathering*, Moshen Mostafavi and David Leatherbarrow write that this detail "reveals what it removes and retards what it quickens."[127] In other words, Scarpa's detail takes a natural phenomena and re-presents it to us, exaggerating some of its aspects while suppressing its destructive effects. Utilizing Cassirer's "reversal" and Merleau-Ponty's deviation from its "pre-ordained direction," Scarpa's detail provides a new consciousness of the effects of water upon buildings, much as Kant's showing-by-refusing-to-show gesture gave us a new appreciation for his sense of humanity.

Both Frascari, in his advocacy for what he calls a "radical anthropomorphism," and Kunze, who has dubbed the effects of this mode of indirect imitation "delayed semblance," argue that metonymy gives us the most fertile procedure for making and understanding architecture. Frascari mentions that the "use of architectural metaphors to explain the content of architectural theories . . . can generate major confusion."[128] That is, regardless of the dominant role of architecture in our conceptual schemas, to employ architectural metaphors to describe architectural situations is simply not very useful. By avoiding the direct correspondence of metaphor, metonymy permits any number of reversals, where effects may substitute for causes, materials for objects, the contained for the container, the abstract for the concrete.[129] Kunze notes, "Where metaphor lends itself to corrupting paraphrase, metonymy is epistemologically empty and, thus, hard to appropriate." Furthermore, metonymical procedures "begin in translation—actually, the failure of translation—and end in image, which is the only means of sustaining an ambiguous relation of polyvalent meanings."[130]

If metonymy is accepted as the "fertile procedure" most indigenous to architecture, several other issues immediately begin to fall into place. For example, when Frascari promotes the detail as the basic metonymical unit of signification/construction, the point where "construction and construing" are chiasmatically united, he also indirectly solves the long-running debate in architecture over truth to materials. As I mentioned earlier in the example of the weathering of building materials, a literal reading of "truth to materials" only means that materials are what they are—a circular proposition that is most unhelpful. From this same proposition we could adopt either the technologist's perspective—that we may do with materials whatever we wish, provided we are clever enough to accomplish it—or the purist's position—that we should always leave materials in as close a condition to how they are found in nature as is possible. Frascari's insight, that architectural details re-present the concrete qualities of substances in imaginative ways, suggests a way out of this situation of equally plausible unacceptable ideologies. Details such as Scarpa's are neither objectively true to their materials, nor mere simulations. They are "authentic lies," poetic constructions made of tangible things that re-present universal qualities in ways that deviate from literal imitation, in order to demonstrate a new consciousness of polyvalent meanings.

The re-presentation of the detail is a metonymical trope not of words but of things, a turning, twisting, or reversal (but not a denial) of straightforward tectonic logic. It is metonymical because it selects only a portion of the qualities of a substance or thing to utilize in its demonstration. It is also metonymical by virtue that this act of selective displacement, far from being reductive in the manner of abstractions, on the contrary allows us to imaginatively re-create the whole out of the part, with no loss of "weight." In a sense, it preserves the whole by making it invisible. Scarpa's drip detail does not show us the destructive effects of weathering, which, because they have been prevented, are kept unseen. Yet it makes these effects known by referring to them indirectly.

The metonymical detail is not a simplification; it is a temporary redirection of our attention based upon the substitution of the part for the whole. A theory of details based upon abstraction would ultimately lead away from material qualities. Abstraction only invites further abstraction, the search for ultimate essences and elementary particles. It cannot provide us with the specular reversal or the ability to agilely leap between the real and the ideal. The metonymical construction, because it is untranslatable, must be experienced, or at least imagined, in its material state to be fully appreciated. It cannot be disembodied into a concept, as there must be a body present in order to demonstrate. Details cannot be separated into categories of aesthetic joints and constructive joints; they must be both. Architecture is free to become both more real and more imaginative.

There are several additional promising aspects of the fertile metonymical procedure. For example, the very particular and concrete situation of the construction does not appear to limit its construing. As Cassirer wrote, by "withdrawing [refusing to act directly] action gains a new scope and a new freedom; it is already in transition . . . from physical to ideal activity." This tells us that we have, in the authentic architectural detail, a built artifact that preserves the essential opposition of our duality of mind, and therefore an example of what Vico would term "poetic wisdom." Unlike architecture that strives towards pure form—which can only exist in a material state as an imperfect approximation, where the actions of time and the elements can only underscore its defects—an embodied architecture can always turn reality to its advantage. Because any particular poetic image points to the ideal indirectly, this also suggests a tentative answer to the question of architectural regionalism. Frascari writes,

> There is no contradiction in saying that architecture builds on the cultural dimension of a place, and then stating that it depends on a corporeal image that does not need a specific place. The first statement applies to the construction of architecture, whereas the second bears on the construing of it.[131]

If Frascari is correct, and I believe he is, then there is no need to assume that regional methods of construction, climatically or culturally influenced building shapes, or the use of local materials must in some way impede the quest for what is universal. His radical anthropomorphism does not depend on the direct imitation of bodily shapes or proportions. Metonymical relations between built and human bodies are not limited to merely visual or objectively measurable similarities. They can include temporal processes and material qualities, such as Scarpa's detail that accelerates change in order to forestall it. There are no universal rules for determining the shapes of architecture, there are only materials that may be shaped into authentic constructions.

Kunze's claim that the construing of metonymy is hard to appropriate suggests another radical outcome. Unlike compositions of shapes that are readily commodified into styles, imagery, or the latest novel fashion, authentic constructions resist the abstract reductions of the market. If there is any architectural strategy that can forestall Manfredo Tafuri's grim prediction that capitalist development will eventually reduce architecture to a "pure economic factor,"[132] it must be the indirect ideality of the detail. As Frascari put it, "a nontrivial architecture is possible only if architects restore the exercise of detailing to its essential position as the guiding concept for the discipline of architecture."[133] Admittedly, within what has become the conventional system for the production of buildings in "developed" nations, the architect or builder's ability to produce authentic details is seriously jeopardized. Some critics have also cautioned that too great an attention devoted to "careful" construction, as was the case in the Arts and Crafts movement, must have the unfortunate outcome of restricting architecture to a status symbol for the wealthy. I would counter that fine materials and extraordinary precision are *not* prerequisites for authentic details, as is demonstrated by innumerable vernacular constructions, but this is the subject for another essay.

Architecture is a poetic way of building so that meanings appear indirectly. Too direct attempts at architectural imitation produce only the kitsch banalities of hot dog buildings, or a Rock and Roll Hall of Fame resembling a record player. The fertile metonymical procedure provides us with a basis for the criticism of these things, as well as of the assumption that the art of architecture lies solely in the creation and manipulation of building shapes. It is not merely a coincidence that as this reductive understanding of architectural possibilities took hold during the Enlightenment, trivial designs for dairy farms in the shape of cows, and brothels organized in plan to resemble gigantic penises, first appeared. Postmodernism, a clear descendent of this tradition, institutionalized Robert Venturi's categories of architectural "ducks" (like the hot dog building) and "decorated sheds" into an erroneous dichotomy. The first term accepts a too literal understanding of construing, the second a too pragmatic vision of construction. Either concept can only serve as a guide for the production of architecture lacking in weight. In order for architecture to become both heavy (significant, nontrivial) and light (imaginative, free), it must turn its attention once more to the details of its construction.

◇   ◇   ◇

Architecture is the only art in which the great struggle between the will of the spirit and the necessity of nature issues into real peace, in which the soul in its upward striving and nature in its gravity are held in balance.

Georg Simmel
"The Ruin"

By "details" Frascari means neither "subordinate parts" nor the orthographic projections of important components of a building conventionally called "details" in architectural practice. For Frascari, a detail is always a joint that impacts construction. This is not exactly the same as saying the detail is always a point of assemblage between different parts of a building. Gottfried Semper's proposal that knots be considered the prototypical details illustrates this. A knot can join several pieces of rope or string together, or connect a rope to some other object, such as an anchor. But it may also join only itself to itself, in which case there is—technically—nothing being connected. If we always insisted on the literal connection of two or more components, neither the knot in a single rope nor the edges and corners of a monolithic concrete structure could be considered details.

The extreme limits of an architectural construction, its edges and outermost surfaces, are certainly joints and usually among the most significant architectural details. The edge of a construction literally joins it to its surroundings. When this joining produces some understanding that goes beyond the merely literal, as when the surface of the Vietnam Veterans Memorial wall becomes a boundary in contact with the realm of the dead, a material and necessary limit of a construction has become a detail. Therefore, we may also classify spires, domes, chimneys and cupolas as details, where the joining of building and sky produces a construing of the building as a vertical being, of its striving upward, or of its need for centrality—while these constructions simultaneously shelter, disperse fumes, or collect sunlight.

The stepped profile of the artificial mountain known as a ziggurat is, I believe, an archetypal architectural detail.[134] The ziggurat demonstrates that it was built in incremental stages, most likely with layers of masonry. The existence of a series of incremental right-angled steps, particularly when they are sized to permit climbing by human beings, is as near to a universal architectural sign of human artifice as we are likely to find. While instances of this stepped profile do occur in nature, they are rare. If we accept the entire profile of a ziggurat to be a detail, we suggest that while a detail is always less than the whole, it is not necessarily small or inconspicuous.

The joint between building and sky, most commonly seen in the roof profile of buildings, is one of the most dominant details in determining our initial reading of a building. As Bachelard would say, this is perhaps the most "rational" part of any building, where the slope of the roof instantly informs us of the nature of the climate. In most regions roof surfaces are sloped to permit gravity to readily draw rainwater off the building. The gable roof, perhaps the most common variety of sloped roof, directs the water to opposite sides of the building. The coverings that allow gable roofs to shed water are not usually themselves impervious to water penetration. Shingles, shakes, tiles, layers of thatch, and sheet metal are only effective in resisting the penetration of water that is running down the surface of the roof. Should high winds or ice dams cause the flow of water to migrate up the gable roof surface, leaks will likely result. A gable roof does not resist the penetration of water so much as redirect it. Generally speaking, the steeper the slope of the roof, the more effective this redirection will be. A gable roof is an indirect means of keeping rainwater out of a building. By taking one aspect of rainwater—its dependence on gravity to find its way to the earth—and basing an entire system of protection upon it, the gable roof demonstrates not only how rain "works," but how it may be cleverly outwitted by human beings. Even when no rain is falling, the gable points to these qualities of rain and roofs. A gable roof, joint between building and sky, with its shingles, gutters, and valleys, is therefore a detail. It is a construction that construes qualities of earth, sky, materials, and human ingenuity.

A flat roof, on the other hand, must be more straightforward in its method of protection. Even though most flat roofs slope enough to guide water either toward roof drains or to the edge of the roof, this slope is not sufficient to always prevent standing water on the roof. Therefore, a flat roof must depend on its covering to be completely impervious to water penetration. Properly installed, a flat roof may be as effective as a gable roof in protecting the building. However, a flat roof does not demonstrate anything about roofs or rainwater (although its flashing details probably do). Its ingenuity lies not in its shape but in the chemical properties of the membrane that covers it. The flat roof is a technical , not an architectural, solution to the waterproofing of a building.[135] Flat roofs were preferred by proponents of the International Style primarily because they looked economical and efficient, which, to some degree, they are. The International Style architects mistook the gable roof for a quaint convention, one incompatible with the machine aesthetic or with a universal architecture stylistically forbidden to vary its shape in response to climatic conditions. The popularity of the gable is not, however, merely a matter of convention; it is also owed to the ability of the gable to "reveal what it removes and retard what it quickens."

I do not mean to suggest that the gable roof is an ideal type of roof, or that it comes to us from the supposedly originary "primitive hut." The gable shape is more likely influenced by the water-shedding characteristics I have described, and by the types of materials we commonly use to frame roofs. Wood boards or timbers can be joined very readily into a structurally rigid triangular frame, which can then be repeated along the building's length to produce the roof structure of a gable. There are climates, and places, where the available construction methods make gable roofs an insensible choice. The igloo is not inferior to the gable; the igloo simply demonstrates the cultural, climatic, and material dimension of a particular place, while still producing a construing, a corporeal image, that is not specific to only one place. The "logic" of an igloo would be readily understood by a citizen of Verona, just as an Eskimo would have no difficulty comprehending the poetic wisdom of the Banco Popolare windows, having once seen them in the rain.

We can find another example of roof constructions chiasmatically joining the universal and the particular in Australian architect Glenn Murcutt's designs for sheet metal roofs that are not, precisely, gables. Murcutt's roof forms take advantage of the ability of corrugated sheet metal to be easily bent in shallow curves so that the "ridge" of these roofs is a curve, not a fold. Because these roofs are not subjected to snow loads, they are thin and light, which is emphasized by the structure that supports them and the way Murcutt designs their edges. The galvanized steel panels (called "galvo" by Australians) that Murcutt employs in his roofs have been popular with Australians since the gold rush of the 1850s. It was the ideal lightweight building material to transport into the remote gold fields, where it could be easily configured into a wide variety of sheds and shacks by unskilled builders.[136] Murcutt often uses galvo roofs to direct rainwater into galvo cisterns, as is common practice in the region. He produces regionally specific corporeal images—from roof-mounted turbine ventilators to roof shapes that demonstrate the peculiarities of climate, culture, and materials—that transcend his particular locale. Murcutt's light, layered construction techniques also demonstrate that architectural weight does not directly depend on massiveness.

Architecture is not something physical that is added to buildings. Because it only appears indirectly, architecture is not contained in objects or things, although it depends on them. This is the snag that has always caught those who wished to argue for some version of Ruskin's equation: "building + ornament = architecture." If, by ornament, we mean the addition of more stuff—extra material, additional steps to the construction process—we will always be confounded by examples of architecture where such ornament is either missing or so integral to necessary features of the construction that it cannot be imagined as separate (it is difficult to maintain that a gable roof is an ornament). Architecture adds imaginative weight to building, but not necessarily actual weight. It is more accurate to say that buildings may possess joints or boundaries, but only architecture contains details. However, just as the demarcation between poetry and prose cannot be precisely established with conceptual rules, neither can the line that separates architecture from building. This makes it very difficult to describe exactly how architecture comes about, which is one reason that I have approached the issue from so many different directions.

Now consider one final example of the radical anthropomorphism of a detail, so that I may conclude this section in a memorable way. One of the most eloquent and elegant architectural demonstrations is the arch. Arches may serve very utilitarian purposes; they may be simple and unadorned by ornament. While beams, which are functionally "synonymous" with arches, show the forces they resist by deflecting in response to their loads, arches gracefully leap across space as though they carried almost nothing; they describe an arc that rises against gravity, in the opposite direction from the beam's deflection. Through a clever trick of geometry, arches convert pulling to pushing and trope material weakness into strength. Structural rationalists have proposed that architectural structures are expressive to the extent they reveal the stresses they endure. If we interpret this as a preference for direct visual evidence of stress, then a sagging beam would be more desirable than an arch. In the spirit of Perseus, an arch refuses to show its stresses directly, while it still gracefully accepts its particular burden. In an arch mute stones are made articulate; heaviness reveals its hidden lightness.

An arch need weigh no more, nor be more complex to construct, than a beam. Yet, the significance of the arch does not lie simply in its shape. In things that are shaped like arches but that lack the arch structure, such as the arch shapes applied to many postmodern buildings, materials are made dumb. These constructions imitate but do not demonstrate. Their construing is merely a matter of convention, and it is at odds with their construction. The architects who employ these devices mistakenly assume that meaning adheres to shapes alone, so that it can be applied directly, like butter to bread. Michael Graves has said, in regard to his use of keystone shapes detached from either actual arches or even arch shapes, "If you eliminate the pragmatic value in any form, you tend to heighten its symbolic value."[137] While such a move may initially produce novelty, it cannot produce, as Graves wishes, an architectural language that relies strictly on convention or the ability to frustrate convention, which is the same thing. As we know from Calvino and Merleau-Ponty, this can only create petrified meanings, lacking in subtlety or ambiguity. While they may be literally light, phony arches and misplaced keystones are weighed down by a conceptual heaviness. They are single-minded and unimaginative. That is, their imagination lies in one dimension only, the play with shapes, and expresses only a small fraction of the depth of things that can be thought architecturally.

The shape of the arch is only an ingenious construction when it responds to the limitations of stone and gravity. True arches demonstrate what Bachelard called the "courage to live in opposition to weight—to live 'vertically.'"[138] If architects dedicate themselves to making authentic constructions, they might rediscover the intense fulfillment that occurs when lives come closer to the earth, without abandoning "the meaning of a healthy straightening up, growing tall, and carrying our heads high."[139] I will let Calvino summarize:

> Marco Polo describes a bridge, stone by stone.
>
> "But which is the stone that supports the bridge?"
> Kublai Khan asks.
>
> "The bridge is not supported by one stone or another,"
> Marco answers, "but by the line of the arch they form."
>
> Kublai Khan remains silent, reflecting. Then he adds:
> "Why do you speak to me of the stones? It is only the arch
> that matters to me."
>
> Polo answers: "Without the stones there is no arch."[140]

◇　　　◇　　　◇

In this essay I have navigated a meandering path touching on many (perhaps too many) examples. The circuitous nature of my journey was, at least partially, an intentional effort to underscore the difficulty of the question of architectural weight. I have attempted to unmask the questionable assumptions behind the apparently rational beliefs about architecture that originated during the Age of Reason. My suspicious attitude towards all forms of abstraction, applied rationality, and what Kant designated "determinate concepts" does not stem from a lack of appreciation for their utility. Instead it reacts to the single-minded way they have usurped nearly complete dominion over the discourse on, and the accepted definitions of, architecture. We need to once again become aware of the limitations of the intelligible universal. There are simply no rules for architectural practice that can be stated with conceptual clarity, because a practice by definition must continually address the unforeseen and uncertain. This does not mean that there is no place for rationality in architecture. It merely means that we should strive for what Bachelard called an "open rationality"—that is, an embodied rationality fully aware of its limits. It also does not mean that "anything goes." There are architectural truths, but they are no longer given by sacred laws or divine geometries. They must be made through the production of authentic constructions. If there are universals in architecture, they will be found in the realm of the imaginative universal, and therefore they will be ambiguously stated. We will need to reconstruct them endlessly.

In order to produce architecture, we must return to exercising those faculties of our imaginations that we have largely ignored since the Enlightenment. Primarily, this means devoting greater attention to the physical and constructional aspects of buildings. Both of these concerns—for the imaginative and actual weights of architecture—can be addressed by the single faculty Bachelard refers to as the "material imagination." In *Water and Dreams*, Bachelard proposed the sculptor's kneading of clay, a mixture of water and earth combined to form a paste, as a basic operation of an imaginative materiality. With a ball of clay in one's palm, Bachelard maintained, one's *hand* would begin to dream. I suggest Bachelard's "dreaming hand" as the attitude that will allow contemporary men and women to create architecture in the often hostile circumstances of our late-modern, technological society. By rejecting the single-minded wish to abandon our bodies, and to cast our commanding but disembodied view over the cosmos, the dreaming hand might once again restore imaginative weight to our constructions.

> [The] working, controlling hand learns the essential dynamic genius of reality while working with a matter that resists and yields at the same time, like passionate and rebellious flesh. It amasses all ambivalences. Such a working hand needs an exact mixture of earth and water in order to realize fully what constitutes matter capable of form, substance capable of life. To the unconscious of the man who kneads the clay, the model is the embryo of the work; clay is the mother of bronze. Therefore I cannot emphasize too much how important the experience of fluidity and pliability is to an understanding of the psychology of the creative unconscious.[141]

Neither the wholesale rejection of reality, not the mindless imitation of it, can ultimately produce architecture that aspires beyond the trivial and utilitarian. What Bachelard has written with regard to the poet, I will maintain as the task of the architect: we must use our capacity to imagine materially in order that we might make reality *sing*. The key to this ability is the architectural version of the poetic trope metonymy, as realized in the production of authentic architectural constructions. When this fertile procedure is creatively employed, architectural details obtain the power to sustain ambiguous relations and polyvalent meanings, by producing poetic images of matter capable of form. "These images of matter are dreamt substantially and intimately. They have weight; they constitute a heart."[142]

The Emerald City:
A Study of Substance and Place

The Emerald City as work-in-progress

Just to amuse myself, and to keep the good people busy, I ordered them to build this city, and my Palace; and they did it willingly and well. Then I thought, as the country was so green and beautiful, I would call it the Emerald City.

L. Frank Baum
The Wonderful Wizard of Oz

For a writer of children's books, L. Frank Baum seems to have been a practical man. I suspect that Baum had doubts about the believability of the city he invented for his most famous story, so he hedged his bets. In his book *The Wonderful Wizard of Oz*,[143] the Emerald City was no more green than any other city. It only appeared to be green because the Wizard of Oz was able to convince its citizens to constantly wear glasses with green-tinted lenses. The cinematic version of the story, which is far more widely known (and which dropped the word "Wonderful" from the title), expunged this unwieldy plot device, replacing it with a magnificent city of (mostly) emerald. The movie's screenwriters appreciated a nuance of the imagination that appears to have escaped Baum: in a fantasy it is better to tell a lie so compelling, so audacious, yet so desirable that we *want* to believe it, than to manufacture a supposedly plausible solution lacking in the ability to excite us.[144] In other words, Baum failed to realize that nearly impossible constructions can sometimes be quite believable. I think the superiority of the celluloid Emerald City over its textual counterpart can be used to demonstrate other aspects of city images and the role materials play in them.

The Emerald City, the capital of Oz, is perhaps the most improbable city in cinema. It is improbable because it is nearly perfect. The Emerald City is magically ruled, not by a common mayor, but by a wizard. In it dreams come true for those who have endured the trials of the yellow brick road. The Emerald City is foremost a refuge, an asylum for fugitives and misfits. It shows us, contrary to our present experience with crime-infested cities, that cities may be places to enhance or restore the quality of human lives. In *The Wizard of Oz* it is the forest—nature—that is dangerous, populated by lions and tigers and bears. Only in the city can one be safe from wickedness. Once in the Emerald City, Dorothy and her companions are groomed, polished, restuffed, and rejuvenated. Recall the joy and relief she and her friends felt upon first sighting the glowing metropolis in the distance. The city is always a goal, particularly appealing to young adults, or to those starting over. It is the end of a journey, the realization of the fondest hope, the place to make it big.

The country, conversely, is only the place from where people come, as in, "I'm an old Kansas man myself." The only request for which the Wizard's bag of tricks comes up empty is Dorothy's wish to return home. We are left to conclude that, once there, no one had ever desired to leave. Dorothy's homesickness is a reminder that not everyone is cut out for the big time. It is generally only the old and defeated that leave the city. They retire to the country, are "put out to pasture," and finally "buy the farm." Still, Dorothy would have never made it back to Kansas without the knowledge gained in the city.

Cities must be big enough to accommodate the dreams of those who seek them. Room for their bodies is far less important. In many cities, there is an inverse relationship between the size of one's dreams and the floor area of one's apartment. The Emerald City may not be physically huge, but it is made to seem bigger in contrast to Munchkin Land, the smallest of small towns where Dorothy began her journey through Oz. There, even the people were tiny. The Munchkins also talked funny. Big ideas cannot be taken seriously when expressed in such high-pitched squeaks as Munchkin-speech. As Peter Gabriel noted in his song "Big Time," in a small town, "they use small words."

The city is the space of possibility. It is a promise, a mixed bag, an open-ended question, and a vast number of niches to be filled. In cities there are too many streets to remember, so they are numbered rather than named. In order for their geography to be grasped, cities must be divided into uptown, downtown, and various "quarters." People in cities have too many things to do, so a real city cannot sleep. Cities are vital and vibrant; they pulse with energy, and they radiate heat and light. In the Emerald City the pace of change is so great that the horse pulling Dorothy's carriage constantly changes color. However, the greatest of cities must strike a delicate balance between stability and flux. At some mysterious point in its growth, the city takes on a character—not a definable structure so much as an image, whereby certain aspects of the city lodge in the memories of its citizens.

A truly extraordinary city, a magical city, must present a striking image indeed. Mere mortals, even mortals of staggering wealth or great power, may build cities of stone, brick, or even steel. Only a wizard could inspire a city of emerald. An entire city of gems—a gem of a city—made of a brilliant, but (usually) small and (presumably) rare, substance, must be a most fantastic place. Of course, all cities are built of what they consider valuable. All cities are capitalist cities in that they are all concentrations of wealth. The Emerald City simply flaunts its wealth more tastefully than most. All cities live on artificial surplus. The dirty little secret of all cities is that they are ultimately at the mercy of the countryside. Economists assume that cities trade services and currency for food and energy, but the real currency of any great city is the dreams it inspires. As centers of commerce, cities exist to exchange, and must exchange to exist. We can exchange most readily that which is unnecessary, therefore cities are fueled by desires, not needs. The city's strongest desire is for what it needs the least—for example, professional sports franchises in American cities. It is as a locus of desires that the Emerald City excels. People arrive wanting what they do not need, and have lived perfectly well without—a brain, a heart, or courage. From the evidence we see, beyond a few cosmetic and transportation services, dreams are the only product the Emerald City produces.

Let us return to the image the Emerald City presents. By "image" I do not mean simply the appearance of the city, but rather the sum total of all we imagine it to be. City images are most often material images, which authors, screen-writers, and planners must concoct with painstaking precision. Any detail that rings untrue or shallow can impair the city's ability to occupy our daydreams. (For example: Baum's version of the Emerald City may be convincing from the *inside*, but how would it serve to convince the neighboring witches of the Wizard's great powers?) Cities are not usually described by their shape, but by conditions of their substance or geography. Therefore, Paris is the City of Light, Rome the Eternal City, San Francisco the City by the Bay, Chicago the City with Big Shoulders, New York the Big Apple (or, as its Mayor Rudy Giuliani once suggested, "the city that can kick your city's ass"[145]). Pittsburgh is known for its steel, London for its fog, Venice for its canals, Amsterdam for its tulips. When a city is identified with a substance, or a substantial condition, that substance or condition will tend to permeate the imaginations of all who arrive there. Therefore cities, or authors who invent them, must choose their substance as carefully as the city's founders chose its location. Joseph Rykwert persuasively presents this principle in *The Idea of a Town*: cities must be as founded in the imagination as securely as they are founded upon the earth.[146]

It is here that we see most clearly the planning error of Baum's version of the Emerald City. Baum's Wizard is too timid; he coerces his citizens to build an ordinary city, whereas his movie counterpart, a confidence man extraordinaire, conceals his lack of true power by proposing to build a city with "the power to stir men's souls." Why emerald? By choosing a substance both elegant and useless, The Emerald City successfully embodies the imaginative principle of excess. Its heirloom quality assures that it will not be easily abandoned. Its floors and walls are much more valuable than anything they could possibly contain, so it appears to have cleverly circumvented the risks of creative destruction inherent to capitalism. Given the value and durability of its material, one almost wonders why there are not more gem cities. Yet, when we consider this question at length, it is evident that not just any shiny stone would do.

A ruby city would have been an inferior choice. The color red has a suspicious past: it is the color of flame and shame, of blood and war, of the heart and the devil. The red light is the symbol of vice. Red is the color of rage and the shade of desire—also of the ruby slippers, which formerly belonging to the Wicked Witch of the East. One could not come by fortune or fame honestly in a ruby city. In it we would find only floozies and flimflam men, get-rich-quick schemes, rip-offs, and robberies. A red city is not so much sought as succumbed to. The temptations a ruby city offers make it no place for the virginal Dorothy and her bumpkin friends.

A diamond city would suffer from excessive transparency. Seen from afar, it could easily be mistaken for a mirage. We could not, from a distance, distinguish a diamond city from a city of glass or of ice. It would shimmer without perceptible substance. We would be perplexed rather than heartened by the sight of it. Could it be another trick of the Witch? How could a city unable to conceal secrets provide refuge? A city of absolute transparency would be a cynical city, a city without curtains behind which to hide, a city unwilling to forget. (Or a city populated exclusively by tabloid journalists.) Such a city would have seen through the phony Wizard from the beginning. A diamond city would be devoid of politicians, salesmen, actors, artists, Gypsies, and children.

A gold city would present problems of its own. The most malleable of metals, gold has little preference for the form it takes. Heavy and dense, but weak, gold could not form the vertical towers and spires of a city meant to be seen from a distance. The precious metal could be gilded onto other structures, or alloyed with firmer metals, but these are unnecessary complications that would lead to an impure city. Gold inspires us to possess it, but offers scant advice as to what should be done with it. Gold is the self-satisfied element. Simply to have it is enough. *Using* it for anything requires far too much effort. Gold is most content stacked in a vault, waiting to be counted by a fat king. Gold is a matter of repose—a horizontal element. It makes more sense to pave streets with gold than to build an entire city of it. And this may be what the yellow bricks were hinting at all along.

What of the more pedestrian substances? A steel city would never have attracted Dorothy. The heat and smoke, brawling and drinking, would frighten a meek Kansas lass. A manufacturing city is always second class—its citizens too hardworking to cultivate lavish desires, its products too useful to excite the imagination. Manufacturing cities send their excess elsewhere, along with most of their dreamers. Likewise, a wood city would be too primitive to be taken seriously—too similar to the forest and, like the scarecrow, too vulnerable to flames. A brick city would again be too ordinary, a place in which to settle down perhaps, but not a place in which to move up in the world. All cities of useful materials would be much too believable for the home of a great Wizard.

If we turn toward the less tangible, a city of light (not *the* City of Light) might offer possibilities. I suspect, however, that we would have gone too far. A city of light would fade in the noonday sun. If our band of heroes had approached their city of salvation at night, how could they have evaded the Witch in her dark forest element. Could we ever trust such a city, not knowing the source of its power? Remember, despite the usefulness of beacons, they are seldom destinations in themselves. Lighthouses and beacons point the way to somewhere else. Furthermore, a city of light would refuse to be pinned down. It would have no ties to the earth, would need no foundation, leave no imprint. Flickering then fading, on then off, particles or waves. A city of light would be too indecisive a city to help Dorothy find her way.

We can almost imagine Baum considering possibilities for the magical city, and then rejecting them one by one as I have. Few architects would take such care in imagining the material alternatives with which to build. Few planners debate the substance most representative of their fellow citizens' dreams. Today's architects and planners, like most members of our technological society, have come to associate materials only with practical purposes, believing them to be merely our mute and lifeless servants. But, as we have seen, materials possess an imaginative life, a personality, and a historicity of their own. When Baum (despite the fact that he resorted to the "green glasses" illusion mentioned previously) finally hit upon a city of emerald, it could not have taken him long to smell success.

Emerald's advantages to this story are legion. Emerald offers us rarity and sparkle, without diamond's suspicious transparency or ruby's implied passion. A green city provides an ideal reflection of nature; a city not in opposition to the forest, but a humanized version of it. It is the city as a dazzling garden, a dream of nature perfected. Because we see only the interior of the city in close-up views, the Emerald City is for us a kind of greenhouse—a hermetically sealed environment ideal for growth, encased not in glass but in gems. What better way to attract a farmer's young daughter than to dangle a reassuringly green bauble in her sight? Emerald, after all, is just stone. What could be more natural than a city made of stone?

The more closely we look, the more sophisticated the choice of setting appears. Besides being the favored hue of photosynthesis, green is also, in the United States, the color of money. How better to again underscore the wealth of the city? Even the vague geography of the city sends subliminal messages. It is clearly located in the heartland. No coast is in sight. It appears to be approximately central to the overlapping territories of the witches. The bad witches come from the east and west, while the good witch comes from the north. The city is approached up a slight slope, all the better to dramatize its desirability. Its spires are not the sharp shards of fractured emerald crystals. These would suggest too aggressive a city. No, the tops of the Emerald City's skyscrapers are gently polished into domes. In contrast to Hugh Ferriss's famous muscular ziggurats, the Emerald City's spires are slender and polite—towers without testosterone, capitalism with a heart. The corridor to the Wizard's inner sanctum is shaped to reverberate the Tinman's footsteps upon the emerald floor. This processional space is vaguely navelike, leading to the Wizard's great throne room. To prevent the imagery from becoming blasphemous, the shape of the ribbed, barrel-vaulted corridor is unlike that of any church. It is more like a giant arched band shell, extruded to an absurd length. This hints that our protagonists are approaching a performer rather than a pope. The clever bogus Wizard has transformed his chamber into a theater, complete with awe-inspiring special effects. Meanwhile, in his vibrant green costume, he resembles nothing so much as a leprechaun.

An Emerald City is most improbable. However, this does not mean it is unrealistic. This is not to say that we are likely to ever see a city extensively made of emerald, only that, if one did exist, it would elicit all of the wondrous reactions suggested in the movie. In other words, as an image the Emerald City is quite realistic, even though the implications of actually constructing it are not. Material images are not opposed to reality, but are imaginative extensions, twists, or distorted mirrors of reality. They are, according to the terminology I have come to adopt, "good lies."

If we did set out to create an emerald city it would not be necessary that it be all, or even mostly, emerald. This is another feature of material images, or perhaps all poetic images. Thanks to the poetic trope metonymy, where some partial aspect or characteristic can imaginatively stand in for the whole, we must only have enough of a substance in order for it to imaginatively spread its effects throughout the whole. As with fairy dust, a witch's potion, Jack's magical beans, or a cell's DNA, a small portion of a magical substance can be capable of engendering mighty constructions.

Material images, like people's nicknames, have unusual standards of appropriateness. Neither arbitrary nor vague, they must inspire, sustain, and accommodate fascination. They have weight because they are both very specific and also open ended. Unlike categories and concepts, they are flexible and slippery. In *Invisible Cities*, Italo Calvino selected titles such as "Hidden Cities," "Thin Cities," and "Continuous Cities" for each of the cities Marco Polo describes. While the titles clearly describe the cities portrayed below them, they could easily be applied to any city, or exchanged between the chapters in the book. The fantastic cities in Calvino's book are the seeds for future generations of imagined cities, and they are the offspring of a single great city. As genetic material for all imaginable cities, they—like the Emerald City—demonstrate the qualities shared by all cities where dreamers dwell.

In a movie intended for children, only a few of the more benign desires that feed the Emerald City are revealed to us. We might wonder: has the Wizard's magic succeeded in keeping all wickedness away? For all her power, the Wicked Witch was remarkably unimaginative. Flying on her broom above the city, she was reduced to threatening Dorothy in sky-writing. How much better it would have been to infiltrate!—to pollute the purity of the sickening emerald pleasantness. Start with that blubbering door man, did he *really* have an Aunt Em himself once? Or, was he swayed, surreptitiously staring through some hidden peephole, by the innocent beauty of young Dorothy? Just how much interest in innocent young beauty might he have? Would he, perhaps, open the gates for a few downloaded photographs? And what of the Wizard? We know, or soon discover, he is a fraud. If he is human, he must have weaknesses. Does he not get lonely? A clever man with a carnival background, he should enjoy a friendly wager now and then. Would he consider a game of cards? Could he be tempted by drink? Sure, he has duped an entire city, but where is the thrill in that, if he is forever trapped in his role? Like the eye of a hurricane, the Wizard himself could be the weak link, the Achilles's heel any *truly* wicked witch would exploit.

By digressing into the realm of wickedness, I may have stumbled upon the most improbable feature of all in this most polished of cities—that it is, in fact, a trifle dull. In a city sanitized for the enjoyment of children, or by the Utopian desires of perfection-seeking planners, much of a typical city's excitement must be purged. This may result in a safer, cleaner city, but such a single-minded place may eventually impair the imaginations (not to forget the political freedoms) of those who dwell there. As material entities, all cities must contain flaws. The stubborn materiality of the city distorts the purely projective aims of bureaucratic planning. Because all the actual cities we know have a seamy side, we can assume that the Emerald City has only succeeded in driving its vices out of sight. What happened to the evil double of this good green city? Is the Wizard's deception intended to stand for all other devious deeds in his city? Only in the Wizard's inner sanctum are we shown a place where everything is not simply as it appears, as if the Wizard has succeeded in inhabiting (or creating) the sole trace of *poché* in this clean and efficient city. Within this hidden space that thwarts vision, from the depths of his vaulted cave and behind his curtain, the Wizard has constructed a terrifying alter ego.

The presence of a double always challenges the easy answer, the plain reading, simple diagram, or static relationship. The imaginative doubling of an image is always dynamic. Doubles continually try to upstage one another. In so doing, they take on different shapes and assume disguises. Frank Morgan, the actor who played the Wizard, also played four other parts in the film: Professor Marvel (the fortune teller back in Kansas), the gatekeeper to the city, the throne room guard, and the driver of the carriage pulled by the "horse of a different color." Could this have been how the Wizard escaped his trap of solitude? Or are we being shown that the division between the Wizard and the citizens of Oz is not as clear as we first assume? Despite claiming he was a "good man," but a very "bad wizard," Morgan's main character finally succeeds in granting the wishes Dorothy and her friends request. The Wizard's familiar lines, spoken while he distributes his gifts to Dorothy's companions—"with no more brains than you have, but they have one thing you haven't got" and so on—are as clear a demonstration as we could wish for that truths can be fabricated, thanks to "the magical series of transfers between theater and reality."[147] The convincing lie has, at least temporarily, the same power as the truth. The Wizard vacillates between displaying great wisdom, as when he grants wishes while simultaneously declaring his lack of the magical power to do so, and ridiculous ineptitude, as when he cannot bring his balloon under control, inadvertently leaving Dorothy behind. It is not possible to say whether the Wizard is extremely clever or an idiot, a "good deed-doer" or a humbug, because he is simultaneously all of these.

The Wizard's real power resides in his charming and garrulous nature; as his carnival background suggests, he is a born salesman. *The Wizard of Oz* shows us that anything is possible for those who are well-spoken.[148] Remember, Dorothy is only able to return home when she has learned to express her desire articulately. However, the story and film also teach us that the power of language is not granted easily. The garrulous Wizard is only able to ward off witches by keeping hidden and silent; Dorothy can put her wish to go home into powerful words only by completing her rite of passage. Because fear had compelled the Wizard to go against his "nature," when he finally speaks his words have nearly magical power. Conversely, driven by fear for the life of her dog, Dorothy puts them both in jeopardy by forgetting where she belongs. The Wizard and Dorothy are also peculiar doubles: he preserves his status by going underground, she gets blown away by the tornado because she cannot. The doubling and re-doubling that exist throughout *The Wizard of Oz*, the ambiguous uncertainty generated by its lies that turn out to be truths, are responsible for sustaining our interest when we watch the movie again and again.

Besides the doubled characters, the film's most obvious doubling concerns the dream, Oz, versus the reality, Kansas. Or is it the other way around? Oz, due to its Technicolor brilliance, certainly seems more real than the monochrome Kansas. Dreary Kansas, landlocked and tornado strewn, is at first only an awful place Dorothy wishes to escape. Later, Dorothy discovers that it is not the objective qualities of a place that make it desirable, but the fact that it has become "home." Because "home" is an imaginative condition, anything for which Dorothy wishes can be found "in her own backyard." Thus, the character of Dorothy acts out the two archetypal contradictory longings that humans have always felt—the desire for freedom and the wish to make a place one's home. These two polar activities of the heart ensure that we can never be absolutely content with a place, no matter how perfect it is. The double resonates with us because we too are doubled, conflicted creatures, forever trying to find a balance between weight and lightness, flight and return, to solve the riddle Milan Kundera calls "the most ambiguous question of all."

Those who have tried to design ideal cities have ignored the impossibility of solving this ambiguous question with finality. The weight of a city comes not just from the mass of its structures, but from the imaginative reading of its substance; not only from its truths, but from the convincing lies (like the myth of its founding) it articulately expresses about itself. The material image of a place gives us a "feel for it," so that we may dream of changing it, carving out our niche in it, and therefore dwelling in it. Too perfect a city, a city that was complete or always truthful, a city without *poché* spaces, cannot offer refuge. This is not to suggest that architects and planners ought to abandon the task of improving cities, only that they should reconcile themselves to the necessity that a living city must contain contradictions. What we imagine a city to be is as important as what it objectively "is." Perhaps the best for which we can hope is to make our cities aspire to the description Dorothy, upon returning to Kansas, offered of Oz: "Some of it wasn't very nice, but most of it was beautiful."

**Active Architecture
from Christo to Christmas Trees**

Christo's 'Wrapped Reichstag' has similarities to
gift wrapping, or the decorating of a Christmas Tree.

There is . . . a totally different experience of time which I think is profoundly related to the kind of time characteristic of both the festival and the work of art. In contrast with empty time that needs to be filled, I propose to call this "fulfilled" or "autonomous" time.

Hans-Georg Gadamer
The Relevance of the Beautiful

For two weeks in July 1995 an estimated two million people assembled in front of a large building in Berlin that had been wrapped in white translucent fabric by the artists Christo and Jean-Claude. (For simplicity's sake, I will refer to Christo and Jean-Claude as "Christo" in the remainder of this essay.) Some had traveled from other continents to be present at this event. Looking upon this unusual construction they would "sit, eat, sleep, dance, [and] listen to drums around the clock."[149] Many of those present entered into discussions concerning the cloth-covered edifice. What was the significance of it? How did it reflect on the checkered past of the city? What relation did it have to the destruction of the Berlin Wall, a less calculated but equally public architectural happening, in which many of the same people took part only a few years earlier? Some claimed that Christo's creation served as a purification rite, not just for the building, but also for the city, or for all of Germany.[150]

Familiar as Christo was with the slow machinery of bureaucratic approval, the time of this project had been unusually long in coming. First conceived in 1971, *Wrapped Reichstag* was in its planning, fund-raising, and, most importantly, approval gathering stages for over twenty years. Christo stated that the reunification of Germany, and the decision to relocate the German government once more to Berlin, made the time right for the project. "I think," he said, in recognition that all the delays and debates had ultimately worked in the project's favor, "all our projects have their own time."[151] It was the subject of the first artistic debate and legislative vote ever undertaken by the Bundestag, the German parliament. Peter Conradi, one of the speakers who defended the project during the debate, asserted,

> This wrapping will insult neither the Reichstag building nor German history, and will be a wonderful cultural symbol of our new beginning in Berlin. Like a prized gift, the Reichstag will become more valuable, not less valuable, after it is beautifully wrapped. *With this act, we want to give a*

positive sign, a beautiful, illuminating signal that fosters hope, courage, and self-confidence.[152]

Comments such as this betray an interest not so much in what the wrapping would look like specifically, but what it might signify: a "new beginning." The Reichstag began its conversion to the new home of the Bundestag immediately after the removal of Christo's wrapping (in a larger sense, Conradi was also talking about the rebuilding of an entire nation). In this respect, the effort produced a positive sign to initiate an important building project. Christo provided a service of divination, such as an augur might have done in ancient Greece or Rome, or as a *feng shui* master could be contracted to perform in present-day Hong Kong. Rather than rely on a ritual sacrifice, the artist employed another equally old but less controversial strategy. If the reality of reunification was weighing heavily on the German consciousness, Christo would veil, in a highly memorable way, one very visible aspect of that reality. If the Reichstag reminded Germans of previous errors and evils, then masking it could free them to dream hopefully of the future. Christo realized that new beginnings call for a disruption in the normal patterns of time, a function that festivals and holidays have always satisfied. The techniques he used to produce his temporal disruption relied on well-established formulae: that when something is hidden it gains an air of mystery, that the place of fantasy—the theatrical stage—is bounded in both space and time through the use of curtains, that all veiled women are potentially beautiful, and that donning a mask, as at Halloween or Mardi Gras, provides license for uncharacteristic behavior. This was a license some of those present joyfully accepted.

> The Reichstag project captured the imagination and may have even signaled a turning point in the city's attitude, a positive outlook that might be taken up by its new planners: for the first time since 1989, Berliners could let go, could experience, even enjoy, one another, could occupy a space they barely knew night and day—a moment whose memory left them wanting more.[153]

It was as much the project's fortuitous timing, as anything else about it, that facilitated these admirable accomplishments. Coming as it did after the reunification of Germany, and before the actual construction of many planned civic projects for revitalized Berlin, it was ideally placed in time to serve as a national (re)building rite. On perfect cue, the artist-prince Christo appeared to reawaken what he called the "Sleeping Beauty" of the comatose Reichstag, with the gentle kiss of his diaphanous fabric.

Whatever one thinks of its artistic merits, *Wrapped Reichstag* addressed a need as old as that of architecture itself: to found the act of building as securely in the imaginations of the people who will undertake it, see it, or use the result of it, as the walls of their structures and cities are founded upon the earth.

What ancient rites remember—and contemporary practices such as ground-breaking ceremonies, cornerstone layings, ribbon cuttings, house warmings, and geomancy still (weakly) acknowledge—is the necessity to mark the time and place of an architectural beginning. By interrupting the apparent continuity of time, ceremonies such as these create places where beginnings can stand out as significant events. Before undertaking an arduous task, we want to be convinced that we are doing the right thing at the right time and place. We need a sign that will foster hope, courage, and self-confidence, as well as insurance coverage. We must be able to imagine success before we can build it. Thus, any construction project, any creative endeavor that involves making, is necessarily double: a work of the imagination shadowing a work made of materials and physical effort. Doing one thing inevitably points to something else, so that a thing made always produces meanings made up. In English, we may detect a vestige of this wisdom in the double meaning of the verb "to fabricate." Both good liars and reliable builders must master the art of fabrication. And so we employ augurs, priests, *feng shui* masters, artists, or geotechnical engineers, who fabricate for us tales of good fortune. Thanks to them, we can dwell securely, comforted by the knowledge that both our constructions, and our faith in them, are well founded.

Despite Christo's proven success as master fabricator, his work raises some doubt as to whether it deserves to be called "art." Contemporary Western art criticism has found it difficult to account for the ephemeral and for works that cross too many disciplinary boundaries. The acceptance of Christo's work by the "art world" is hampered by his practice of producing constructions that fall outside the conventional gallery system for the display of art. Those accustomed to the conventions of museums and galleries—the well-established modes of display, the rather tidy divisions between painting, sculpture, and architecture, or between the "spatial" and "temporal" arts—often find photographs of the various "wrappings" incomprehensible. In his work Christo leaves behind few objects—except for his preparatory drawings, often used in raising funds for the projects—that can be sold as commodities. No one can really possess a "Christo collection." Christo's creations tend to polarize public opinion as to what art "is." Yet people who become involved in the projects, who witness them first hand or assist with their construction, even those who profess no previous interest in art whatsoever, tend to assume the attitude of religious converts. A Christo project challenges the supposed disinterest of the art viewer. To remain a mere spectator in the presence of an on-going Christo construction is to feel left out. Like a camper who happens upon another pitching a tent in a strong wind, the detached viewer who merely observes the process feels a tinge of guilt. A rare opportunity to be of service, to feel useful, and to connect with one's fellow human beings has been missed. A Christo project provides beleaguered contemporary men and women the rare chance to create something, to be a productive part of a community. Here, art theorist Suzi Gablik describes Christo's use of what I call the "Tom Sawyer effect" to gathers helpers to finish *his* fence:

> His own projects . . . take place outside the art world and often require legal battles, material production in factories, and the mobilizing of thousands of volunteer labor forces. Getting it all together is a collaborative effort on the part of many people, and the energy for the work is drawn as much from the community as it is from the artist himself. When *Running Fence* was constructed in California, a twenty-four-and-a-half-mile length of white nylon had to be stretched across land belonging to ranchers, most of whom were initially hostile to the project. Part of Christo's "work" involved winning them over; it took nearly a year to convince sixty families to let their land be used, but in the end they gave him not only the desired permission but also immense support, promoting press conferences themselves to defend the project publicly.[154]

Wrapped Reichstag, the product of a similarly arduous winning-over process, seems to have changed the way many Germans regard the Reichstag, as well as their attitudes toward the general reconstruction of Berlin. One could speculate whether the hope and self-confidence Christo's wrapping rite produced will make architect Norman Foster's work reconfiguring the Reichstag into a modern home for the legislature any easier. The good will may just as easily raise the stakes; high expectations generated by the event could easily lead to disappointment in the building. No matter what its lasting effects, the Reichstag wrapping is certainly a part of architecture—has always been a part of architecture—even though architects have not hurried to receive it as such. For the last four hundred years architects have become progressively more infatuated with dreams of unobtainable permanence, and with the abstractions of timelessness and ideal form. Fearing architecture's, and their own, mortality, architects have turned from the tangible and the temporal. This is a flight we must reconsider, as Christo has done:

> [The] temporary character of the project is also an esthetic decision to challenge the immortality of art: if art is immortal, if building things in gold, steel, and stone is really immortal and will make us live forever, probably it is more courageous to go away than to stay. All our projects have a strong self-effacing relationship. The fabric conveys that fragility of the work that will be gone. Our projects have a very strong nomadic quality, like the nomadic tribes that build their tents. By using this vulnerable material, there is a greater urgency to be seen—because tomorrow it will be gone. . . . Nobody can buy those works, nobody can own them, nobody can charge tickets for them. Even ourselves, we do not own these works. The work is about freedom, and freedom is the enemy of possession, and possession is the equal of permanence. This is why the work cannot stay.[155]

I am unable to judge the sincerity of Christo's denial of ownership, or the appropriateness of his use of the word "freedom." What I can state with certainty is this: whenever two million people gather peacefully to devote most of their attention to a building, those who claim to practice architecture should take notice. While popular appeal is undoubtedly insufficient grounds for determining the significance of a cultural event, the apparent spontaneousness of the gathering, as well as the wrapping's marginal position with respect to both the art world and popular culture, ought to give us pause. Architects should be clamoring to study this phenomena even if for the most self-serving motives.

Instead, *Wrapped Reichstag* has barely appeared on the radar screens of the architectural media. It is rare that Christo is invited to speak at architectural schools or professional conferences. We have decided that architecture is about objects and not events, about forms and not forces. What is most easily fixed and conceptualized is now assumed to be the essence of architecture. Because it is easier to describe forms than motions, motions have been all but ignored by architectural theories. This is not merely the fault of architects. Nearly irresistible cultural forces have influenced these choices, and in many ways architects had no choice at all. Coerced or not, architects have decided to exclude from their domain not only "happenings" of the Christo sort, but also the comparatively mundane work of making a building.

I am not claiming that architects care too little about the construction quality of the buildings they design, but that, for most of them, the activity of building has become either neutral, irrelevant, or meaningless. It is not considered a matter of "design." Architecture as it is now practiced and taught in most of the world is primarily an art of visual composition and secondarily an exercise in functional space planning. (Depending on the market niche sought, these priorities are sometimes reversed.) Because the first is usually taken by the public to be merely a matter of fashion, and the second simply common sense, we are beginning to see—in the nations that have granted professional status to architects and have thus restricted the right to offer architectural services—challenges being raised to these privileges. The word "architecture" in its most expansive sense is today more likely to be applied to the underlying structure of computers than to the art of building. Whenever someone is acknowledged as an "architect" in the public consciousness, you can be nearly certain that he or she is a politician or diplomat who has just orchestrated a complex legislative maneuver.

These signs are cause for concern, not just for architects, but for anyone who believes that building ought not be reduced to its lowest common economy-driven denominator. However, the signs of the times are not strictly negative. In the work of many architects and, especially, in the best work of students everywhere, I have detected a reason for optimism. Whenever I have discerned, in the attitude of an architect or student, an artist, craftsperson, or builder, a sincere interest in the temporal life of a work of architecture, I have found traces of what the philosopher Gaston Bachelard referred to as "weight" and "heart." Of course it is important that these designers and builders were gifted and clever and dedicated—this cannot be discounted. Their talents would lend credibility to any issue upon which they might choose to focus. Still, I take from their work something in addition to an appreciation of its depth. I also find in it an indication of where the best hope for meaningful architectural practices currently lies. The finest work that I know refuses the fashionable preoccupation with the certainties about architecture—its shapes, concepts, and objects, which I characterize as its "nounness"—while paying greater attention to its acts, timing, and material conditions, its "verbness."

This workmanlike stuff of architecture, which includes making it, preparing for it, cleaning it, painting it, and planting flowers around it, has spent the last two centuries toiling like Cinderella—unmentioned and confined to the ideological cellar. With the place-making, home-making, community-making activities hidden away, the shape-shifting "ism" sisters have been getting all the attention. Whatever the differences in their outward appearances, neoclassicism, the International Style, postmodernism, and deconstructivism all remain fixated on objects and shapes. Definitions such as Walt Whitman's "architecture is what you do to it when you look upon it" have been forgotten. Whitman asked, in "A Song for Occupations," "Did you think it was in the white or gray stone? or the/ lines of the arches and cornices?"[156] I hasten to add, recalling the concluding line from Italo Calvino's dialog about the arch in *Invisible Cities* ("without the stones there is no arch"[157]), that those stones and lines are necessary to provide us and Whitman with architecture upon which to look.

I am *not* suggesting that architecture can be reduced to a type of imaginative experience without tangible support. Even in its purely imaginary state, architecture always involves imagining bodies and things, events and substances, growth and decay. Nor am I claiming that architecture can exist as a verb alone. Its active verb processes and stable noun attributes are the yin and yang of architecture. But we have been paying too much attention to its nounness so, to restore a balance, I wish to extol its verbness. Our object fixation has become a detrimental single-mindedness that must be dispelled if we are to appreciate the imaginative richness of architecture.

My explorations have led me to both expand and narrow the kinds of practices I classify as architectural. I do not, as my inclusion of *Wrapped Reichstag* makes evident, restrict the creation of architecture to the activities of the professionals licensed to design buildings. In this essay particularly, I have been forced, perhaps by the shortcomings of my own imagination, to stray rather far from the conventional limits of the subject. For example, pressed for an illustration of meaningful building, I am unable to suggest anything better than the Amish barn raising—another subject rarely featured in architectural periodicals. Nothing else I could imagine shows us so clearly that timber joinery and cooperative effort may also facilitate the binding together of a community. Barn raisings make places and give shape to a civil society, and so I feel justified to count them among the concerns of architecture. In a similar vein, hoping to find an even simpler instance of the indissoluble connection between making and meaning, I am compelled to write of Christmas trees.

◇　　　◇　　　◇

Any activity of production involves the transformation of matter for a purpose clearly defined somewhere between society and the individual. The maker and the object to be created are tied together by an intimate relationship which does not disappear at the conclusion of the production process.

Giuseppe Zambonini
"Notes for a Theory of Making in a Time of Necessity"

The way that something is made leaves behind a residue that affects how we are likely to understand it. This is most obvious in things we have made ourselves, but it extends even to things that have been anonymously produced for us. I first recognized this aspect of things due to the influence not of an architect or craftsperson, but of a former roommate who was, of all things, an accountant. His lesson still serves as the best example I have of the importance of the manner of making. After sharing a house for a few conflict-free months, my roommate and I faced the approaching Christmas season. As I already owned an artificial Christmas tree that I had purchased for a former workplace, I suggested that we put it to use in our house. I even jokingly suggested that, with an entire house at our disposal, we should be able to find room to store the artificial tree, covered with a large plastic bag, in its fully decorated state for future Christmases. What a great labor-saving idea. We would simply retrieve the tree from its hiding place, put it where we wished, plug it in, and *voila!*—we were ready for Christmas.

He was aghast. Never mind saving the artificial tree from one year to the next, he informed me; we would not be using the accursed simulation at all. I was instructed that the proper spirit could only be produced if the tree was first, until very recently, happily growing, and second, painstakingly selected by us only after perusing the inventory of a number of vendors in our area. He would have preferred that we find and fell a tree on our own. The expediency of a purchased tree was acceptable only because our urban location and late start made the complete do-it-yourself method impractical. Once the tree was obtained we would, after securing the services of female companions, proceed to merrily decorate it to the accompaniment of seasonal music and drink. This was the *only* way that the Christmas spirit could be produced, although he allowed that married couples and families might follow a slightly modified recipe. Shortcuts of any kind were characterized as detrimental to the "spiritual" cause.

      While I have tried to portray this episode in an amusing way, I take its lesson very seriously. A Christmas tree does not mean what it is supposed to mean unless careful attention is paid to how it is produced. The process cannot be rushed. The time of making and the aura of meaning are inextricably linked. The time spent making a Christmas tree is of a different kind than the time most contemporary women and men spend at labor or leisure. As with many ritualized activities, there is a deliberate slowing down that occurs during the decorating of a tree. When decorating a Christmas tree, we all become patient artisans. Or, if we cannot, we are consigned to some peripheral task, such as procuring snacks or untangling the strings of electric lights. Children, who are apt to make the process more difficult, must nevertheless be suitably included. It is a ritual that calls to mind innumerable memories of past trees, of relatives now gone, and of houses and apartments we occupied long ago. The tree, its wonderful fragrance, and the tree-making ritual provide a locus for our shared memories. Tree decorating should be a social activity, in part because shared creation strengthens social bonds. Joseph Rykwert has written of building, and I believe it pertains as well to Christmas trees, that it "is, after all, the group activity par excellence."[158] It is a most unfortunate circumstance that requires someone to decorate a Christmas tree alone.

      Helping friends decorate their tree is a gift you give to them, a favor of your time and effort. Assuming that all goes as planned, you will receive some compensation for your trouble, not only through the gift exchange that the holiday brings, but in your reciprocal enjoyment of the activity. Presumably, you are owed similar assistance, if not now, then in the future. Therefore, the making of a Christmas tree has much in common with a barn raising. Within Amish society, assisting in the erection of another family's barn is also a gift that will eventually be returned to you and yours. There is a simplicity in this arrangement, as well as a notable corporeality. Each participant gives his bodily presence, as in the phrase, "When I needed you, you were *there*."

Moving to a new residence is yet another activity in which many friends are enlisted to help. What would otherwise be a somewhat disagreeable (but hopeful) experience also becomes a social ritual. Jokes are told, past moves are remembered, an impromptu feast is arranged, and the first beers are spilled on pristine floors. Such disorganized "christenings" are usually followed by a more formal house warming, once the family has settled in. In the wide realm of making, Christmas tree decorating, barn raising, and the arrangement of a new home represent a primitive stage where bodily presence cannot be separated from meaning or result.

Borrowing from the writings of Ivan Illich, and noting that these activities usually include a feast, another term for them would be "convivial."[159] The joyful conviviality of these creative volunteer activities is significant because it reveals the need for an economic theory of making. We will eventually have to address the question of economics if we wish to understand how making is situated in the present world.[160] For now, I will note only that the examples I have used, including *Wrapped Reichstag*, appear to invert several of our usual economic assumptions. The Amish may be prohibited by their beliefs from contracting outsiders to build their barns and from using heavy machinery to assist them. But even if these prohibitions were momentarily lifted, they would be unlikely to opt for the labor-saving methods. They would decline them, recognizing that they were being offered the equivalent of a pre-decorated Christmas tree. In the convivial economy of meaningful making, in a particular instance of what Lewis Hyde calls a "gift economy"[161] more effort is often better than less; slow may be better than fast. One cannot send a stand-in, hire a professional, or write a check. Offers to pay will be politely (or not so politely) turned aside: "I don't want your money," and "What are friends for?" Whitman writes,

> I bring what you much need, yet always have,
> I bring not money or amours or dress or eating . . . but I bring as good;
> And send no agent or medium . . . and offer no representative of value—but offer the value itself.[162]

What we are after in these productive activities is a kind of "economic" increase, a profit, not in terms of quantifiable wealth, but to the intangible imagined "feeling bond" between the participants. The power of the ritual decorating of the tree, of the activity itself, is such that the actual appearance of the tree is secondary. Even the lovely scent of pine matters less than the actions of those who bring the Christmas tree into being. The infamous "Charlie Brown tree," a sickly, misshapen tree selected out of pity in the *Peanuts* animated Christmas episode, makes just this point. This does not mean that great care is not paid to the appearance of the tree, only that, in the final analysis, the care means more than the appearance.

A Christmas tree is more important as a ceremony than it is as a thing. The thing can be simulated, the ceremony cannot. So it is with most ceremonies. Sincerity and effort are required, but perfection in the result is not. A minor stumble by one of the groomsmen does not ruin the wedding; dropping the class banner does not invalidate the graduation. Should one of the corners of the Reichstag fabric have come undone, this would have been quickly remedied with little impact on the work. Therefore, we can also find in ceremonial behavior some of the same improvisational qualities we see in play-acting. There is always some play within the play.

This is not to say that religious rituals and ceremonial rites are not carefully and precisely choreographed, or that the exact movements of the participants do not matter. However, because these activities involve fallible human beings, unpredictable materials, unforeseeable weather conditions, and other serendipitous circumstances, the occurrence of chance happenings must be allowed for in some way. Otherwise, the ceremonies would degenerate into either monotonous mechanical motions, identical each time, or risk becoming complete failures, simply because some minor deviation had occurred. Instead, successful ceremonies incorporate into their fabric the chance to turn or trope a novel turn of events into a significant sign.

"Trope" is a term for the poetic use of words that causes them to turn into a meaning, often technically incorrect, other than what they would normally have; it is a play on words, making use of metaphors, metonymy, synecdoche, or even puns, homonyms, and associations.[163] I intend using it in the wider sense of an imaginative way of framing things or events so that they may be read in a poetic way. For example, in the ceremonial rites the ancient Greeks conducted at their temples, the sacrifice of live animals would have undoubtedly lent an air of uncertainty to the proceedings (just as children do at Christmas). By incorporating the unpredictable behavior of the animal into the ceremony as a series of signs that required interpretation, the ceremony became more, not less, meaningful. This process did not conclude even with the sacrificial victim's death. The animal body was taken apart, read for further signs, and then symbolically reconstructed on the altar.[164] The sacrificial rites of the ancients were precisely structured to allow infinite adaptability and interpretation. This was done by creating a time when all present were receptive to signs—"pregnant moments" when every second was potentially saturated with meaning.

The ability to turn the unexpected to an advantage is vital to all arguments I might wish to make in favor of architecture's verbness. If the reader will allow me to add the ancient Greek sacrifice to the decoration of a Christmas tree, the Amish barn raising, and any number of ritualized social activities that involve making, I can propose a number of lessons for architecture. These are the lessons of the Christmas tree.

◇   ◇   ◇

LESSON I   Making and meaning are inextricably bound together; one cannot be understood without the other. The problem with artificial Christmas trees is not merely that they are poor simulations of the real thing, or even that they are artificial. All Christmas trees are artificial; there are no naturally occurring trees with lights and garland. Artificial trees (at least those that are designed to be convenient and time-saving) err in that they try to make easier and speedier a process that owes its worth to just the fact that it is neither easy nor quick. The logic of the artificial tree stems from a reductive misunderstanding of the function of Christmas trees. Christmas trees are not simply decorations; they are ceremonies. To understand all forms of artifice, all authentic human constructions, we must pay sufficient attention to how they are made.

Even though he makes beautiful drawings, Christo's most important skill appears to be his Tom-Sawyer-like ability to convince people, lots of people, that his projects are worth contributing to. (Unlike Tom, Christo does not exploit the generosity of others in an effort to minimize his own labor. However, both rely on the same principal—the fulfilling sociability that comes from participating in creative, sociable work—to achieve their somewhat different goals.) He intentionally chooses projects that require public support, including the assistance of many volunteers, to go forward. Christo is primarily a maker of secular ceremonies, not things. The gigantic scale and public nature of his works make them unavoidably theatrical. Their significance lies in the area of illicit commerce between what is made and what is made up.

Wrapping buildings, bridges, and islands in fabric, or hanging lights and glass balls on fir trees, are all seemingly foolish activities. It is only when we are willing to treat their underlying silliness as what Michael Taussig calls "public secrets" that we can trope these activities into socially meaningful constructions.[165] No useful critique of Christmas trees or Christo's creations is possible without addressing the conditions of their making. The forms of Christo's work, like the pattern of blood vessels a priest would read in a sacrificed animal's liver, are not irrelevant; however, they only have meaning within the temporal confines of the ceremony and its preparation.

◇   ◇   ◇

LESSON 2   The unpredictability of materials, site conditions, weather, and the builder's, the priest's, the augur's, or your friends' skill should not be unfortunate obstacles to the possible perfection of a ritual or building design. On the contrary, they may add to the meaningfulness of the endeavor. In other words, mistakes, contingencies, and unforeseen events are only detrimental to making when they cannot be troped into meaningful signs. The role of the architect is similar to that of the mentally agile augur, geomancer, or priest: to be clever enough to accommodate the unexpected and turn it to an advantage. Thus, the comic strip character Charlie Brown, otherwise the epitome of a loser, displays the makings of a great architect. By troping an emaciated twig into the most spiritual of Christmas trees, Charlie demonstrates how architecture comes to be. The fascination with the found object in the work of many twentieth-century artists, such as in the contents of Joseph Cornell's boxes, also demonstrates this ability to trope chance occurrences into meaningful relationships. Carlo Scarpa's preference for modifying existing buildings and incorporating architectural spoils into his works provides another example. So too, does Frank Lloyd Wright's swerving of a concrete trellis beam around an existing tree at Fallingwater.

Wright's move is, of course, something of a scam. The trellis beam was only in conflict with the tree because Wright put it there. The meaningfulness of architecture relies to some extent upon our willingness to entertain these public secrets, to not blow the whistle on them, or declare "bah humbug!" to decorating the tree. You *could* inform the burly ex-Marine, who is tearfully pressing a note into one of the seams between the black panels of polished stone at the Vietnam Veterans Memorial, that his deceased buddy is not really there, that his attempt to transmit a message this way is both pathetic and absurd. I would not advise it. In their encounters with buildings, many people are willing to be deceived, assuming the architect is a skillful enough spellbinder to meet them half-way. Architecture always gives us a little more than what is literally there. This is why Hermes, messenger and trickster, was considered the patron god of Greek craftsmen. But the architect cannot succeed before an audience of Scrooges or little dogs who are always sniffing behind curtains. Persons who have lost the willingness to use their imaginations are immune to architecture. These are people who would buy pre-decorated Christmas trees.

No construction will ever be perfect, and the architect can never guarantee that he or she can fool all of the people all of the time. What an architect can strive for is the production of an open work, a work that leaves room for the willing perceiver's imagination.[166] Here architecture has a distinct advantage over less massive, less tangible forms of artistic production. The large scale of a building's production requires that the making be social work. The necessarily unfinished nature of all buildings (which constantly weather and are maintained, altered, renovated, and adapted to other uses), like the temporariness of a Christo creation, assures that architecture is always a work in progress, and therefore always open to reinterpretation.

When a construction strives for perfection or permanence, it becomes a noun, something to possess and consume, as opposed to something that is done. But we cannot *have* architecture, we can only fabricate it. Of course, the situation of absolute timelessness is an impossibility. Contrary to anthropomorphic theories that would have architecture imitate the idealized shapes or the proportions of human bodies, architecture is most "human" not because of what it looks like, but because it is imperfect, in progress, and mortal, like us. To the degree that Christmas trees or buildings may aspire to lasting significance, they do so indirectly, by functioning as "time machines." They show us that architectural permanence is neither a material nor conceptual matter. Permanence and stability are instead "poetic constructs, anchored in collective memory and reinforced by rituals and customs."[167]

◇   ◇   ◇

LESSON 3   Disregard for the conditions of architecture's making, which has become the conventional mode of professional architectural practice, alienates architects from possibly the richest source of architectural meaning: the active engagement with the limitations imposed by material and social circumstances. If architecture appears only indirectly as a kind of ghost haunting our constructions (as I have argued in my essay "The Weight of Architecture"), it makes little sense to search for it exhaustively in objects and things. Architecture can only be captured objectively by reducing it to something less. Usually that will mean conceptualizing it into forms, types, functions, or sets of rules—none of which will contain the architecture. We will be able to steal closer to our illusive prey if we pay more attention to its situations, changes, and processes of becoming. This is why the philosopher Gaston Bachelard maintained that the study of motions was more important than the study of forms. Bachelard would advise us that to understand architecture we must "investigate its mobility, productivity, and life."[168]

Vernacular Architecture
and the Economics of Dwelling

Dwelling on the Boundary
Jefferson inhabits his bed between rooms
Monticello

I consider conviviality to be individual freedom realized in personal interde-
pendence and, as such, an intrinsic ethical value. I believe that, in any society,
as conviviality is reduced below a certain level, no amount of industrial
productivity can effectively satisfy the needs it creates among society's members.

Ivan Illich
Tools for Conviviality

Think of a scale beginning with works such as Christo's wrapping projects and the decorating of a Christmas tree, where effort and event are primary and the object disposable and secondary, continuing to works such as a barn raising, where the object ascends to greater longevity and an importance roughly equal to the activity.[169] The scale would extend past this point to partially industrialized production, such as more conventional building, and finally, on to fully industrialized manufacturing. (At this end of the scale the thing produced commands all our attention, while the process that created it is assumed to be meaningless.) This essay will focus on an area nearer the scale's middle—the phenomenon known as "vernacular architecture."

For much of the twentieth century architects have been attracted to architecture that seems to appear almost naturally in certain groups or societies. Most would include Amish barns in this classification, as well as Shaker structures, Pueblo dwellings, Italian stone *trullo* houses, and Yemeni high-rise mud houses, to name but a few. Too often architects' interest in these constructions fails to extend beyond issues of appearance—including massing, typical shapes, or materials used. I would like to add to these concerns a discussion of the social aspects of the ways these buildings are made and occupied.

When people join to make a vernacular building, as when people gather to decorate a Christmas tree, perfection of the final product does not appear to be the goal. The examples of vernacular buildings mentioned above are not representations of some ideal prototype. To the contrary, their minor imperfections and lively improvisations appear to be a major part of the "charm" we find in this work. While the creators of these buildings do face limits, they are generally determined by climate, the availability of materials, terrain, and cultural tradition, rather than by any explicit theory. The builders work from highly adaptable rules of thumb, rather than fully conceptualized principles that can be stated in the abstract. Just like ritual animal sacrifices, novel conditions, when encountered, are troped into solutions that reaffirm the basic beliefs of the builders. These subtle refinements to the established construction techniques are arrived at empirically, in response to necessity. A society that continues to produce vernacular architecture never sets off on a quest for additional improvements, never instigates an independent speculative enterprise dedicated to finding "the best way" to build. If my brief list of examples can be taken as a representative sample, I would be led to conclude that vernacular building is unconcerned with progress and not overly committed to efficiency; it is building as group craftwork or group ceremony.

Vernacular architecture is but one instance of the broader field of vernacular production. These production practices are as varied as the societies in which we find them. However, they have one thing in common: they are always, for want of a better term, "premodern." This distinction is based upon an ideological, not chronological, understanding of "modernity."[170] The fact that vernacular production continues to exist in contemporary times, albeit in a fragmented manner, proves that vernacular practices cannot be adequately bounded in historical terms. Just as vernacular architecture cannot be identified by appearance alone, neither is it accurate to portray it as unsophisticated or ancient. For the purposes of this essay I will characterize the ideological basis of modernity—and this is exactly what vernacular production rejects, or remains ignorant of—as having two components: modern economic relations are organized under the assumption of scarcity, and modern production processes are dedicated to ever-increasing levels of efficiency. While traces of these assumptions or goals may exist in vernacular production practices, they are always subordinate to other goals having to do with the experience of the productive process.

In the shift from premodern to modern societies, certain cultural assumptions are inverted. Edward Tenner, a chronicler of technological ironies, has characterized modern medical technology as "doing better but feeling worse."[171] Extending this reasoning, I think it would be accurate to describe premodern societies as "doing worse but feeling better." Premodern societies privilege meaning over utility. Members of these societies "feel good" because their dreams are as powerful as their methods are ineffectual. This is why vernacular production is always partially ceremonial. To the premodern, the creation of meaning is more important than the creation of an artifact. Modern societies, through their extraordinary technical ingenuity, have inverted this relationship between the virtual and the real. Modern production processes are no longer ceremonial, they are certain. Yet this very efficiency, this success at manipulating the physical world to suit our ends, has contributed towards lessening the significance of our achievements. Thus, our "feeling worse."

Vernacular architecture must then, according to my definition, combine both limited and relatively inefficient production practices with the will to imbue its creations with an "aura" of significance. Such practices are literally, from a modern perspective, backwards because they do not seek to progress beyond their moderate levels of efficiency. The economies in which such architecture flourishes also operate in an inverted manner: instead of being dedicated to growth, they strive to maintain the status quo. Economies of subsistence are driven by the assumption that the gods will (usually) grant the gifts necessary for the society's survival. A cooperative distribution of gifts occurs where moderns would expect to find competition for scarce resources. While a premodern society may develop an abstract exchange economy, particularly for trade with outsiders, the economics of their building activities will be closer to a gift or shared favor "convivial" economy. That is, out of necessity social interdependency will likely characterize the members of a premodern society. Therefore, even simple economic exchanges will be partly ceremonial. Economic relations are "convivial" in that the feeling an exchange creates is as important as the fact of the exchange itself; this attribute distinguishes them from either modern free-market or state-controlled national economies.

There is another aspect of the societies that produce vernacular architecture especially of interest to us at present—they are very close to the environmentalists' ideal of sustainable societies.[172] Nearly everyone in the society will have an appreciation for architecture because they make it, and their architecture will quite literally give shape to the community. While we may find in these societies rare instances of environmental destruction or degradation of their natural surroundings, these will be the exception. Usually, their intimate dependence on nature will be fully understood. Not only will the buildings they produce be friendly to the environment, they will demonstrate the manner of this friendliness through their form and method of construction. Wind direction, rainfall, runoff, solar radiation, evaporative cooling, and many other natural effects will be visibly incorporated into the design strategy. In other words, the limitations and stresses imposed by the environment will not be simply overpowered by technology, but will be re-presented in meaningful forms. Sustainable buildings actually serve to increase the understanding of, and appreciation for, the environment.

Well-being within a group where relations remain largely convivial is not predicated on growth or progress. Growth is only necessary in a predominantly abstract economy of commodity exchange. In a convivial society, much of the work one does is immediately and noticeably tied to self-preservation. However, there will also be tasks that, because of their size, will be beyond the ability of a single person or family. Constructing houses, churches, or fishing boats (vernacular *naval* architecture) will require additional help. These tasks are made possible through the assistance of relatives and friends. Their help is not paid for, it is a gift. For the sustainability of the society it is necessary that this sort of gift be passed on, reciprocated, when another is in need. As long as the type of help that is necessary to build big or complex structures circulates evenly around the community, everyone is likely to be satisfied. Scarcity will never develop because wants will not become virtually unlimited, but remain at sustainable levels. The gift of convivial assistance is perpetually renewable.

Nearly every member of the convivial society is likely to be adequately sheltered by structures that are often ingenious and sometimes beautiful. Because building, the group activity *par excellence*, promotes social bonds, dwelling—feeling at home—is rather naturally its result. The forms of dwellings (the object, the noun) exist in a reciprocal relationship with the form of dwelling (the activity, the verb). This is not to say that vernacular architecture must be simple or crude. While it may seem to contradict much of what I have just described, vernacular architecture may be found within contemporary capitalist economies, and it may be technologically sophisticated. This is possible because vernacular production need not reject the preference for efficiency and certainty in total, but only to the extent that some room remains, some trace of ceremony and conviviality, for the creation of a compelling aura to occur. Vernacular production is foremost an attitude toward making. Paradoxically, in contemporary society the pockets of uncertainty necessary for vernacular production may be most often found at the leading edge of technological progress. In this region of excitement and unpredictability, creation retains its "mythical" status, as when Silicon Valley techies whisper in reverent tones of the sacred founding of Apple Computer in the confines of Steve Jobs's garage.

When Le Corbusier extolled the virtues of the engineer's art in *Towards a New Architecture,* he was praising what I would call "engineering vernacular." The ocean liners, airplanes, and automobiles Le Corbusier then photographed were still partially experimental. Their production and operation had not yet become certain. The engineering behind them—like that behind Silicon Valley computer innovations in the seventies and eighties—was still that of a practice, as opposed to a technique. Thus, one was able to see in these planes and ships some of the astonishing ingenuity (as well as a restraint noticeably lacking in most early twentieth-century architecture) typically found in vernacular artifacts. Le Corbusier erred, at least in this polemic text, by attributing too much of the appeal of these engineering feats to the cold reason of technical rationality. His enthusiasm for industrially mass-produced housing, for example, overlooked the consequences of transforming a "machine for living" from an artifact to a commodity. Nevertheless, his praise of engineering vernacular reminds us that it is possible to produce vernacular artifacts, even high-tech vernacular, wherever pockets of uncertainty survive.

With this essential clarification made, I can begin to enumerate several ways in which the rejection or ignorance of modernity might play itself out in a hypothetical convivial society. The members of this society, having not yet converted their time into money, organize their activities in harmony with natural rhythms—the planting of crops, the migration of animals and fish, etc. They construct buildings during the period between planting and harvesting, when the primary activity of their existence can be suspended safely. As a convivial activity, building is enjoyable work, more or less like decorating a Christmas tree. There is no need to rush, so care is taken to decorate the buildings. Their completion might be, strange as it may seem to us, intentionally delayed by foundation rites, feasts, fasts, and ceremonies, as well as by taking undo care in the process itself. Perhaps these delays are timed so that the completion of the buildings falls on a holy day, marks the onset of the harvest, or allows them to receive newlyweds or a newborn. What to a member of a commodity-based economy would be considered useless work, wasted time, and rampant inefficiency is essential to the culturally conservative agenda of the premodern builder.

Also perplexing to the modern outsider would be the way that all of the care and ingenuity would fail to produce anything approaching perfection. Huts would be round but not perfectly circular; roofs would be gabled, but the slope might vary from one end to the other. The Navajo hogan exhibits these traits. This structure—usually consisting of corbeled logs covered with mud and thatch—was round and sometimes domelike, sometimes conical. The hogan was precisely organized. Its opening always faced east, the source of all goodness. A centrally located fire, with a smoke hole above it, divided the hogan into its north (male) and south (female) sides. On its west side, directly across from the opening, was the place of honor reserved for the matriarch or patriarch of the family group. However, it never seems to have occurred to the builders of the round hogans to make them exactly circular. Such an idealization would serve no purpose to the Navahos, other than to make their dwellings needlessly difficult to construct. It would not make them noticeably sturdier or add in any way to their meaning.

There is another reason why geometric perfection is rarely equated with excellence in vernacular construction. Because people in these societies build their own dwellings, sometimes with the help of children, parents, and friends, their standards of acceptable building practice are inclined to be flexible. One does not tell a lifelong friend, as one might a contractor, to "tear it down and do it over," unless one wishes to lose one's lifelong friend. In such a society, it would make little sense to strive for the exact imitation of an ideal model, which could only serve to erode rather than strengthen social ties. The preference for the conceptual ideal, the unattainable perfect thing—and therefore the preference for the noun—leads to what Ivan Illich calls "the corresponding impoverishment of the social imagination."[173] By making perfection or permanence the overriding goal, one declares war on reality, as well as on the good-natured incompetence of one's peers. Of course, in the construction of a temple, church, or shrine, the standard of workmanship would likely be raised far in excess of that required for more rudimentary buildings. Even still, minor screw-ups, botched jobs, material flaws, and construction errors would, whenever possible, be troped into meaningful improvisations.

This was one of Victor Hugo's chief complaints towards the

academically trained architects who, in their misguided striving for perfection, "mutilated" the great Cathedral of Notre-Dame. These "architects of good taste" failed to appreciate that Notre-Dame was a hybrid work, a building whose corporeal makeup was experimental, improvising, transitional. Hugo wrote,

> These hybrid constructions are by no means the least interesting to the artist, the antiquary, and the historian. They show us to how great an extent architecture is a primitive thing, in that they demonstrate (as the Cyclopean remains, the pyramids of Egypt, the vast pagodas of India demonstrate) that the greatest products of architecture are not so much individual as they are *social works*; rather the children of nations in labor than the inspired efforts of men of genius; the legacy of a race; the accumulated wealth of centuries; the residuum of the successive evaporations of human society—in a word, a species of formation.[174]

It makes sense to see vernacular architecture as social work rather than the product of individual genius. A dependence on individuals of "good taste" would impair a culture's ability to endlessly replicate, and endlessly adapt, its buildings after the "geniuses" had passed on. Hugo's characterization of Notre-Dame as a "species of formation" is one of his many references in *Notre-Dame de Paris* to the building as a living thing (later "killed" by the injuries inflicted upon it in the sixteenth, seventeenth, and eighteenth centuries). The Gothic cathedral, and the products of vernacular building, are buildings forever in the process of becoming. They demonstrate that architecture is as much a verb as it is a noun.

We have already seen that convivial ways of making, as concerned with the process as the product, proceed at a relatively unhurried pace. This is a natural result of the fact "vernacular labor" costs nothing, except for the expectation of future reciprocity.[175] (Certainly, this was not true of the Gothic cathedral; however, the honor of serving God undoubtedly kept the costs of labor lower than they might otherwise have been.) With materials, this is not likely to be the case. While materials may be free for the taking, they are also likely to be in limited supply. Therefore, vernacular constructions often exhibit an economy of material that even modern technologists can appreciate. The intimate relationship between the lives of the villagers and their natural surroundings would dictate that they not squander nature's gifts. This cleverness in using materials wisely could be directly attributed to a previously mentioned attitude—the tendency to see the natural world not as an endless repository of resources to be plundered, but as a somewhat unpredictable source of gifts. We are all familiar with the amazing variety of uses that Native Americans made of the buffalo. As we see time and again, in any convivial society, the gift of nature is not simply consumed but is sacrificed or otherwise troped into a reaffirmation of the peoples' spirit and way of life. In this manner, a gift received from nature or the gods becomes a sacrifice, and thereby a gift returned. Again, this insistence on combining an imaginative construction with an actual one, so that something made unfailingly produces made-up meanings, is a feature common to all premodern building construction.

◇   ◇   ◇

The functional shift from verb to noun highlights the corresponding impoverishment of the social imagination. People who speak a nominalist language habitually express proprietary relationships to work which they have. . . . Not only what men do but also what men want is designated by a noun. "Housing" designates a commodity rather than an activity.

Ivan Illich
Tools for Conviviality

The type of imagination found in a society that maintains an economy based primarily upon the exchange of gifts parallels, I believe, some other qualities of imagination that affect the types of things they build. Take, for example, Michael Taussig's description of Charles Darwin's 1832 encounter with the native peoples of Tierra del Fuego, South America. The Fuegians appeared to share everything equally among them. Even a shirt given to one would be immediately torn into pieces and distributed to all. While the Fuegians seemed to respect private property, they did so only after all goods were equally shared. Until then, by European standards, they were brazen thieves. According to Darwin, they "asked for everything they saw, and stole what they could," splitting the articles so that "no one individual becomes richer than another."[176] But this is not all Darwin observed.

> They are excellent mimics: as often as we coughed or yawned or made any odd motion, they immediately imitated us. . . . They could repeat with perfect correctness each word in any sentence we addressed them, and they remembered such words for some time. . . . All savages appear to possess, to an uncommon degree, this power of mimicry. I was told, almost in the

> same words of the same ludicrous habit among the Caffres: the Australians,
> likewise, have long been notorious for being able to imitate and describe the
> gait of any man, so that he may be recognized.[177]

Despite Darwin's condescending tone, his recognition of the highly developed mimetic faculty among the Fuegians was accurate. There does seem to be a connection between the heightened capacity to imitate and the reliance on an economy of gifts. It is as if these primitive peoples, who appeared childish to Europeans, lived in a state of civilization closer to what Vico's "ideal eternal history" would term an "Age of Heroes," than to our "Age of Men." They preferred imitation to abstract indication. Vico wrote,

> Children excel in imitation; we observe that they generally amuse them-
> selves by imitating whatever they are able to apprehend.
>
> This axiom shows that the world in its infancy was composed of
> poetic nations, for poetry is nothing but imitation. . . . The arts are nothing
> but imitations of nature, and in a certain way "real" poems made not of
> words but of things.[178]

Could it be the capacity to produce "poetic" constructions made of things, such as vernacular architecture, is somehow facilitated by a childlike heightening of the mimetic faculty? We might suppose that the apparent naturalness we find in vernacular architecture stems, in part, from the sort of embodied imagination that takes pleasure in imitation, and in the embodied exchange of gifts. Taussig concludes "that there is indeed an intimate bond between the spirit of the gift and the spirit of the mime."[179]

Without the will to detach the value of a thing from the thing itself, premodern societies cannot conceive of prices (at least not within the group), the need for growth, or the necessity for "progress." We moderns tend to see gifts as material expressions of generosity, but to a society that depends on gift exchange to eliminate scarcity, the gift is "an impossible marriage between self-interest and altruism."[180] The social being of the gift is a two-headed beast, a shotgun union between opposing forces, a clever cultural trope that conceals greed beneath magnanimity. Lewis Hyde maintains that gifts have an "erotic life," by which he means that gifts serve to produce attractions and unions between members of a society.[181] The gift itself is a chiasmatic union of *eros* and *logos*, producing a clever form of self-preservation that binds the individual to the group. This is why Ivan Illich defines a convivial situation as that leading to "individual freedom realized in personal *interdependence.*"[182] It is not by accident that suitors in most societies approach the object of their affection bearing gifts.

If a totally free market did exist (the closest approximations we have are stock markets and commerce conducted via the Internet), in it the value of things would have to be determined by *logos* alone, and exchanges of goods or services would not produce social bonds. In social groups such as the Gypsies, who reject anything remotely approaching this form of economy, or with peoples who have never "discovered" it, such as the Fuegians before they encountered Europeans, there is still the tendency to speak "poetically." These groups will not likely have a written form of language or, if they do, it will be limited in its use. Neither will they have a widely used system of mathematical notation. In a recently published study of Gypsy or "Roma" culture, Isabel Fonseca reports that reading is still a highly suspect activity with the Gypsies. Even today, most European Gypsies are illiterate, and Gypsy merchants avoid written accounting records (and therefore taxes). Fonseca repeats the tale of a young Belgian who lived with the Gypsies long enough to learn to speak Romani, as he described his despair at the thought of returning to his native language.

> I would no longer express myself in the wild, archaic "Romanes," unfit for small talk. I would no longer use the forceful, poetic, plastic descriptions and ingenious parables of the Rom or indulge in the unrestrained intensity and fecundity of their language. Old Bidshika once told us the legend about the moon's being dragged down to earth by the sheer intensity, weight and witchery of the Romany tongue. And it almost seemed that it could be true.[183]

Gypsies stubbornly protect the primacy of their spoken poetic language while resisting other forms of acceptable capitalist behavior, such as serving as wage laborers. Recall that the rise of literacy in Europe paralleled rather closely the growing dominance of capitalism. Some historians now claim the spread of literacy throughout Europe during the Renaissance was driven primarily by commercial interests, not by the pure "thirst for knowledge" that was trumpeted in our high school history books.[184] The emergence of a new class of citizen, the bourgeoisie, was facilitated by this group's mastery of "the stylus, quill, and counting board."[185] Simultaneous with these developments, vernacular architecture grew gradually scarce on Western European soil. This would seem to fit with Victor Hugo's declaration in *Notre-Dame de Paris* that "the book will kill the building."[186]

You might object that the last illustration I have chosen, the culture of the Gypsies, is inappropriate because the Gypsies do not produce a vernacular architecture, or—due to their migratory habits— much of anything else we could identify as "building." Recall however, that I am concentrating on imaginative practices, not building styles or techniques. If one insists on maintaining that architecture exists only as things, objects, and shapes that can be described geometrically, then few, if any, examples of Gypsy architecture will be found. If on the contrary one holds, as I do, that architecture is an imaginative activity, a manner of making, a poetic way of framing objects and events so they become meaningful, then a Gypsy architecture most certainly does exist.

In European cities, Gypsies tend to inhabit the spaces we might refer to as the urban *poché*, much as homeless people do in American cities. In these unseen, under-utilized, and un-programmed spaces, often in the face of the most abject circumstances, Gypsies find the freedom to *dwell*. Accomplished squatters, they erect camps with what Fonseca describes as a "shanty-accretive aspect."[187] Some live out of abandoned cars and buses; others literally inhabit the gaps between the structures of their inhospitable *gadje* (non-Gypsy) neighbors. There is a long tradition of migrating Gypsies traveling in caravans of elaborately decorated wagons, pitching tents, setting up portable shops, or arranging spaces to provide for impromptu musical performances. Gypsies are adept at transforming the waste products of *gadje* societies into adornments to their dwellings. They seem to have a preference for the most brightly colored, most tasteless, kitsch items (Fonseca writes of one woman's fondness for Day-Glo plastic fruit trees), which are re-presented as meaningful ornaments—much as our poor ancestors fashioned homemade ornaments to decorate their Christmas trees. Gypsies are dedicated rebuilders and recyclers; they do not recognize the fundamental capitalist concept of disposability. Like hermit crabs, they prefer to reuse their living quarters rather than create them from scratch.

Fonseca describes a young Albanian man's intentions to move his family into an abandoned high-rise apartment building without plumbing or services. He talked of repouring the concrete floors, painting, and stenciling "the walls with flowers as Gypsies everywhere loved to do."[188] What Gypsies gain by inhabiting the places no one else wants is the freedom to live as they please. It is instructive to compare the freedom to dwell obtained by Gypsies, through forsaking the material comforts most non-Gypsies demand, with the lack of autonomy accepted by modern apartment tenants, who are often forbidden to own pets, raise children, redecorate, or hang pictures wherever they wish. In the modern age, Ivan Illich writes, "the ability to dwell is the privilege of the dropout."[189] Gypsies, like all vernacular builders, require a suitable imaginative dimension to their building and dwelling. Fonseca, quoting the Polish poet Jerzy Ficowski, reports how otherwise assimilated Gypsy workers in 1950s Poland rejected the worker housing that had been provided for them.

> The year 1952 witnessed an event which is inconceivable for non-Gypsy observers. Some families from block 37 betook themselves to a wooded spot in the neighborhood of Nowa Huta, to live there in crude huts made of planks. They said that a house was like a prison to them.[190]

Gypsies rejected the worker housing because it was presented to them finished, complete, as a product, *a noun*. As such, it left them no opportunity to make anything out of it, either imaginatively or in fact; it left them no room to dwell. The situation of the Polish Gypsies recalls Adolf Loos's story of the "Poor Little Rich Man," who commissioned an architect to design every aspect of his house. Because the resulting house was perfect, the rich man was unable to change or add a thing, not even to bring his birthday gifts into it. Not only could he not hang another picture, his architect instructed him, "you can't even *move* a picture." Lacking the willingness of Gypsies to abandon material comfort for the ability to dream, the rich man suffered a sad fate.

> Then a transformation took place in the rich man. The happy man suddenly felt deeply, deeply, unhappy. He imagined his future life. No one was allowed to give him pleasure. He would have to pass by the shops of the city impervious to all desires. Nothing more would be made for him. None of his dear ones was permitted to give him a picture. For him there would be no more painters, no more artists, no more craftsmen. He was precluded from all future living and striving, developing and desiring. He thought, this is what it means to go about life with one's own corpse. Yes indeed. He is finished. *He is complete!*[191]

Earlier, I mentioned Hugo's claim that the misguided efforts towards perfection had mutilated, and eventually "killed," the Cathedral of Notre-Dame. Here, Loos implies that a perfect and complete house may transform a client into a corpse—if not literally, then in spirit. What is it the Gothic and vernacular builders, and the Gypsies, recognize about dwelling, that the rich man's architect did not?

The failure to participate in the construction of an artifact—like paying someone to decorate your Christmas tree for you—inhibits your ability to imaginatively make it "yours." As Illich has written, "most people do not feel at home unless a significant proportion of the value of their homes is the result of the input of their own labor."[192] In Martin Heidegger's well-known essay "Building Dwelling Thinking," he proposed a reciprocal relation between the three activities of his title.[193] By "dwelling" he meant not just to have shelter and an address, but to feel at home on the earth. In order to dwell, we must build; in order to build, we must be capable of dwelling. According to Illich, "dwelling in this strong sense cannot really be distinguished from living."[194] Vernacular architecture cannot really be distinguished from vernacular dwelling, and therefore from vernacular *living*. Indeed, Marco Frascari often defines architecture as the union of the art of living well with the art of building well. Even those who do not literally make buildings must occasionally engage in thinking about building-dwelling as they make subtle changes to their environments. In the late 1980s film *Planes, Trains and Automobiles*, the traveling salesman Del Griffith always places a picture of his wife on the nightstand of whatever sleazy motel he temporarily occupies. It is only by this act, which he might have learned from the Gypsies, that Griffith is able to dwell. When architecture strays too far from these activities of social imagination, it begins to be an area of technical specialization, an obscure object of perfection, a commodity. Instead, I would agree with architect-educator Stephen Parcell, who writes, "Lifelong immersion in an architecturally permeated world" qualifies us all as "architects since birth."[195]

It is only by uniting the imaginative aspects of building with the practical ones that dwelling becomes possible. According to Gaston Bachelard, the chief function of a house is to shelter daydreaming; "The house protects the dreamer, the house allows one to dream in peace." Bachelard might have been describing the Gypsies with the phrase, "housed everywhere but nowhere shut in, this is the motto of the dreamer of dwellings." And he may have had Loos's poor little rich man in mind when he wrote,

> Maybe it is a good thing for us to keep a few dreams of a house that we shall
> live in later, always later, so much later, in fact, that we shall not have time

> to achieve it. For a house that was final, one that stood in symmetrical relation to the house we were born in, would lead to thoughts—serious, sad thoughts—and not to dreams. It is better to live in a state of impermanence than in one of finality.[196]

Bachelard counseled that understanding is more readily gained by studying motions than studying forms. Therefore, the lack of a characteristic form to Gypsy architecture should not cause us to overlook it. The forms of Gypsy houses have radically changed over the centuries, simply because the leftover products and spaces produced by *gadje* civilization have so noticeably "progressed." The Gypsies' *manner* of dwelling has, however, remained constant. By virtue of the ability to "dream dwellings" they can migrate from one hostile circumstance to another, always finding the means to make themselves "at home." Meanwhile, the authentic ancestral home of the Gypsies remains the subject of ethnographic dispute, a dispute the adaptable Gypsies willingly exploit. There are advantages to not being "from" anywhere. With no verifiable historical origins, and no homeland, the Gypsies are free to make wherever they happen to be their home.

Gypsy culture also played a significant role in *Notre-Dame de Paris*. Victor Hugo's famous novel (written in 1830 and set some 300 years earlier) is, in part, a celebration of outmoded misfits. His heroes are pre-Renaissance architecture, the young Gypsy woman Esmeralda, and the misshapen Quasimodo. Hugo wistfully wrote of a golden age of architecture, before Johannes Gutenberg's printing press, when thought was "never written out in full except upon those books called buildings."

> So, too, see how from the time of the discovery of printing architecture gradually decayed, withered, and dried away. How plainly we see the water sinking, the sap drying up, the thought of the time and of the people withdrawing from it! The sense of chill is almost imperceptible in the fifteenth century; the press was still too weak, and could only draw off somewhat of the superabundant life of mighty architecture. But with the dawn of the sixteenth century the disease of architecture becomes apparent; it has ceased to be the essential expression of society; in distress, it becomes classic art; from being Gallican, European, indigenous, it becomes Greek and Roman; from being real and modern, it becomes pseudo-antique. It is this decline which is known as the Renaissance, or revival. And yet it is a magnificent decline; for the old Gothic genius, that sun which is setting

> behind the gigantic presence of Mayence, for some time longer pierces with
> its last rays all this hybrid heap of Latin arcades and Corinthian columns.
>
>   It is this setting sun which we take for the light of dawn.[197]

Hugo never used the term "vernacular architecture," yet I believe he was
mourning the obsolescence of something very similar. See how the
authentic buildings produced by the architecture he supports, in
opposition to the neoclassical and what he calls the "theocratic," are
described. Could this not just as easily serve as a suitable definition for
the vernacular?

> They belong to this age. They have a human quality which they perpetually
> mingle with the divine symbolism under whose inspiration they are still
> produced. Hence edifices pervious to every soul, every intellect, and every
> imagination, still symbolical, but as easy to understand as Nature herself.[198]

Hugo recognized and wrote of a startling aspect of the modernity many
took to be the light of a new dawn. While most characters in his novel
experienced the withering away of places "pervious to every soul," only
society's effluvia—the Hunchback and the Gypsies—are able to feel at
home, to dwell in the poetic sense Heidegger described. Quasimodo
dwells in the masonry *poché* of the great cathedral; Esmeralda and her
clan in the seedy underworld of Paris. At first glance neither has built
anything obvious, which might seem to sever the Heideggerian
connection between building and dwelling, if we did not accept the more
flexible understanding of building demonstrated by the motel-dwelling
Del Griffith. For these dreamers of dwelling do, in fact, make
imaginative constructions. Quasimodo, in his childlike way, constructed
a maternal persona for the grand Notre-Dame. He inhabited the
structure as a son would cling to his mother, and he animated it with
friends of his imagination—gargoyles, sculptures, and his beloved bells.
Hugo wrote of the "almost consubstantial union of man and edifice,"
where the cathedral had served, in the different stages of Quasimodo's
life, as "egg, nest, home, country, universe."[199]

In just the same way, the constructions made by Esmeralda and
the Gypsies, as I described them previously, are a form of building,
simply one less obvious than we have come to expect as "architecture."
The Gypsies are also master fabricators in another sense—they are
excellent liars. Fonseca reports that their lies are mostly intended to
amuse. For Gypsies, lying is an art. As their surrounding environments
are both inhospitable and dull, and because they fear outsiders knowing

them too well, Gypsies spin tales that are more entertaining than the truth. In Hugo's novel, the Gypsies produced elaborate social fabrications—bogus royalty including the "King of Tunis," "Duke of Egypt," and "Emperor of Galilee," along with a "Court of Miracles" to administer a thieves code of honor and the laws of the lawless. When poet and outsider Gringoire appears before the court, facing execution, he attempts to persuade it that his status as bard and playwright should qualify him as one of them. "'I don't see,' said he, 'why poets should not be classed with vagabonds. Aesop was a vagrant; Homer was a beggar; Mercury was a thief.'"[200]

Gringoire was right. There is a strong affinity between the poet and the thief. By mentioning Mercury, who is the Roman counterpart to Hermes, Gringoire invoked not only the patron deity of thieves, but also of craftsmen and merchants, as well as the protector of gates and boundaries, and the maker of marital matches. How can this strange grouping of godly affinities and responsibilities be explained? I can begin by observing that the earliest markets were usually located at the boundary between two communities. The markets in ancient Greece were neutral territory, designated a sacred place, agoras on the boundary, which would contain temples to various gods, most notably the god of the boundary himself—Hermes. Thus Hermes came to be associated with trade. Vico tells us that merchant, merchandise, and commerce all retain a vestige of the name of Mercury. At the boundary it was difficult to insure that exchanges between two primitive groups, neither of whom answered to a greater authority common to both, were always the result of mutual consent. As Norman O. Brown writes, there could be no legal distinction between legitimate and illegitimate appropriation: "There is only simple appropriation." Brown mentions "theft by consent," where one party openly takes the property of the other, under the assumption that the other will later respond in the same manner.[201] In this situation, it is difficult to distinguish theft from the exchange of gifts.

The peculiar mirror-image relationship between gift and theft is also evident in the contemporary practice, common to many American universities, of stealing some symbol or ritual object from a rival school. The victim of such a theft (who is always intentionally made aware of the perpetrator's identity) is then obligated to steal the object, or perhaps a similar object belonging to the other, back again. The thefts are never taken seriously, so as to be reported to the authorities. Instead, the two parties enter into a unique social relationship of friendly hostility and "one-upmanship." Brown reminds us that "'stealing' meant originally stealthy or magical action," where "magic is needed to overcome the distrust of the stranger and break down the taboos of social intercourse."[202]

It was Hermes's association with such forms of cleverness, such craftiness, that endeared him to those who skillfully worked with their hands. I have invoked the example of Hermes-Mercury to underscore the complexity both in all forms of human exchange (gifts, marriage, sex, speech, barter, trade, theft) and of human artifice (language, poetry, art, architecture, crafts, lies, markets, laws, governments). According to Georg Simmel, the most significant outcome of all forms of exchange between humans is "that the sum of values is greater afterward than it was before."[203] In the gift exchange, the university's mock thefts, or even the lovers' embrace, this increase is to the intangible feeling-bond between the individuals. In the commodity exchange, the increase takes the more readily measured form of profit. In either case, the society depends on the continuation of the exchanges for its survival.

Hermes was both a facilitator and promoter of *all* forms of exchange, but he was no mere transparent conduit through which messages flowed. He was lustful and cunning; thus he was not above allowing his own desires to color his messages, or influence the terms of the bargains he might strike. Hermes knew of our tendency to blame the messenger for the message, particularly when his duties involved conducting dead souls to the underworld. To protect his own interests, Hermes needed to be skilled in the art of rhetoric, so that his words could both conceal and reveal his intentions. The mythical figure of Hermes gives a body to language, and to other types of exchange. We moderns tend to think of language (and economic markets) as disembodied systems, so we mistakenly assume that the purpose of language is to convey meanings that are absolutely clear. On the contrary, the possibility of lying is built into languages, just as the possibility of a swindle is an inherent risk of buying and selling.

Hermes was also a god of sustained action—of making and trading and moving from place to place—but it was seldom his mission to end up anywhere in particular. He had no "theory," no metaphysical foundation, to guide him in his tasks. His nimble-minded swiftness, contempt for rules, and eternal roaming of roads and boundaries allowed him to make his home anywhere, never to be shut in. Without the need to maintain a consistent point of view, Hermes always looked at any situation from at least two directions. In his preference for exchanges that increase the sum of values, Hermes recognized that illegitimate appropriations may be necessary at times to sustain the flow of exchanges, just as poetic lies may be needed to insure that a message will have suitable impact. This is the sense in which I intend to promote the "verb" aspects of architecture; I do not support an architecture of change and approximation in opposition to an architecture of immutable perfection. To idealize change, as in the economist's concept of growth or the technologist's imperative of progress, is to accept a conceptualization every bit as burdensome as the ideal of permanence.

Hermes points to an understanding of architecture that encompasses both its truths and its lies. Architectural making always involves something real and something "really made up." Architecture is a boundary condition, between the practical and the imaginary, the visible and the invisible. Neither this, nor my observations regarding the absence of a "perfection imperative" in vernacular architecture, should be understood to mean that architects cannot be inspired by the purity of abstract geometries. Once more, we must look beyond building shapes to evaluate the success of such architectural practices.

Consider Thomas Jefferson's home, Monticello. It was designed in the classical idiom and in concert with the principles of Andrea Palladio. Monticello is organized into symmetrical wings, each connecting to a central octagonal volume, which is capped by a dome. The fact that Jefferson's house was conceptually complete, as an abstract composition of ideal shapes, did not make it uninhabitable, unlike the inhumanly complete house of Loos's rich man. Jefferson was, evidently, a much better architect than the one the unfortunate rich man commissioned. Jefferson knew how to select aspects of the house that could, while fully constructed, suggest multiple possible uses, thereby multiple interpretations. The most telling example of this is Jefferson's famous bed, which he located in an alcove that formed the boundary between two rooms, so that he might roll out of it in one direction to enter his study, and in the opposite direction to place himself in his bedroom. By inhabiting the boundary, Jefferson, like Hermes, could keep his options open; he was not forced to live in a state of finality. While his house may have appeared to be complete as a composition and a construction, it was incomplete, and so inhabitable, as a dwelling.

The gift, the convincing lie, the poem, the work of architecture—all are social constructions combining something literally and materially true with an imaginative dimension that cannot be real or true, or even complete. This is why there is no contradiction in the ancient Greek craftsmen's worship of Hermes, the god who refused to establish a point of view, so that his "truths," like the craftsmen's, were always convincingly made to fit the situation at hand. There are "good" lies, such as gifts, where the material benefits to the recipient overshadow the eventual expectations of the giver, thereby producing a social bond. Vernacular architecture produces good lies. There are also "bad" truths, such as to claim that the Fuegians ruined the perfectly good shirt Darwin's companions gave to them, when one of them might have worn it proudly, but only at the cost of eroding the integrity of the Fuegian community. Vernacular builders everywhere exhibit the preference for good lies over bad truths.

We have come full circle. I began with twentieth-century architects' interest in certain "poetic" ways of building they came to call "vernacular architecture," a phenomenon most commonly found in groups at least partially isolated from the cultural assumptions of modernity. I noted that the cooperative efforts of these peoples usually took the form of a gift exchange, and recognized a correspondence between the spirit of the gift and the spirit of the mime. I observed that the heightened mimetic faculty, a "childlike" attribute, influenced the tendency to speak and build poetically, and identified some of the conditions that would disrupt this influence, most notably the spread of written language, whereby ideas would become intangible, but inflexible. I invoked Loos and Bachelard to demonstrate the impossibility of dwelling in a perfect building, and Hugo to describe the "death of architecture." And I have tried to show how, following this death, it is increasingly difficult for any of us to dwell in the world, unless one happens to have the mind of a child, a poet, or a thief.

So what now prevents us, all "architects from birth," from building poetic edifices "as easy to understand as Nature herself?" Why, given all the attention architects have devoted to vernacular building (or the Gothic), do we so seldom reproduce its effects? Shall we blame Gutenberg and his press? Or the academically trained architects Hugo accused of "mutilating" Notre-Dame? Should we fault all architects, as Bernard Rudofsky, the author of *Architecture Without Architects*, once did?[204] Or only modernists, as Tom Wolfe and Prince Charles more recently have? Who killed architecture? Was it Enlightenment theorist J.-N.-L. Durand, in the laboratory, with his grids? Is capitalism the culprit, as Manfredo Tafuri and many others have argued? How *did* we move from buildings, and building practices, "pervious to every soul, every intellect, every imagination," to obscure "books" of architecture, which only the initiated can decipher? I propose a somewhat new, although not entirely original, solution to this mystery. *We* murder architecture, whenever we subscribe to the bad truth that it is merely a technique, a commodity, or a noun.

◇   ◇   ◇

An economist is a man with an irrational passion for dispassionate rationality.

John Maurice Clark

It is now possible to proffer a characterization of the general attitude of post-Enlightenment modernity: it is the belief that there are neither "good lies" nor "bad truths." With this attitude, modern scientists (as well as others, such as journalists, whose existence would not be possible without the underlying metaphysics of modernity) began their task of presenting us with an "objective" picture of reality. Through their efforts, the world would become progressively demythologized and disenchanted. The Age of Heroes must end when miracles are rationally explained and skeletons are dragged from every closet. Good lies (such as art, architecture, religious beliefs, gift exchanges, and the aura of heroes), which had made the weight of mortality and imperfection bearable to primitive peoples, were supposed to be rendered obsolete by the creation of devices and procedures able to extend our lives, cure our illnesses, shelter us effectively, and provide for our bodily pleasures. Technologists proposed to substitute *actual* improvements to the material conditions of human life, for the *imagined* superstitions, myths, or poetic lies that formerly granted us psychological, but not necessarily physical, comfort. They operate under the secure assumption that the former are unquestionably superior to the latter.

Like the elder sibling who informs a younger child, "There ain't no Santa Claus, but it doesn't matter, you still get the gifts," technology strives to erase the lies—but not their benefits—from our lives. The price technological progress extracts from us, in return for its undeniable material improvements, is the degradation of all forms of imagination not immediately tied to its own agenda. Only with great difficulty can we simultaneously entertain convivial lies alongside scientific truths, which is, obviously, why the Catholic Church persecuted Galileo. In a technological society the majority of individuals will presume that the efficient cause is the only legitimate cause; all other endeavors of imagination will be labeled "foolishness." Once we accept the hypothetical Cartesian doubt on which modern technology is founded, all else following this decision proceeds with apparent rationality. Bachelard would likely call this form of thought a "closed rationality," rational thought unable to rationally explore its own consequences.[205] The economist's "irrational passion for dispassionate rationality" is a member of this species of thought.

The members of a technological society have made the decision (even if they are unaware of it) to privilege one way of thinking, based on one set of assumptions about the world, over all others. Hermes would caution us against making such an irrevocable choice, which is why philosopher of technology Jacques Ellul characterizes this decision as "a wager."[206] While the technological wager sets in motion an endless search for the most efficient means to meet all conceivable ends, this quest is severely constrained by the conceptual foundations of technology itself. Concerns unrelated to the efficient cause must be, by definition, excluded. This lack of flexibility gives to modern technology a conceptual rigidity betrayed by our preference for a "nominalist language" and our tendency to convert activities to instruments, concepts, or commodities; that is, "dwelling" is replaced by "housing." The "impoverishment of the social imagination," which Illich maintains must be the result of this "functional shift," falls outside the scope of legitimate technological concern, primarily because imaginative social constructs defy the precise conceptualization technological thinking demands.

Let us look at a simple instance of a technological improvement to a building, and its social effects. Earlier in this essay I described the central position occupied by the fire within the Navaho hogan. During the Middle Ages, European houses gradually progressed from similar centralized open fires combined with smoke holes, to a centrally located fireplace and masonry chimney. Besides durability and noncombustibility, the massive masonry chimney also provided the probably unforeseen benefit of a thermal mass, which could store the heat from the fire, radiating warmth even after the fire had gone out. Even for the wealthiest nobles, who could employ numerous servants, the job of simultaneously tending several fireplaces around large mansions, castles, or palazzi was a daunting one. Thus, parts of houses would often be cyclically heated during the course of the day. The rooms left unheated for certain periods, such as the bedrooms at daytime or the dining room at night, would then, during the coldest weather, become temporarily uninhabitable. An unintended by-product of this cyclical pattern was that the family would be forced to inhabit a common space within the house during most of the daylight hours. In the peasant houses, which were likely to contain only a single room and single fireplace, this was even more the case. Privacy for the peasant could only be had at the expense of warmth. Family members were forced to gather together simply in order not to freeze. Since the same fire was used for cooking as well as heating, the hearth was both literally and symbolically the heart of the home. Travelers and guests would immediately be ushered into the warmth and glow of the home's fire.

Beginning with Benjamin Franklin's enclosed stove in the late eighteenth century, we have witnessed continual refinements to the means of heating our buildings. Modern high-efficiency furnaces evenly heat entire houses, using far less fuel than the old fireplace, and require no tending. There is no question that, from the standpoints of efficiency, convenience, and comfort, the modern centrally heated home is superior to houses heated by fireplaces. What are the social effects of this improvement? In the uniformly heated modern house there is no comfort-related reason for the family to gather together. If the parents work and the children go to school, the only remaining family gathering is likely to occur around the evening meal. After this, the family members will all retreat to "their rooms," to complete homework, make phone calls, engage in hobbies, watch television, or surf the Internet.

Accompanying this freedom, and this privacy, there may come symptoms of a breakdown in the sociability of the family: the parents barely speak to each other, or to the children; the children feel isolated, jealously guard their "turf," exhibit anti-social behavior, etc. None of this, surely, *has* to happen, but the conditions facilitated by the improvement to the house's heating system significantly increase the possibility that it *can* happen. By removing a certain form of abjection, a type of lack with regard to our control over the environment, the furnace eliminates our need to gather together and to form social bonds as compensation for the inefficiency and inconvenience by which we stay warm and alive. The fire*place* was an architectural feature of the home, whereas the furnace is merely an invisible machine. In Illich's terms, the fireplace is a "convivial tool" for heating a home; it accomplishes its task of providing warmth and at the same time promotes sociability. The furnace is a technique that is, at best, neutral in its effects on sociability, but is more likely detrimental to it.

To the social imagination, there are qualities of fireplaces that might cause us to prefer them over the modern furnace, even though they are less convenient and efficient. This is why Lisa Heschong, in her book *Thermal Delight in Architecture*, takes issue with standards of "thermal comfort" promoted by the American Society of Heating, Refrigeration, and Air-conditioning Engineers.[207] ASHRAE's preference for a uniform temperature throughout all the enclosed areas of a building removes the architect's ability to influence social gathering by providing islands of "thermal delight." In the same spirit, Kenneth Frampton has bemoaned the role air-conditioning has played in removing climatic factors from the influences on architectural form.[208] Frampton might also have mentioned the social effects of air-conditioning, whereby people are influenced to seal themselves within their homes, as opposed to sitting on their front porch, taking a walk on the shady side of the street, or visiting the local swimming hole. In nearly every technological innovation we could examine, we would find similar trade-offs. An immediate and readily quantified material improvement will be accompanied by a delayed and difficult to define negative impact on our social, ethical, or erotic imaginations.

Architecture is a way of building that produces convivial tools like fireplaces, front porches, wind-catchers, and (perhaps Heschong's most "delightful" example) porch swings, where the gentle motion of the conversing couple creates enough air movement to comfort them on a summer evening. Such clever architectural details combine a true and ingenious construction with an intelligible sign—a "good lie"—that not only promotes sociability, but demonstrates qualities of materials, human nature, and the environment. In this sense, the term "sustainable architecture" is actually redundant, because it is inherent in the nature of architecture to prefer convivial constructions to technical fixes that may be highly efficient, but meaningless. The ethics of an alive architecture demands both soundness and utility from what has been made, and an imaginative conviviality from what has been made up. As it was Hermes's role to sustain all forms of exchange, it is architecture's role to sustain the meaningfulness of places and constructions, so that in all the encounters between bodies and buildings, "the sum of values is greater afterward than it was before."

When faced with the temptations of technological improvements, extremely cohesive and self-secure groups, such as the Amish or the Gypsies, may refuse the material benefits in order to preserve their ways of living-dwelling. Convivial economies can exist side by side with commodity-based economies, as was the case in Europe during the Middle Ages and much of the Renaissance, and as the Amish still do within the United States. In the United States groups of ethnically similar immigrants have often formed extended families who pool their resources to invest in such things as the college education of the next generation. In Europe, Gypsies maintain hostile or predatory economic relations with outsiders, and convivial relations within their clans. Within the smaller society of the family, the gift—not currency—exchange remains the dominant economic mode, even in modern economically advanced countries. We see this pattern again and again. Within the group, where social relations remain paramount, the exchange is based on gifts. At the boundary between groups, gift, theft, and commodity exchange all vie for dominance; since the sixteenth century, the commodity has usually come out on top.

Once commodity exchange becomes the dominant mode of economic relations, value first becomes lodged in things (commodities) that are used up (consumed) when we make use of them. Because the success of a market economy depends on continuous growth, those who participate in it will be rewarded for their zeal to transform all formerly convivial processes into techniques and commodity exchanges. The mechanisms for doing so are well known—advertising and marketing are foremost among them. For those modes of making and using that resist commodification, such as the work of poets, artists, and other "foolishness," the market economy will offer primarily disincentives. We push this type of "uneconomic" behavior to the margins of our society, primarily because it does not fit the conceptual underpinnings of our economies. (For example, contemporary economic theories have virtually nothing to say regarding the difference between those who gain intense fulfillment from their work and those who consider their jobs as a necessary evil.)

This has affected architectural production in significant ways. For example, the aspect of architectural practice known as "design"—which, despite the best efforts of Enlightenment theorists like J.-N.-L. Durand, most often proceeds in the same unpredictable and uneconomic manner as other forms of artistic production—has been pressured to become more businesslike. Architectural firms now rely on vaguely defined terms such as "schematic design phase" and "design development phase" to assure their clients that there is a method to their madness, and that design production operates in the well-organized manner of an efficient machine. The design phases guarantee the client certain *products*, but no one knows if any of them will contain architecture. The unquantifiable verbness of architecture increasingly is ignored in favor of the readily commodified products of its nounness.

Building, the act of making upon which architecture depends, is similarly affected by the conceptions of a market economy. Its communal and craft aspects, as well as the social bonds they produce, face gradual extinction. Building has become more industrialized, and the builders themselves progressively less skilled. Today the most valuable construction-related skills are managerial, not productive, as is borne out by the rise to prominence of the construction manager.[209] One of the first steps a construction manager usually takes is to apply the technique known as "value engineering" to an architect's working drawings. During this process, the value engineer will suggest changes to the architect's design in order to make the building less expensive to construct. There is generally a tacit agreement between value engineers and architects that the shape of a building will not be altered; thus value engineering further institutionalizes the contemporary assumption that the worth of a building lies only in its appearance and in the ways that it instrumentally fulfills its functions. (Lawrence D. Miles, the "father" of value engineering, designated these concerns, respectively, as the "esteem" and "use" factors of a given commodity.[210]) Value engineers are less sympathetic to the "irrational" attachments some architects have for traditional materials and craft-based methods. To the value engineer a replica of a carved limestone panel, cast in fiber-reinforced concrete, is unquestionably superior to its "authentic" counterpart, given that it looks identical to it, while it is also quicker and easier to produce. Like their predecessors, the efficiency experts, value engineers simply apply, rigorously, our contemporary economic assumptions to a given production process—in this case the making of buildings. Value engineering assumes that "value" is a neutral designation of worth, but the concept of "value" already presupposes that anything "valuable" can and should be treated as a commodity.

Less direct in its association to architecture, but equally influential to the way buildings are received, is learned consumer behavior. Consumers, always wanting more, bigger, and better things, are unlikely to find long-term satisfaction with a work of architecture. In this regard, Joseph Rykwert has written that the task of architecture—"to make every building an integrating, reconciling, and cleansing form," to promote a sense of well-being, and to make people feel at home—opposes the agenda of advertising.[211] Rykwert suggested that, in a perverse sense, architects might have something to learn from advertisers.

> Consider American advertising, a highly organized and still growing industry. An increasing proportion of the huge sum—large enough to float most European countries—which is devoted yearly to persuade Americans to spend more than they need, goes onto motivational research and its variants. Which means that it is being spent to harness the findings of psychologists to selling methods; translated into realistic terms, it is the deliberate sharpening of neurotic tendencies—anxiety and inferiority, loneliness fears, auto-eroticism, repression, infantilism and all the others—so that they may be assuaged and averted by some quite superfluous product which the advertiser offers.[212]

Rykwert argued that by adopting the methods of advertising, while reversing its aims, architecture might be better equipped to fulfill its role in an economically hostile environment. In the forty years since his article was published, the prevailing trend has been in the opposite direction. The planning of a retail store now capitalizes on all our carefully researched behavioral tendencies, neurotic and otherwise, to turn every store into an efficient mechanism of consumption. Supermarkets place healthy, desirable foods, such as fruit juices, across the aisle from the cookies, forcing parents to endure what retail consultants cynically refer to as the "whine factor."[213] Rykwert was not claiming, nor am I, that the mechanisms that promote ever-increasing consumption are evil. My conviction is that a free-market economy, and the mechanisms it creates, are merely techniques to promote economic exchanges; in other words—they are technological improvements over less efficient convivial forms of economy. Like all other technological improvements, a "free market" requires that certain social costs be tolerated in return for the material benefits it provides. While tales such as Charles Dickens's *A Christmas Carol,* and countless other morality plays, have held the heartless individual businessman (rarely businesswoman) up for scorn, the wholesale comparison of economic systems is a more complicated matter. It would be overly simplistic to portray the convivial or premodern societies we have known as good, and consumer economies as bad. Social benefits are maximized in a convivial economy, whereas material benefits are maximized in an economy of commodity exchange.

A gift economy is therefore "socialist" in the most literal sense of the word. Economies of commodity exchange begin as "materialist," but eventually progress to the stage where economic power is most readily represented in less tangible goods, and therefore demand the more flexible designation "capitalist." In the gift economy, value is never completely detached from activities or things, so property retains its mythical and erotic dimensions. The freedom to make economic choices can only be obtained indirectly, by means of a kind of manipulative generosity, a delayed or displaced value. (The effective limit of this procedure is determined by the point where gifts begin to be interpreted as bribes.) In *local* markets, goods as well as buyers and sellers retain their corporeality, so that these situations continue to promote social interaction, much like the pure gift economy. In a market*place*, factors other than the maximization of profit (such as the friendliness of the grocer or the beauty of the butcher's daughter) continually come into play.

I agree with Jacques Ellul, in distinction from critics such as Manfredo Tafuri, that it is not capitalism per se, but the overuse of instrumental logic, that fuels "the devaluation of all human activities and tendencies other than the economic," so that "all values [are] reduced to money values, not only in theory but by practice."[214] In this, I accept Ellul's contention that "Marx carried out an encircling maneuver" around capitalism, but did not depart from those aspects of bourgeoisie thought that established the primacy of economic relations over all others. The rise of *homo economicus* is but one manifestation of the growing dominance of what Kant called the "determinate concept," and Vico the "intelligible universal." While gift exchanges and free-market bartering predate the Enlightenment, neither large-scale Marxism nor corporate capitalism would be possible without many of the assumptions upon which modern thought is based.

Any economic system that seeks to orchestrate exchanges on the national or international level is eventually forced to resort to overly reductive conceptual assumptions. This fact is demonstrated in that we often find convivial economies within the family, tribe, or village, but not within nations. Economically speaking, there can be no "global village" because economic relations in a village are always largely convivial, and village economic markets are bounded in time and space.[215] It makes little difference, at least as far as the production of architecture is concerned, whether a pervasive and all-encompassing economic market, where all values are reduced to money values, is "free" or state-controlled. It is the lack of a definable boundary, the absence of any region where the *logos* of economic value does not hold sway, that leads to the devaluation of all other human activities. Both the capitalist corporation and the state-controlled bureaucracy are disembodied timeless entities unaccountable for their actions in the way mortal human beings must be.

It is important to remember that modernity has simply reversed the relative importance that premodern societies established between the real and the imagined. Where primitive societies countered their meager ability to dominate nature by constructing imaginative "worlds" of great sophistication, we have responded to our success in controlling natural forces by becoming less imaginative in ways that are not strictly technical or entrepreneurial. Both tendencies have always been present in human societies, which is why all societies have employed techniques and conducted economic exchanges. This is also why traces of premodern economic behavior still persist in our late-capitalist economies. Tipping waiters and cab drivers, or haggling over the price of an automobile, are vestiges of a time when economic exchanges were as much social as material transactions. So is the practice among groups of friends where everyone volunteers to buy a round of drinks in a tavern. According to our prevailing economic assumptions, there is no difference between four friends who each take turns buying a round of drinks, and another four who equitably split a total bill at the end of the evening. However, the first practice is more convivial; it allows each person to momentarily deceive themselves into believing they are distributing gifts to their friends.

Dwelling is the imaginative counterpart to physical living. While a living body can be defined by any of a number of technical considerations, such as the presence of respiration or brain wave activity, dwelling requires that this person "feels" at home. Making a suitable place for oneself in the world is, like the convivial relations among friends sharing drinks at a bar, largely a matter of what one believes. Therefore, a useful economics of dwelling must be able to account for the made up as well as the made. An economist of dwelling must utilize poetic measures as well as quantifiable ones, because only poetry can establish the exact dimensions of something as ever-changing as the house of our dreams. "A house that is as dynamic as this allows the poet to inhabit the universe. Or, to put it differently, the universe comes to inhabit his house."[216] Resorting to numbers and geometric calculations alone, to calculate the value of this house, this *home*, should now stand out in all its absurdity. We might as well try to put a price on the universe.

Despite the best efforts of all involved, the construction of nearly all buildings exceeds their initial budgets. While not an excuse for errors, faulty planning, or price gouging, an economics of dwelling would probably reassure us that this is how things should be. Most important works of architecture prove to be more difficult to build than originally anticipated. Persons moving from apartments into homes of their own frequently underestimate the costs associated with maintaining a house. Their calculations often ignore the time that will be spent tending lawns, shoveling snow, or patching the roof—time that could easily be spent on pursuits that would generate additional income for the family. Yet the client who commissions an adventurous design from her architect, or the first-time owner of a single-family house, seldom regret these decisions. Whether they recognize it or not, they come to learn that architecture is not a commodity that can be delivered efficiently. When we "buy" architecture we acquire a priceless gift in addition to the building or landscape we have created. Architecture creates a universe where we can safely dwell.

Gendered Words, Neutered Spaces,
and the Trouble with New Urbanism

Morning in Santa Barbara

It therefore makes sense from our standpoint of a philosophy of literature and poetry to say that we "write a room," "read a room," "or read a house."

Gaston Bachelard
The Poetics of Space

Architecture has always been a marginal enterprise, precariously poised between fantasy and utility, between dreaming and surviving. The tenuous position of architecture in contemporary America is unique only in that it constitutes a historically unprecedented form of abjection. Since architecture, and other forms of imaginative activity, have always thrived in conditions of uncertainty,[217] architecture's present cultural irrelevance cannot be blamed solely on the conditions of our late-modern technological society. We architects have been slow to adapt from dealing with hardships imposed by the natural environment (the form of adversity to which architecture has traditionally responded) to addressing obstacles originating in the conditions of late modernity itself. While the conditions of architectural production are now radically different than those encountered by premodern builders, architects have not modified their strategies in order to adequately engage this new reality.

Professional architects today are simultaneously too powerful (they employ nearly omnipotent building technologies that allow them almost total freedom to construct any building shape they might choose—for example, the practice of Frank Gehry) and not powerful enough (they are mostly prohibited, by unrealistic budgets and insufficient time, from telling the "good lies" necessary to allow their clients to imaginatively dwell in their creations). Architects, as well as most other artists, enter the new millennium vacillating between enthusiastic infatuation with technology and the nostalgic desire to withdraw from it. Neither approach permits architects to balance the often competing concerns of fantasy and necessity. Architects can neither abandon nor ignore technology because it is no longer simply a collection of techniques for making buildings, it is the determining characteristic of the site or situation on which they must build. Therefore, architects in the twenty-first century must artificially create appropriate forms of uncertainty, voluntarily chosen areas of powerlessness, to substitute for the material hardships of vernacular builders, so that they might emulate their success.

Perhaps architects could learn from the ways that a similar set of obstacles, in the arena of language, have been dealt with by successful authors and poets. When Victor Hugo complained that the invention of the printed text had killed architecture, he misled us with a less-than-precise identification of both the victim and the perpetrator. The victim was not architecture, but one manner of making architecture; the assailant not the book, but one way of thinking, encouraged by the book. Hugo correctly sensed that printing technology had a profound effect on our languages. The conversion of vernacular speech to the nationalist "mother tongues" paralleled the replacement of vernacular building with industrialized construction. As Hugo understood, this shift in the nature of languages (and buildings) made them less active, less substantial, less poetic. Yet this loss of freedom of expression has remained concealed behind the societal and personal autonomy we gained in our progress to modernity.[218] With an adequate income, we have the ability to buy what we want, live where we choose, select the jobs we prefer and the schools we wish to attend. All of these freedoms share an inherent limitation: they are available to us only if we accept, and can afford, our roles as consumers. Compared to other possible roles—maker, poet, politician—the role of the consumer is largely passive. The shift in our language from verb to noun announces the transition to a less active mode of engagement with our environment. Ivan Illich has called this "the industrial corruption of language."

> Fully industrialized man calls his own principally what has been made for him. He says "my education," "my transportation," "my entertainment," "my health" about the commodities he gets from school, car, show business, or doctor. Western languages, and above all English, become almost inseparable from industrial production. Western men might have to learn from other languages that ownership relations can be restructured in a convivial way.

Illich mentions that only salaried employees "say they *have* work; peasants say they *do* it." He then continues,

> In a society whose language has undergone this shift, predicates come to be stated in terms of a commodity and claims in terms of competition for a scarce resource. "I want to learn" is translated into "I want to get an education." The decision to do something is turned into the demand for a

> stake in the gamble of schooling. "I want to walk" is restated as "I need transportation." The subject in the first case designates himself as an actor, and in the second as a consumer. Linguistic change supports the expansion of the industrial arena.[219]

This corrupted or nominalist form of language reflects the "devaluation of all human tendencies and activities other than the economic." We begin to lose sight of the possibility for convivial relations, or any alternative to the industrial, or by now postindustrial, mode of production because our language ceases to grant us the means for expressing these thoughts. In this regard contemporary English, the officially sanctioned language of the global economy, is nearly the opposite of the poetic Romani spoken by Gypsies. Isabel Fonseca, in her study of Gypsy culture, confirms this by noting of Romani, "Its function is to express sociability rather than to exchange ideas."[220] With the atrophy of the mimetic faculty, caused by its devaluation and subsequent disuse, the poetic potential of language—the possibility of producing tropes, multiple meanings, ambiguities, play with sounds—is gradually abandoned in favor of a strictly literal communication code.

English has become the chosen language of international business not only because it is the language of the world's premier economic power, but also because it is (in its written form) both alphabetic and lacking in word genders. By excluding genders, pictograms, and poetic effects, the English taught in business writing courses moves toward the purely instrumental notation offered by mathematics. Native English speakers do not consider the lack of gendered words to be of any significance. However, as Gaston Bachelard points out, what is lost in this lack is one manner of making distinctions, one mode of imitation, one faculty for portraying nuances. For example, Bachelard, who wrote in French, maintains there is an important distinction to be made between the dream (*rêve*, masculine) and the daydream, or reverie (*rêverie*, feminine). He believes word genders address the "need to make everything feminine which is enveloping and soft." His specific example does not interest me so much as his more generalizable remarks on it.

> [The defense of gendered language is] a very insignificant remark in the eyes of philosophers who speak the language of the universal, a very insignificant remark in the eyes of thinkers who hold language to be a simple instrument which must be forced to express all the subtleties of

> thought with precision. But how would a dreaming (*songeur*) philosopher who ceases to reflect when he is imagining and who has thus admitted to himself the divorce between intellect and imagination, how could such a philosopher, when he dreams about language and when words are coming out of the very depths of dreams (*songe*) for him, not be sensitive to the rivalry between the masculine and feminine which he discovers at the origin of speech? Already, by the gender of the words which designate them, the dream (*rêve*) and reverie appear to be different. Nuances are lost when one considers dream and reverie as two varieties of the same oneiric phenomenon. Rather let us keep the clarity which is the genius of our language.[221]

Bachelard clings to his gendered words because he will not deny himself any of the possibilities of language. He prefers the language of "natural poetry" to the "language hammered out by authoritarian prosodies." He intends to use the substance of language itself, not merely what is said but how it is said, to seduce or inflame. Whereas the modern legal contract or construction specification must avoid ambiguity at all costs, for the poet the ability to suggest multiple readings is the hallmark of success.

The "divorce between intellect and imagination" is required in the nominalist mode of language in order to insure precision, and to convey authority. The inapplicability of the poetic mode of expression to the efficient production demanded of *homo economicus* is amusingly parodied by Gabriel García Márquez in his novel *Love in the Time of Cholera*.

> Florentino Ariza wrote everything with so much passion that even official documents seemed to be about love. His bills of lading were rhymed no matter how he tried to avoid it, and routine business letters had a lyrical spirit that diminished their *authority*. His uncle [and boss] came to his office one day with a packet of correspondence that he dared not put his name to, and he gave him his last chance to save his soul.
>
> > "If you cannot write a business letter you will pick up the trash on the dock," he said.[222]

Ariza struggles, and ultimately fails at his task. Resigned to defeat, he claims, "Love is the only thing that interests me." Even if inspired by love, poetic expression must be devalued because it is an instance of a "tendency other than the economic."[223]

Saul Bellow's novel *Humboldt's Gift* recounts the disposition of the United States—aggressively capitalist, progress-oriented, and English-speaking—to proudly kill off its finest poets (no doubt an extreme form of devaluation). Bellow's character Charlie Citrine ticks off the names of the dead: "Edgar Allen Poe, Hart Crane, Randall Jarrell, John Berryman." He mentions that America is "too tough" for these weaklings, as is proved by their "childishness, madness, drunkenness, and despair."[224] Citrine observes that, unlike the rest of us, these men refused to become "unfeeling bastards" in order to survive. So it is ultimately with sympathy that he says "look at those good and tender and soft men, the *best* of us. They succumbed, poor loonies."[225]

The apparent freedom offered in an advanced capitalist, technological society is therefore a freedom of very limited depth. We partake of this freedom under terms demanding our strict conformity. With the loss of the mimetic mode of expression, language, and all else, loses its substance. Early oral contracts used the bodies of the involved parties as corporeal guarantees.[226] Illich tells of the eventual substitution of the testament for the solemn act whereby a father placed a clod of soil into the hands of his chosen heir. In old Hollywood westerns, the Indians were always skeptical of the white man's written treaties. The Indian chief would only come to terms when faced with an "honorable" white man whom he believed to have "iron in his words." Swearing as he "grasps his beard or his balls," the honorable man, Illich writes, pledges "his flesh as a troth" to insure his fidelity to the contract. When the written contract replaced a man's spoken oath, "a conditional curse called upon himself in the event he should become unfaithful," a living, breathing document was superseded by one intangible and indestructible.[227] A person's name in a society where the mimetic faculty was still active was probably an imitation of their body, or what it did— "smith," "weaver," etc.—so the existence of one's "good name" was immediately tied to the well-being of one's body.

As I suggested at the beginning of this essay, the dematerialization of language has been accompanied by the abstraction of substance and space. Leon Battista Alberti, in 1435, utilized projective geometry to construct linear perspective, the rational technique for reproducing appearances. During the Renaissance, as perspective became the dominant way of "seeing" reality, space was progressively mathematicized. However, this mathematization did not at first become fully instrumental. Geometric forms and formal orders still retained their symbolic association with the structure of the cosmos, and with the perfection of God. Because of the widespread interest in the science of optics, it was also commonly known that linear perspective was a technique of approximation—that its monocular viewpoint, and the differences between the flat picture-plane and the curvature of the human retina, could compromise the "realistic" quality of the perspective drawing. Besides its nearly magical ability to produce illusions of reality, perspective implicitly shattered the concentric harmony of the Aristotelian cosmos. But this would remain largely unnoticed until around 1500, when Copernicus nudged the earth out of its privileged position in the universe.

Also during the Renaissance more flexible Arabic numerals, which included the all-important zero, gradually replaced the computationally cumbersome Roman ones. Measures of time were made uniform, and town clocks proliferated in all settlements that could afford to have them. Calculations were further idealized in the form of algebra, which could express mathematical relations free of the weight of particular numerical values. All this apparently rational progress was paralleled by a nearly equal fascination with numerological mysticism. Alfred Crosby writes, "Astrology was more popular during the Renaissance than during the Middle Ages, employing hundreds of number smiths and astronomers in the production of horoscopes of increasing mathematical sophistication."[228]

In architecture, this impulse took the form of a hybrid project— the mathematical-mystical idealization of architecture. It operated by founding a system of correct, harmonious, or absolute geometrical proportions upon objectified measures of the human body, on musical scales, or on the discovery of seemingly magical computational outcomes, such as the Fibonacci series. The analogy between building and body had, perhaps, always existed, and even Vitruvius had couched it in terms of ratios and rhythms, but here something new was added—the desire to forever fix these relationships so that they might be included as equals among the mathematically expressed discoveries of astronomy and physics.

Swept along in the tide of enthusiasm for abstraction, some of the most talented architects of the age professed their devotion to these "rational" rules. This enthusiasm for rules mirrored the grammatical standardization of language; it attempted to replace the embodied limit-conditions of vernacular building with universal laws, just as the poetic expression of vernacular speech and symbolic geometries had been

replaced by the rules of grammar and mathematics. In the hands of
Andrea Palladio (or centuries later, Thomas Jefferson) such rules might
contribute to an architecture that was notable for its appearance of rigor,
and orderliness, as well as, in its geometric perfection, its symbolism of
the divine structure of the cosmos. These triumphs had the unfortunate,
and still lasting, effect of lending credence to the rules, rather than to the
individual genius of the architect who applied them. For idealized human
proportions took the *shapes* of bodies, not the miraculous condition of
their being alive, to be their most significant quality. As Hugo later
recognized, this dogma of perfection overlaid the stones of Renaissance
architecture and its descendants "like a second petrifaction."[229]

Not all Renaissance architects were convinced of the utility of
the rules of proportion. Michelangelo criticized Albrecht Dürer's catalog
of human proportional "types" for idealizing that "for which no fixed rule
can be given," and for neglecting to address human movement.[230]
Michelangelo's commitment to qualitative proportion, in not only the
shapes of bodies but their age, led him to controversy when his *Pietà* was
first displayed in 1499. David Leatherbarrow writes that the sculptor
"balanced the thirty-three year old body of the dead Christ on the lap of a
woman who appears to be . . . in her early twenties, perhaps late teens."[231]
Michelangelo was forced to defend his work with an appeal to the
qualitative principle of decorum; in order to convincingly portray the
eternal purity of the Virgin, he was forced to tell a "good lie," depicting
her as an innocent young woman. To have shown her in middle age
would have been to produce a literally true work, but one that rang false.
Michelangelo, whom Hugo considered to be the last great architect,
made frequent use of similar selective distortions throughout his
incomparable artistic career. Unfortunately, his defense of a flexible
understanding of proportion, and emphasis on bodies that moved and
aged, was overpowered by the idealism and mysticism of his
contemporaries. By substituting a mannequin or a mummy for a living
being, these architects sucked a little more of the waning life force
from their buildings.

More than a century later, René Descartes postulated an infinite,
three-dimensional, immaterial space. In Descartes's space without
qualities, there could be no distinction between sacred and profane, no
"auras," no bodily awareness of up and down. Improving on what was
only a latent feature of linear perspective, Descartes freed the gridding of

the universe from its association with visual appearances (although not from the ideological implications of the "cone of vision"), producing a wholly instrumentalized space. In Cartesian space, one could now provide a precise description of location, size, or shape—an undeniable boon to navigation, the study of ballistics, as well as to the expansionist dreams of the powerful. In it, the intellect would finally triumph over the imagination, for if all previous spatial conceptions had been to some degree anthropomorphic, Cartesian space denied human qualities. Where the anthropomorphic space of vernacular societies had suggested that everything, including a village or tribe, had its own body and therefore bodily limits, Cartesian space freed the intellect to conceive of such abstractions as "endless growth." Geometry, which heretofore had always been to some degree symbolic, became instead analytic. Drained of its imitative possibilities, Cartesian space is de-poeticized; populated with disembodied intellects having no reliable knowledge of one another, it is antisocial space. It is also static, given its preference for easily described shapes and regular movements, where spatial relationships can be substituted for temporal and material ones.

To most contemporary readers, accustomed as they are to living and imagining in Cartesian space, Gaston Bachelard's *The Poetics of Space*, first published in France in 1958, initially seems at once strange and vaguely familiar.[232] The spaces Bachelard describes are saturated with qualities. They may be mysterious, as is the space concealed within a box, or personal, as the space one "occupies" in a bureau or wardrobe; they can be contradictory, possessing "intimate immensity," or at once fragile, and yet sheltering and secure, as in the image of a nest. In reading the book, we begin to see that poetic space is the space in which we lived in our childhood, when our legs rejoiced at running upstairs, when we feared venturing into basements, and when we could project ourselves into miniatures, "dreaming dwellings" in flowers, toys, and shells. In *The Poetics of Space*, as well as in his other books dedicated to exploring the "material imagination," Bachelard revealed himself to be a dreamer of words. His philosophy gives us one of many examples we might find where Hugo's division between living and dead language begins to get complicated, because the words of Bachelard's dreams were most often *written* words.

Somewhat like a Gypsy finding space in which to live in an unfriendly town, Bachelard located niches and pockets of printed language where poetry was still alive. He did so by seeking out other exiles, and by reading them with the open imagination of "eternal childhood." Thus he championed writers and poets many dismissed as madmen, such as Poe, and especially Lautréamont, author of the poetic masterpiece of animal aggression, *Les Chants de Maldoror*. Bachelard felt these men, as well as others more commonly praised—Rainer Maria Rilke, Paul Claudel, Charles Pierre Baudelaire, Friedrich Nietzsche—were able to give poetic resonance to their words, so that even though they appeared fixed on the page, in the imagination of the reader they took wing. Such literary images were, Bachelard believed, rooted in the material imagination, which could never be totally finished, for "becoming is the phenomenon of substance and substance is the phenomenon of becoming."[233] Bachelard even found a poetics of substance in the *act* of writing. Not content to consider writing as an instrument of communication, he mused over "the great universe of the blank page," rejecting the supposed neutrality of the chemist's ink, in favor of ink that *dreamt*. He was convinced, "When my pen leaks, I think awry."[234]

Bachelard preserved the convivial function of language by promoting the dynamic imagination of matter to a higher value than the comparatively static imagination of forms. As opposed to Hugo, who was pessimistic about the effects of the book, Bachelard was optimistic that neither the industrial corruption of language, nor any other corruption, could ever incarcerate the dedicated "word dreamer."

> As soon as we put language in its proper place, at the height of human evolution, it is revealed in its double effectiveness: it bestows on us the virtues of clarity and the powers of dream. Really knowing the images of words, the images that exist beneath our thoughts and upon which our thoughts live, would advance our thinking in a natural manner. A philosophy concerned with human destiny must be an openly living language. It must study the *literary man* candidly, because the literary man is the culmination of meditation and expression, the culmination of thought and dream.[235]

Since the Renaissance, literate peoples have adopted a previously unknown mind-set: they have become dreamers of words. They, like Bachelard, could find the spaces within mass-produced texts to imaginatively dwell. In this regard, their adaptation resembles that of the nineteenth-century city dwellers Georg Simmel described in his essay "The Metropolis and Mental Life." Simmel wrote of urban residents' ability to turn inward, of the "essentially intellectualistic character" of their existence.[236] Bachelard argued, in opposition to Jean Paul Sartre, that the power to live in the imagination need not lead to a withdrawal, not to closing-off the self from reality, but could instead produce an ability to "sing reality."[237] To the degree one is able to manage it, the imagination "does not deny reality *per se*, but only the ossified and habitualized crust of reality." Neither does it "annihilate the real world; it mobilizes its potencies of transformation."[238]

Even if we concur with Bachelard's lofty opinion of the literary mind, as opposed to Hugo's skeptical view, it is easy to see that the colony of the truly literate is ever shrinking. Those "poor loonies" who are able to transform reality through the force of imagination are under siege. This is why Illich characterizes the literary world as an island. On this "Island of the Text" they are, Illich warns, increasingly threatened "by the betrayal of those clerics who dissolve the words of the book into just a communication code."[239] The best defense they can mount, in order to preserve the "double effectiveness" of their words, draws its power from the substance of language itself.

In a very similar way, whenever architecture, after the printing press, has made a place for itself on this island of literate imaginations, it has done so by devoting attention to the imaginary substance of its own becoming. It is in this task that Bachelard's praise of the virtues of literature and poetry can be of use to architects. In stating this I am not promoting yet another version of the well-known "architecture as text" metaphor, so much as suggesting a mode of imaginative practice. The familiar text metaphor has often rested on the aspects of writing that are immutable, suggesting that architecture ought now imitate a language devoid of life, rather than the objectified body it emulated during the Renaissance—one corpse merely being substituted for the other.

An architectural practice that makes suitable use of the material imagination is more flexible, more open, than one depending on the imagination of forms alone. Here is a particularly relevant fragment of Bachelard's argument for the primacy of the material imagination:

> When I began meditating on the concept of the beauty of matter, I was immediately struck by the neglect of the *material cause* in aesthetic philosophy. In particular, it seemed to me that the individualizing power of matter had been underestimated. Why does everyone always associate the notion of the individual with form? Is there not an individuality in depth

that makes matter a totality, even in its smallest divisions? Meditated upon from the perspective of its depth, matter is the very principle that can dissociate itself from forms. It is not the simple absence of formal activity. It remains itself despite all distortion and division. Moreover, matter may be given depth in two ways: by deepening or by elevating. Deepening makes it seem unfathomable, like a mystery. Elevation makes it appear to be an inexhaustible force, like a miracle. In both cases, meditation on matter cultivates an *open imagination*.[240]

This passage comes from Bachelard's second book on the imagination of substance, which has been given the English title *Water and Dreams*, but which Bachelard would no doubt have preferred to be known by its French name *L'Eau et les Rêves*, expressing so much better the essentially feminine character of water. Here Bachelard's prejudice in favor of not only gendered words, but gendered substances, again appears. He concludes the book by rhapsodizing on "a lovely round word that rolls over stones." In all his books he respected the conventional gendered associations of the four elements—fire and air tending to the masculine, water and earth to the feminine—that had long existed. However, he added a noteworthy refinement. In the paragraph repeated above, Bachelard cites two ways matter may be given poetic value: "by deepening or by elevating." Deepening, in his philosophy, was associated with the feminine; elevating with the masculine. Both operations are possible in *every* substance, as his two later books dividing the feminine earth into "reveries of repose" and "reveries of will" make evident. Bachelard would continually refine his position, finally arguing in *The Poetics of Reverie* that the imagination was essentially androgynous, but composed of two opposite inclinations, the feminine *anima* and masculine *animus*.

The androgyny of the imagination results from the presence, in varying degrees, of each inclination in every human being. So while we might generalize about the tendencies of men and women to imagine in certain ways, Bachelard thinks in terms of certain hours when we might dream in one or the other mode. "In each human being the clock of masculine hours and the clock of feminine hours do not belong to the realm of figures and measurements." He goes on to state that the masculine clock (and no pun was intended) "has the dynamism of jerks," while the feminine "runs continuously in a duration which peacefully slips away."[241] Here I will hazard an interpretation of Bachelard's

underlying sensibility: by privileging the imagination of matter over that
of form, the imagination of depth over surfaces, of reveries over dreams,
Bachelard betrays that his true sympathies lie with the *anima*. He
confesses as much when he declares, in *Water and Dreams*, that he could
not be "rational" about water, as he had attempted to be in his earlier
study *The Psychoanalysis of Fire*. Water images, it seems, carried him
away; he often granted them his "unreasoning adherence." Bachelard is
most easily seduced by all things "enveloping and soft." This is the
dominant psychology of his *work* which, he informs us, may or may not
reflect the psychology of the *man*.

What does this tell us about the imaginative construct we call
"architecture"? Let us return to vernacular, or pre-Renaissance,
architecture. Its substance is, directly and obviously, of the earth; it often
begins by digging into the earth; it encloses, shelters, and protects.
Funerary constructions, which literally surround the corpse with earth,
play a dominant role in this type of architecture. Vernacular architecture
is produced primarily through communal, sociable actions, rather than
competitive ones. The conclusion is obvious, and it is reinforced by all
the romance languages that assign the word a feminine gender—
architecture is feminine. Better still, *architecture is maternal*. If the most
common cosmological schemes assert that *we* are earth ("dust to dust"),
and if the analogy between bodies and buildings holds, then buildings,
even those not literally or directly "of" earth, must be *imagined* as earth,
and therefore are, again, maternal. Even in the present, we are inclined to
maternalize anything that nurtures or shelters us, hence referring to our
school as *alma mater*. In describing the inherent maternity of the house,
Bachelard cited the poet O. V. de Milosz: "I say Mother. And my thoughts
are of you, oh, House."[242]

In her intriguing study "The Walled-Up Bride: An Architecture
of Eternal Return," Manuela Antoniu demonstrates that, for masonry
constructions in Eastern Europe, the legendary ideal sacrifice, the soul
most able to stabilize a construction, was that of the master mason's
wife.[243] Antoniu mentions that in some versions of the regional legend of
mason Master Manole, his wife is permitted an opening in the wall for
her breast, so she can continue to nourish her child as, it is implied, will
the monastery in which she is entombed nourish her community. Even
the metonymical substitution of a shadow for the sacrificial victim's
actual body ("captured" by measuring it with a piece of string, which is

then immured in the foundation), once practiced in the same geographic region, suggests a maternal sacrifice, due to the association of darkness with enveloping mystery, and therefore the *anima*. "[For] architecture there is something deeper here than metaphor and analogy.... The womb is not just an archetype of inner space, and the mother's body not simply a representation of the first house; rather they are inner space and first house in themselves."[244]

As Bachelard advised, we must be cautious not to confuse imaginative tendencies with the physical features of human bodies. That is, we should not confuse gender with *sex*. However, just as the social construct "architecture" is bound to the materials and processes of its becoming, so the social construct "gender" is bound—loosely but inevitably, with great flexibility from culture to culture, and place to place—to the corporeality of male and female bodies.[245] Illich notes that while both men and women may "make themselves at home through every move," only women experience the "housing" of another human within them.

> The culture may be matriarchal or patriarchal, the greater share of power in the hands of women or men, but only for women does to live and dwell mean to engender bodies, to leave behind a trail of new life. In one culture men may build shelters, make fences, or terrace a hill; in another, these tasks are assigned to women. But only from women does bodily life come into the world. No matter how the local mythology depicts the creator of the world—as mother, father, or androgyne; no matter whose name the children carry—mother's, father's, or uncle's; the special space (and the time that corresponds to it) that sets the home apart from nest and garage is engendered *only* by women, because it is they who bear living bodies.[246]

Unlike Cartesian space, vernacular space is always explicitly gendered. Universal space obscures the distinction, experienced with far greater profundity by those who bear living bodies, between inside and out; universal time negates the biological rhythms of the female body. Thus, the de-gendering of space and time is inherently sexist, because its disorienting effects on the lives of women are more pronounced than its effects on men. Such sexism is not necessarily the result of willful patriarchal oppression; it is caused by the imposition of supposedly universal categories that negate the particularity of male and female lives. Following this line of thought, "treating everyone the same" is a sexist ideology.[247] Gender on the contrary, both in language and in society, "implies a complementarity within the world that is fundamental and closes the world in on 'us,' however ambiguous and fragile this closure may be."[248] You will recognize that "closing the world in on us" is approximately the definition of making the suitably bounded *places* Heidegger thought necessary for dwelling. Because the instrumentalization of space dissolves the closure of gendered places, it is both inherently antifeminine, and antiarchitecture.

In sympathy with Bachelard's use of the substance of language as an antidote for the overuse of instrumental reason, I would like to explore another way of looking at the processes that have been dissolving the boundaries necessary for architecture. Universal space ignores the quality my colleague Donald Kunze calls "intransitivity" that is so characteristic of human experience.[249] In the space-time of our bodily experience, it seems to take longer to reach a desirable destination than to return from it, vertical movement is more pronounced than horizontal, night-time is fundamentally different from daytime. These incongruities, which would remain invisible to transitive measuring techniques, can be accurately described only through our poetic ability to measure intransitively. Here author Ken Kesey describes the swelling up of the evil "Big Nurse" as she enters the mental ward, in *One Flew Over the Cuckoo's Nest:*

> She's swelling up, swells till her back's splitting out the white uniform and she's let her arms section out long enough to wrap around the three of them five, six times. She looks around with a swivel of her huge head. Nobody up to see ... so she really lets herself go and her painted smile twists, stretches to an open snarl, and she blows up bigger and bigger, big as a tractor, so big I can smell the machinery inside the way you smell a motor pulling too big a load.[250]

Kesey equates the size and proportions of the nurse's body with power, much as medieval paintings used the size of the figures depicted to signify their relative importance. Using a system of intransitive measure like Michelangelo's qualitative ages, Kesey is able to tell a good lie that more truthfully characterizes Big Nurse's sinister power than an accurate description of her body would have done.

Not coincidentally, there are certain activities—certain verbs— within the English language that intrinsically resist the objectifying influences of the industrial corruption of language. They are called "intransitive verbs"; one such verb, architect-educator Paul Walker Clarke informs us, is "to dwell."

> A simple linguistic analysis reveals the distinction between *dwelling* and
> *housing*. *Housing* is the gerund of the transitive verb *to house,* while *dwelling*
> is the gerund of the intransitive verb *to dwell.* With the transitive verb, the
> action passes from a subject to an object, as in "The state houses people."
> An intransitive verb is one whereby the action is an inherent attribute of the
> subject and is not transferred to an object. "People dwell." Dwelling is an
> inalienable attribute—a right—of people and individuals. Dwelling cannot
> be accomplished for one by another. This relation is so sacrosanct it is
> embedded within the syntax of our language.[251]

Unlike the homogenized modernist space-time Illich derisively calls
"spime," the intransitive space and time of dwelling are bounded by
concrete limits. Along with gender, we can add other aspects of
difference—age, mortality, human fallibility, qualities of site, gravity, and
materiality. Cultural constructs arising from material conditions of
difference are signs of a heterogeneous world where the fact that women
cannot always be interchanged with men, night equated with day, up
substituted for down, old for young, or stone for steel "blocks the
emergence of any universal category."[252] By providing areas of
intransitivity, these limit-conditions allow architecture to establish
bounded places resistant to the universalizing tendencies of advanced
technology-advanced capitalism.

     Imaginative conditions that defy transitive measurement
brought about in response to these and other limit-conditions are
therefore a prerequisite for architecture to occur. Vernacular architecture
succeeds because the physical limits placed upon it are compensated for
by the nearly unlimited social and material imaginations of its builder-
dwellers. Vernacular builders re-present the very particular material
limits of their existence as good lies that transcend their specific
situation. While an architecture where *anything* is possible—such as that
conceived as a purely compositional exercise, a manipulation of
abstract shapes in immaterial space—may provide for the hypertrophy
of the formal imagination of its designer, it can only alienate the un-
indoctrinated who might attempt to build it or dwell in it. Architecture
predicated upon *any* system of uniform abstract measure—the avant-
garde architect's abstract immaterial space, the neoclassicist's
demythologized proportions, or the developer's heavily leveraged time
that is money—is an architecture devoid of social imagination.

     Tellingly, the avant-garde approach shares many conceptual
assumptions with what might at first seem its logical opposite, the

socially conscious tradition of Utopian planning. Consider, for example, the most recent manifestation of this impulse, new urbanism. Though new urbanists pursue many laudable social goals, and have achieved some success providing a commercially viable and environmentally superior alternative to conventional suburban sprawl (exemplified in projects such as Kentlands and Seaside), the movement's ultimate influence is likely to be compromised by its overly simplistic conceptual foundations. When avant-garde architects claim to disrupt the societal status quo by instilling "unease" with their disturbing, dislocating shapes, and new urbanists claim to produce social harmony by carefully prescribing sidewalks, picket fences, and house facades, each accepts an insupportable degree of spatial determinism. Andres Duany, a pioneer of the latter movement, reductively uses the word "vernacular" to refer to an American traditional style of housing with pitched roofs and porches. Duany's efforts to produce "communities" through carefully constructed codes are founded on his contention that he "can code anything."[253] But the authoritarian prose of a code is only suited for describing transitive measures—shapes, colors, materials, minimums and maximums—not the intangible qualities of places and social bonds.[254] Descartes, too, maintained that his methodology could describe anything with certainty, including matter, which he believed to be adequately characterized by the wholly transitive measure of its "extension."

Avant-garde architects[255] and new urbanists are able to specify the bounding of their projects in geometric space, but they do not address the intransitive phenomena of the time of building-dwelling. The weakness of this geometric worldview is, according to Bachelard, that "when a geometrician speaks of volumes he is only dealing with the surfaces that limit them." In fact, the "geometrician's sphere is an empty one."[256] Duany would not find it possible to impose a vernacular economy upon the urban professional occupants of his new towns, or to "code" them into building their own homes, while helping their neighbors do the same. It is unlikely he would even be able to forbid the installation of air conditioners. As economist David Harvey asks, does not the new urbanists' approach perpetuate the fallacious assumption "that the shaping of spatial order is or can be the foundation of a new moral and aesthetic order?" Harvey writes that new urbanism repeats the fundamental error of all Utopian planning by "privileging spatial forms over social processes."[257]

It is not that the shapes of porches or the patterns of streets do not affect the viability of a community; it is that their social impact can never be predicted with certainty, due to the inherent intransitivity of social, cultural, and material processes, not the least of which is the ineradicable ambiguity of language. In partial recognition of this, the "imagineers" behind one of the latest new-urbanist-inspired ventures, the Disney Corporation's development of Celebration, Florida, have attempted to bolster the architectural scheme (pedestrian-friendly streets, mandated front porches, fiberglass classical columns, and imitation wood siding) with traditional-sounding street names, a carefully consumer-engineered town seal (a little girl running down a town street with her dog), plans to organize Boy Scout troops and other social activities, and a company-owned town newspaper.[258] But like the ersatz building materials, one might doubt the authenticity of the social bonds organized after the model of an amusement park. Architect Lucien Kroll has questioned the assumption that dwelling can be purchased like a club membership, complete with "prefabricated friends."[259]

Like friendship, dwelling cannot be "coded" because it is a *delayed* imaginative condition that can only arise after a suitable period has been devoted to the activities of building and thinking. This explains Illich's observation that most people could not feel at home unless a substantial portion of the effort to build their house was their own. The work of building-dwelling imposes spatial and temporal limits, a kind of intransitive measuring, that allow us to close the world in on ourselves. When Heidegger, inspired by a poem of Friedrich Hölderlin, wrote " . . . Poetically Man Dwells . . . ," he asked, "What is the measure for [such] human measuring?" He concluded that this "strange" measuring could only be accomplished poetically; that, in fact, poetry was in essence just this sort of "taking measure."

> Man's taking measure in the dimension dealt out to him brings dwelling into its ground plan. Taking the measure of the dimension is the element within which human dwelling has its security, by which it securely endures. The taking of measure is what is poetic in dwelling. Poetry is a measuring. But what is it to measure? If poetry is to be understood as measuring, then obviously we may not subsume it under just any idea of measuring and measure.[260]

Heidegger denied that unambiguous quantitative or transitive measures truly touched "the nature of measuring," much as Bachelard maintained that the "clocks" of our masculine and feminine imaginings did not "belong to the realm of figures and measurements." Codes, which rely on "normative prescriptions" cannot guarantee dwelling, or "prevent the production of trivial designs,"[261] because they can rely only on objective truths, which tend to have "bad" social ramifications when taken alone. As Heidegger wrote, "The poet, if he is a poet, does not describe the mere appearance of the sky and earth."[262] The sociability necessary for dwelling requires the poetic telling of good lies, like the delayed gratification and displaced self-interest that is the assistance of friends (an assistance that, since it is voluntary, cannot be "coded"), or the convincing foundation myth.

Merely reproducing the appearance of vernacular architecture does not establish the poetic measures necessary for dwelling. Vinyl or cement-board siding, fiberglass classical columns, and other "no maintenance" materials so popular with contemporary housing developers are too expedient, too convenient to require (and promote) kindness among neighbors. These elements are bad lies because, while they may look "traditional," they discourage the convivial behavior that characterized vernacular building-dwelling traditions. It is not that the phony columns and simulated wood sidings are "untrue to their materials," but that the fictions they present, relying on mere appearances alone, are too shallow to permit the thorough poetic measure-taking of one's home or neighborhood. Just as with the developer-organized scout troops and developer-controlled newspaper in Celebration, simulated vernacular shapes and prefabricated social organizations are shortcuts past the time-consuming social work necessary for authentic dwelling.[263] A community is not a commodity. Communities are contentious living and breathing entities; they cannot be purchased by passive consumers. No-owner-involvement construction methods and no-maintenance simulations of traditional building materials repeat the mistake of artificial Christmas trees: they assume that we can drastically reduce the time and effort that were historically necessary to produce a certain artifact, but accurately simulate its appearance, and no one will notice the difference.

Urban planners need to recognize the limitations on what can be coded, and developers on what can be prefabricated. Codes *can* be effective if the circumstances are right. In contrast to the town of Celebration, Santa Barbara (named for the patron saint of architects),

California was able to create what Charles Moore called its "Mediterranean dream" when it was substantially rebuilt following a 1925 earthquake. Not just any dream could have been coded in Santa Barbara. In their wisdom, the town's planners chose a dream that fit, in an exaggerated way, the historical circumstances of the town's founding. One of the earliest buildings in the region really was a Spanish mission. Beyond this plausible connection, Santa Barbara was able to make its fiction convincing by building low-rise structures with masonry in a climate that was suitably similar to that which it imitated. The low walls that enclose properties, the open arcades and courtyards of Santa Barbara, and the outdoor rooms that do not need to be roofed, all promote a relationship with space and climate both uniquely fit to this particular place and reasonably similar to their Mediterranean predecessors. As Moore observed, this goes beyond matters of "style"; it is "fundamentally created by a characteristic relationship between people and enclosure."

> These walls, open stairways, balconies, and arcades throughout the town serve to symbolize, as much as actually to invite the movement of people between indoors and out. They are an affirmation that the public realm is as much to be lived in as the private. By encouraging and dramatizing the act of public inhabitation, the builders of Santa Barbara have made a stage for daily action as rich as any devised by Hollywood.[264]

Pre-1980s Santa Barbara gives us an example of how the normative prescriptions of codes can be leveraged by climate, historical circumstance, and suitable building practices into the realm of good lies and poetic measurings. The comings and goings between public and private spaces in Santa Barbara was partially facilitated by its enviable climate, which makes air conditioners virtually unnecessary (in suitably designed buildings). The shaded arcades and courtyards with fountains provide social gathering areas of "thermal delight" within the town. Thick masonry walls promote thermal comfort by absorbing the heat of the days, and then returning it during the cooler nights. Some of the more recent developments in Santa Barbara, beginning with an air-conditioned behemoth hotel in the late 1980s, demonstrate the inability of codes alone to prevent trivial or socially damaging designs. Santa Barbara also shows us that all socially good lies must have a tangible connection to the truth. The fiction that is the town's image could not have been "coded" without the assistance of climate, history, and white stuccoed masonry walls.

We must be much more circumspect than the new urbanists regarding the power of codes, or any prescriptions that rely on transitive measures alone. David Harvey warns that, even if vernacular processes *could* be coded, the clannishness and distrust of outsiders that still characterizes most remaining tribal societies might have to come along with them.[265] In an odd sort of reversal, the nostalgic withdrawal advocated by communitarianism (the philosophical movement most closely allied with new urbanism) risks replicating some of the least desirable communal aspects of vernacular societies. At the same time, the movement's idealized communities seem most effective as retreats from, not solutions to, late-capitalist development. In *The Fall of Public Man*, Richard Sennett wrote,

> All too often, what is "self-evidently wrong" about a social system is self-evident precisely because the critique fits nicely into, and does little damage to, the system as a whole. In this case, the celebration of territorial community against the evils of impersonal, capitalist urbanism quite comfortably fits into the larger system, because it leads to a logic of local defense against the outside world, rather than a challenge to the workings of that world. . . . And this is why the emotional logic of community, beginning as a resistance to the evils of modern capitalism, winds up at a bizarre kind of depoliticized withdrawal; the system remains intact, but maybe we can get it to leave our piece of turf untouched.[266]

Sennett (writing in 1974) went on to say that the modern sense of community "seems to be about fraternity in a dead, hostile world." Yet there is an unfortunately small space to be traversed between fraternity and xenophobia. The nostalgic wish to retreat from the impersonal modern world can lead to a romanticization of the gated compound, the ghetto, of blood, or of race. Mixing and intermingling of different types of people is necessary, Sennett believes, to give the modern citizen "that sense of tentativeness about his own beliefs which every civilized person must have." Such sentiments reveal their author to be an inhabitant of the Island of the Text. Sennett knows that the skillful use of language can prevent conflict with others.

Similarly Bruce Krajewski writes, "In its ability to make otherness seem familiar, language makes otherness less threatening, often dissipating the compulsion to rid one's self of otherness through violent means."[267] In this regard the place-bound market remains exemplary as a space of interdependent social interaction that promotes tolerance of others. In contrast to the gated community, the retreat I have been calling the Island of the Text is not simply a space of isolation, but a protected enclave from which "literary man" can engage the world on his own terms, in order to mobilize its potencies for transformation.

This, finally, is the rub: how do we forge some conditional truce between the forces of instrumental reason and the embodied imagination? How do we establish what Bachelard called a "regular filiation" between the real and the imaginary, so that we are neither overwhelmed nor isolated? How do we safely navigate between the universal and the particular? How do we balance the need to form a community with the greater obligations of town, state, and national citizenship? In the realm of architecture, at least, the best hope appears to lie with indirect, very particular, place-bound solutions, a view that squares with architect Vittorio Gregotti's belief that "specific conditions are increasingly emerging as the only possible elements on which to base a project."[268] Because of the incredible pace of social change with which we must now live, all settlements of a general nature fade into oblivion as soon as the deal is struck. Architecture must always exist in an endless process of negotiation with the world it occupies. Architectural practices must constantly adapt to the situations in which we find ourselves living. Soon, these practices may be less identifiable by the artifacts they produce, or by the titles their "practitioners" adopt, than by the single constant that has always delineated the space of architecture: practices are "architectural" when they concern themselves with supporting our physical and imaginative need to dwell.

> She-Architecture can teach us to forget about self-celebration, about overstressed apotropaic emulations of an original conception, and celebrate instead the fertile voids that house our private and public life and the beauty of their inner space.[269]

The Contradictions Underlying
the Profession of Architecture

Loos used
simple, unadorned materials,
not wishing to rely on what he saw as the irrational 'Awe of Work'

The seeming inability of the architect to create space that gathers the order of
the cosmos and becomes laden with culturally relevant meaning is as much a
fault of contemporary culture as a properly architectural or formal problem.

Alberto Perez-Gomez
"Abstraction in Modern Architecture"

In discussions about architectural practice much confusion has been
generated by the failure to distinguish between architecture and
architecture as a profession. The former is an activity that is as old as
humanity itself, while the latter is a much more recent way of practicing.
When this manner of practice began to dominate Western Europe, the
design of buildings was removed from its former place within the
building trades guilds. The professional architect primarily came into
being in order to create a "space" where architectural practices could be
insulated from the direct influence of the newly emerging capitalist
market, as well as from the modern tendency to convert uncertain
practices to efficient techniques. From the outset the professional
architect has been party to a sort of truce, a compromise, with the societal
development we know as "modernity." Yet this compromise has always
been beset by a number of contradictions. Some of these are inherent to
the general nature of professions; others, of greater interest to me, are
intrinsic to the architecture profession itself.

I will begin with the separation of the design of buildings from
their construction and maintenance. In societies producing vernacular
architecture, each of these stages in the life of buildings was apt to be
carried out, anonymously, by the same person or group. While Victor
Hugo, Bernard Rudofsky, and others have, with some justification,
pinned the responsibility for the "death of architecture" on the
emergence of "name" architects who replaced the anonymous master
builders of the guilds, we could just as readily argue that Leon Battista
Alberti and his literate descendants deserve a place in the peculiar
modern enclave where reason and poetic wisdom are held in precarious
balance—the refuge I have taken to calling the "Island of the Text." The
architecture profession attempted to negotiate a similar protected space
apart from, but still adjacent to, the growing capitalist market. This
requirement of "proximate distance" meant that the profession of

architecture has had, since its birth, an affinity for the concentrations of capital within urban areas. The architect has always been a creature of the city. Unlike the guilds, however, the architecture profession was able to secure on its protected island only the portion of building production known as "design." This was due in part because the newly literate architects did not generally emerge from the class of the building trades (or, if they did, their aspirations to move in the same social circles as their patrons would influence them to downplay this fact), and also because their growing faith in the powers of instrumental representation and rationalized production caused them to believe the skilled builder would eventually become dispensable. This professional definition of the architect's job assumed the means of building construction to be neutral. Construction was left adrift, protected initially by the remnants of the craft guilds, and eventually by the far weaker building trade unions. While the guilds had blurred the distinction between the employer and the employed, the trade unions represented only wage laborers; where the guilds had preserved their monopolies through secrecy, the unions were faced with the impossible task of restricting the practice of skills that had become (theoretically) accessible to anyone who could read.

When the architect's job began to exclude the potential significance of building production, the division between "mere buildings" and architecture arose. This is not to say that the professionalization of the architect necessarily entailed excluding a concern for methods of construction, as Filippo Brunelleschi's ingenious design for the falsework needed to construct the dome over the Cathedral of Florence attests. However, the new practice paradigm did institutionalize the belief that the means of a building's production were without consequence to whatever meanings might be associated with the building. The process of construction had once served to produce both social bonds and tangible signs of sociability, but now building was merely the means by which to realize the architect's design—much as printing was the means to produce an author's text. Design, in turn, became more abstract, more visual, devoting more concern to supposedly universal principles than to material or social processes. Contrary to what is often asserted, the difficulty with this arrangement has less to do with the fact that the duties of the master builder, formerly held by one party, were now divided among at least two, than with the ideological exclusion of building processes from the province of design.

Brunelleschi's practice is as good a place as any to locate the "emergence of architecture as a self-conscious individual practice . . . inseparable from the rise of the burgher class in the last half of the fifteenth century."[270] It was then that the title "architect" was revived from the Greek term for "chief builder," a turn of events that owed more to the nostalgic Renaissance fascination with all things classical than to the ancient title's appropriateness for the newly emerging professional role. From Italy the title and the mode of practice spread first to France and, by the mid 1600s, to England. The split between architect and builder was institutionalized in the French Academy of Architecture (founded in 1671), marking "the creation of a proper professional elite."[271] Even so, not until the end of the nineteenth century, with the advent of professional licensing, did the definition of "architect" finally become stabilized. During the Renaissance, architects who had been trained as builders continued to compete for prestige and commissions with artists and aesthetes, leading not only to confusion, but also to competitive hostilities, the most pronounced being the scandalous feud between Gian Lorenzo Bernini and Francesco Borromini (contributing to the latter's suicide). For dilettantes such as Alberti, painters such as Raphael, and sculptors like Michelangelo and Bernini to practice architecture, it was necessary, first, that rudimentary knowledge of construction could be acquired through scholarly study, and, second, that the builder retained sufficient skill to compensate for the architect's ignorance. The popularity of Vitruvius's ancient architectural treatise, and the numerous imitations it spawned, was due to the new profession's hunger for a written body of knowledge with which to legitimate itself. Even today, few professionals evidence such a love of books as do most architects.

Renaissance architects equally stressed, along with the importance of texts, the importance of drawing. Their manner of using drawings to describe buildings led to what Dalibor Vesely has called the "conflict of representation."[272] Whereas Medieval builders had worked primarily from secret rules of thumb that allowed them to transform sketches and incomplete ideas into templates for stable constructions, Renaissance architects needed to present their buildings to both clients and contractors as finished "projects." This novel conception was significant to architectural practice in two ways. First, the building-as-project was necessarily a concept propelled into the future by the force of the architect's imagination. The general preference among architects for designs Robert Venturi classifies as "heroic and original"[273] is, to an extent, a side-effect inherent in the willful concept of building-as-project. This was Daniel Burnham's reasoning when he advised architects to "make no little plans." Burnham realized the architect's ability to persuade others to build and pay for these futuristic dreams depended upon proposing plans with the "power to stir men's souls." Brunelleschi's design for the dome of the Florence Cathedral was so original as to be unbuildable until he devised a method to accomplish it. Only by conceptualizing the building as a futuristic project could it become legitimate for architects to design structures that exceeded the capabilities of existing building techniques. The professional practice of architecture thereby severed its connections with vernacular or craft traditions, and allied itself with the progress imperative of modern technology.

Second, to describe these virtual buildings to a builder who by the late eighteenth century was assumed to be merely an automaton (and I underscore the falsity of this assumption) required producing increasingly unambiguous drawings through the instrumental techniques of projective geometry. Translating this nominalist prose, the builder was to faithfully follow the instructions of the architect. After several hundred years of practice under this convention, its full effects began to be known. Previously, construction drawings had been approximations of the far more complex entity known as "the building," which could only be realized through an imaginative but tradition-bound social process we call "construction." Because the logic of building and the logic of drawing are not identical, Medieval buildings could not be produced through simple objective translations of drawings. It was necessary for the builder to reinterpret and improvise in order to make the drawings buildable.

The late-twentieth-century professional architect's drawings, on the other hand, are assumed to be complete, although abstract, representations of the ideal building, of which the constructed building is an approximation. In other words, in the master mason's sketch, the drawing was an incomplete representation of a building, but in the modern architect's working drawings, buildings have become imperfect representations of drawings.[274] The logic of the drawing has superseded the logic of building, resulting in buildings that aspire to be like drawings. This contradiction is perhaps most evident in the work of architecture firms, such as Coop Himmelblau, who attempt to translate the gestural freedom of early design sketches directly into buildings that look like these sketches. During construction, the uninhibited freedom of such drawings will often translate into a building that is very difficult to construct, and so the logic of the building stands in direct contradiction to the logic of the drawing that inspired it.[275] The profession's growing taste for idealized compositions in immaterial space, lacking any analogous relationship to processes of construction, is also partially an inherited result of the descriptive methods required by the building-as-project. Taken to its extreme, this impulse would result in works such as those of Étienne-Louis Boullée, whose career consisted primarily in producing unbuildable theoretical projects.

Another issue architects faced as their profession developed stemmed from the increasingly secular nature of their clients. As Renaissance architects came to be recognized as individual artists, this progress was mirrored by the emerging individuality of their clients. In addition to the Church and the aristocracy, the sixteenth century added the wealthy merchant to the stock of the architect's potential customers. The secular nature of the merchant's endeavors and his awareness of his mortality combined to present the architect with a previously unheard-of building program that can only be seen, in hindsight, as a mixed blessing. The individuality of the merchant client meant that the architect could cultivate a professional relationship with a single "man of vision," who might become a life-long patron. Where the merchant in his business was entirely dedicated to economic motives, in the construction of his villas and palaces, as in his donations to the Church, he was apt to be motivated by loftier goals that were fueled by the desire for immortality. This had the benefit, for the architect, of exempting his practice from the harsh economic realities of everyday building. The long-term effect of the architect's nearly total devotion to the needs of the wealthy and powerful has resulted, however, in the architect's continued estrangement from the bulk of building volume.

As secular life increased in importance, and as our societal tendency to think in terms of concepts began to predominate, the client's desire for immortality took the form of a demand for permanence in the structures he commissioned. Since the concentric organization of the plan, or the proportions of a facade, could be described according to instrumental concepts that were assumed to be everlasting, this conceptual permanence was projected onto the material construction of the building. Historically, extreme durability had only been an explicit architectural goal for a limited number of buildings—churches, temples, palaces, and fortifications. Now, the client's (and architect's) dreams of immortality, coupled with the objective representational techniques architecture adapted from science and commerce, promoted permanence to a general requirement for architecture. "Timelessness" became a prominent fixture among the idealizations of the profession. Architecture had become a noun, and it was merely a small step through the frictionless economic space of our rapidly dematerializing markets from project to *product*.

The institutionalization of the ideals of permanence and perfection therefore came from outside, as well as inside, the architectural profession. The widespread societal desire for permanence owes much of its existence to our nostalgic wish for stability in the face of continual progress and creative destruction. Philosopher Karsten Harries has labeled this peculiarly modern anxiety "the terror of time."[276] Modernity has co-opted the supposed opposition between permanent and temporary, offering up the ideality of the former as a conceptual counterweight to the reality of the latter. Capitalist development values permanence solely as an assurance that relatively unpredictable material processes, such as the decay of buildings, will not interfere with market-driven processes, such as planned obsolescence. This is why "consumer engineering" experts prefer "style obsolescence" to other types that are more difficult to control. "Styles," as they say, "wear out faster than gears."[277] The heterogeneous world of material change threatens to undermine the homogeneous space-time of materialist development, and therefore must be neutralized.

When building materials are conceptualized as permanent, they can be safely ignored. Thus, Henry-Russell Hitchcock and Philip Johnson, in their text to the 1932 International Style exhibition at the Museum of Modern Art, extolled brick for its permanence, but recommended using mortar the same color as the brick to suppress the evidence exposed masonry always gives of its own becoming. They yearned for an "ideal" material like stucco, "but elastic with a wide color range."[278] Their wish was realized nearly fifty years later in the creation of "Exterior Insulation and Finish Systems" or EIFS—a synthetic stucco that has become the favorite material of both architects and developers who place primary emphasis on building imagery. The preference for materials lacking temporal qualities has also been institutionalized by contemporary building codes, which are uniformly hostile to vernacular modes of construction, and to all building methods that derive their durability from sustained maintenance, such as traditional adobe construction.[279]

The current professional fixation with permanence and geometric perfection appears as an aberration among the themes that have inspired builders since before recorded history. Contrary to this relatively recent prejudice, historical evidence suggests that the prevailing tendency of architectural practices has been toward *sustainability*, not material permanence. As an ethos for practice, sustainability has the advantage over material permanence of being both possible and far more sociable in its effects. A festival structure, adobe building, or nomad's tent is sustainable because it is continually, perhaps endlessly, rebuilt.

Another innovation that changed the practice of architecture—along with the timelessness inherent in the architect's instrumental drawings and the permanence preferred by clients and building codes—was the rise of industrialized builders. As builders became "contractors" they could no longer quantify the feelings of pride building well had always produced; they could market their services only upon more readily measured aspects, such as a structure's stability or the efficiency by which they had erected it. Or else they might represent the ostentatiousness of a building simply through the quantity of labor required to produce its ornate near-perfection, leading to Adolf Loos's lament that lay persons in the early twentieth century evaluated buildings strictly on the basis of the effort that appeared to go into making them. This stood the social function of craft on its head, reducing it to a labor-intensive means to produce symbolic capital. But it was also the vestige of a time when building was social work, and the buildings that required the most work were the most socially significant. Loos was protesting that this form of "taking measure" was no longer applicable to architecture produced by partially industrialized building specialists. The same nostalgia led to industrially produced parodies of hand-crafted building ornament, another contradiction Loos sought to expose in his essay "Ornament and Crime."[280] The contradictory aims of efficient construction and the appearance of permanence ultimately led to the Modern Movement's preference for building materials (like EIFS) that were "not supposed to weather,"[281] just as efficient construction combined with appearances designed to appeal to our "awe of work" led to postmodern functionalist boxes, sheathed in the nostalgia of thin stone veneers.

As much as it has sought to deny it, the profession of architecture has never been free of such wider societal influences. The greatest autonomy has been granted to architects in the areas the rest of society have cared least about, such as in purely cosmetic decisions, in theoretical projects, or in entries into "ideas competitions." Of course, the architect could not aspire to professional status by slavishly serving the whims of the client. Philip Johnson's oft-quoted assertion that architects in the 1980s had become "whores" serving "corporate johns" would, if accurate, mark the end of the professional aspirations of architects. As professionals, architects had always professed to understand the clients' needs better than their clients.

The architect's more thorough understanding was assumed to include the interests of those citizens who might not pay for, but who would use or otherwise be affected by, the building. Just as authors, after the printing press, learned to write for an audience of anonymous "model readers,"[282] architects, after architecture became a profession, learned to design for anonymous "building users." Without the quality standards of the guilds and the high skill of the builder, the architect had to insure the safety and satisfaction of these unnamed building occupants. This responsibility for the public welfare helped to justify the licensing of architects. Because they dealt with concerns more noble than profit alone, architects were fit to join the professional ranks as near equals to jurists and clerics. Unlike Johnson's whores, professional architects were expected to place the best interests of society above either their clients' or their own. Like more established professionals, architects maintained at least the illusion of autonomy in that they were engaged, retained, or consulted, but never hired.[283] Yet even in architects' socially beneficial role, another contradiction lurked. For while the portions of architects' practices concerned with safety and practical needs could be easily measured, and therefore economically justified, the fulfillment of the their artistic aims rested solely on the shaky foundation of the client's approval.

The production of architecture always seems to generate complex problems uniquely its own. In her essay "Can Architects Be Socially Responsible," Margaret Crawford observed that professions depend on the creation of a protected market and on the "assurance that membership in the profession would provide both social status and visible economic advantages." But, she continues, architecture has "failed to satisfy many of the underlying social assumptions necessary for successful professionalization."[284] One reason for this is that the public, those anonymous "architects from birth," continue to modify, add to, redecorate, and repaint their homes and businesses without the professional advice of architects. This has led to a conflict of dwelling. Ivan Illich wrote that successful professions must "disable" the public's ability to perform certain duties, which then, by law, become the province of the profession alone.[285] But since dwelling is so fundamental a human need, and "cannot be accomplished for one by another," the ultimate success of the architectural profession would entail disabling the ability of the public to dwell—obviously a contradictory situation that places the profession of the architect in irresolvable conflict with architecture itself! When Loos wrote his tale of the poor little rich man who commissioned an architect to design his house, only to find that his architect had finally determined every aspect of his existence, he described, in an exaggerated way, the underlying ethos of the professional architect.

Another unavoidable conflict within the architectural profession is the competition with other building producers. In contrast to medical professionals—who, until recently, were nearly as effective fortifying their particular island (by disabling all other healers) as the guilds had been—architects have never properly distinguished how their involvement with building production is distinct from that of builders and engineers. Unlike the contractor and engineer, whose services are valued and reasonably well understood, architects have been unable to convince the majority of their economically motivated clients that their services cannot be adequately expressed in terms of cost, function, and marketable imagery. The reason for this is quite simple: the former two groups can define their activities in ways that are amenable to the sort of transitive measurement demanded by the capitalist market, while architects, if they remain committed to the intransitive activity of dwelling, cannot.

The architecture profession's well-earned reputation for overspending budgets ought to be counted as a mixed blessing when seen in this light. Architects, with notable exceptions such as Samuel Mockbee's Auburn-University-based Rural Studio, have been slow to adapt their practices so that limitations originating in societal conditions, like absurdly low budgets, become constraints to be imaginatively troped into authentic constructions. In fact, absurdly generous budgets, such as that available to Richard Meier for his design of the Getty Center in Los Angeles, and overspending as a general strategy of practice run the risk of impoverishing the ingenuity by which buildings are made, thereby promoting wastefulness. Meier's use of concealed stainless steel sheets as a waterproofing membrane behind the open joints of some stone cavity walls at the Getty could serve as a symbol of such unimaginative excess.[286] The point is that while architecture may be either cheap or expensive, it cannot be "cost-effective." The transitive measures that allow us to establish cost-effectiveness of commodities cannot account for the imaginative something extra, the gift, the aura, the *significance*, that architecture gives to human lives.

A similar distortion occurs if we try to portray architecture as a functional technique to produce safe and secure buildings. Architecture is not "problem solving" because the problem to which architecture ultimately responds is our need to dwell, and this is not a solvable need. However, the functionalist perception of the architect's job continues to dominate the opinions of our clients. To the extent the contemporary architect's work impacts the health and safety of the public, they have been forced to cede authority over these "problems" to the bureaucratic controls—building codes, lending criteria, minimum standards, etc.—so beloved by technological society. Ironically, the lack of attention devoted to safety among architects (either too concerned with compositional matters or too deferential to the economic interests of the client) accelerated the proliferation of these controls. Nevertheless, health and safety issues remain the last finger in the dike protecting the architect's professional island from the flood of opportunistic competition. However, because of our societal preference to define these issues narrowly by their "problematic" aspects, it is becoming difficult for architects to claim that engineers or builders cannot follow a building code as well as they do. The same is true of "function." By allowing function to be reductively defined by objective measures, and by erroneously proposing that form was entirely derived from it, or—alternatively—totally separate from it, architects *themselves* made form, in the first instance, a secondary and derivative quality and, in the second, either irrelevant or simply a matter of fashion.

When Robert Venturi, in *Complexity and Contradiction*, offered his well-intentioned advice that architects "stick to their jobs" (that is, the appearance of buildings), he was proposing a strategy even more pernicious than the form of specialization eventually adopted by most other professions.[287] While it could be argued that the reductive thinking behind architects' specialization according to building types stifles innovation into the ways buildings are actually used, it is not unlike the specialization by case type employed by lawyers and doctors. An architect who only designs hospitals could still, theoretically, embrace the full range of issues building production has traditionally encompassed: structure, services, materials and methods of construction, program, maintenance, etc. Venturi's proposal was, in fact, more akin to the division of labor advocated by efficiency experts like Frederick Taylor. The decorated functional shed, particularly when the design of the shed is turned over to the engineer and other function specialists, is a surrender to the questionable assumptions, such as Taylorism, underlying the production of commodities in our technological society.

Venturi was advising architects to devote suitable attention to what he knew they could still control, which was the appearance of buildings. Yet, by severing what a building looked like from all material and social limits that might constrain its appearance—budget, program, region, climate, materials—the visual appearance of the building was reduced to a communication device, and the possibility of building poetically evaporated. This form of practice, which many of our star architects have adopted (not just those we designate "postmodernists"), presents yet another major problem to the architect as aesthete. Even freed of the need to wrestle with the more material issues of building, architects, unlike painters and most other artists, must convince someone else to pay for the construction of their compositions. Crawford notes, "Architecture's expensiveness inevitably binds it to the sources of finance and power, making it very difficult to achieve the autonomy from bourgeois standards that art had fought for since its emancipation from aristocratic patronage."[288]

Besides this lack of autonomy, the application of the ideal of "disinterested pleasure" to architecture—as advocated by Kantian aesthetic philosophy, and facilitated by the modern practice of accepting projective drawings or photographs as accurate depictions of architecture—further widened the schism between the building as an aesthetic object and the building as a material becoming. The social nature of architectural practice was additionally endangered by Kant's emphasis on individual artistic genius. Kantian aesthetics downgraded the importance of the mimetic faculties, as well as the circumstances of artistic production, and endorsed a split between creative endeavors that were either "purposeless" or "purposeful." Influenced by the sort of thinking found in Kant's *Critique of Judgment*, architectural theorists have often mistaken the lack of readily defined transitive relationships between the practical and the useless—or, for that matter, between form and content, function and form, building and design, practice and theory, shape and substance—as evidence of the lack of any relationship whatsoever. These erroneous dichotomies—as well as the equally misguided counterreactions, such as functionalism, they spawned (which assumed the same pairs of terms had direct projective relationships to one another)—have haunted architecture ever since.

We can see one manifestation of this difficulty in the works of contemporary avant-garde architects. An extreme degree of arbitrariness is inherent in their dependence on formal rules entirely of their own devising, compared to the tangible limit-conditions engaged and imaginatively troped by vernacular builders. This arbitrariness restricts them from producing edifices "pervious to every soul, every intellect, and every imagination."[289] This is not to assert that the architect does not have, like the author, considerable ability to define within the work the rules by which the project is to be engaged. It is not the arbitrariness of form alone that denies relevance to these works, it is the arbitrariness of form combined with the meaninglessness of construction. The forms of the artist Christo's wrappings are also somewhat arbitrary, but they become significant by the social processes of their realization.

The great quantities of verbiage that often attach themselves to the works of avant-garde architects could be attempts to substitute ideological persuasion for more traditional processes of socialization. Similar to the importance title and framing (both in the literal and figurative senses) have acquired as painting has evolved into a fine art, textual support has become increasingly necessary to justify the compositional strategies of professional architects. Hugo was not quite correct: the book did not entirely kill the building; however, buildings that aspire to the status of art now require an explanatory book. But because these persuasive attempts are seldom offered in terms accessible to "plain folks," their effects are far more limited than the time-honored methods of socialization—building and dwelling—had been. Ideologies are always less convincing than skillfully told stories, because the ideologue is restricted to the language of (apparent) truth, while the storyteller and vernacular builder may additionally resort to good lies. Architecture has always been a partially self-socializing practice, because building was unavoidably social, and because the making of a building required the troping of material circumstances into intelligible signs. True architectural details always "tell tales."[290]

A conflict of construction arose, however, when architects began to consider the design of a building purely as a matter of shape composition. When construction is reduced to a technique of efficient production—when gravity, the availability of materials, local customs, climate, and issues of constructability are excluded from the province of design, and when construction's traditional social function is eliminated—we are left with a vacuum where architectural designs cannot be properly socialized. This gap cannot be adequately filled by the explanations of architects alone, so other largely unconscious "irrational" judgment criteria are sucked into the void.

Loos was speaking into this void when he brought to light many of the contradictory assumptions we continue to employ when we evaluate architecture, such as our tendency to valorize the evidence of extensive effort. Once industrialized production transforms meaningful social work into efficient labor, the amount of effort that goes into the production of a building should also, logically, become irrelevant. Yet, as Loos was writing this was not the case. In 1898 hearts still "beat with reverential awe at the sight of a polished granite wall."[291] Now, at the end of the twentieth century, after decades-long exposure to simulations of hand-crafted building methods, the public's awe of work may have finally begun to wane.

However, within the architecture *profession* this tendency is as strong as ever. It exists in the "cult" of the architectural design studio in the United States and in all other regions where architectural education is based on the studio model. Architecture students in these areas pride themselves on the quantity of time they put into their studies. In architectural studios, a model made of wood is more highly regarded than a formally identical model made of cardboard. Why? The awe of work perhaps? If, as the prevailing architectural theories since the

Enlightenment have held, a model is merely an abstract miniature of a building, a purely instrumental representation, we should judge it only in terms of its accuracy. As Loos would tell us, if we are to behave as true moderns, we should praise not the most labor-intensive, but the most efficient means of building models. However, architects continue to hold the wood model in higher esteem, in part because they feel that it is evidence of greater commitment on the part of its maker. We analogously attribute quality in the model to quality in the design of the building the model purports to objectively represent. One's cleverness in making a model is taken as proof of one's cleverness in designing a building, even though the modern circumstances of building production have almost totally severed any relationship these two skills might have once shared.

The architectural profession's tendency to be influenced by the awe of work ironically connects it with another culturally conservative movement that is its inverse: the practice of Freemasonry. Faced with the collapse of the guild system, Freemasonry, which probably began in Scotland at the end of the sixteenth century (although Freemasons claim a lineage extending back to the builders of Solomon's Temple), was an attempt to preserve the social function of a building craft while gradually eliminating its practical or "operative" aspects. While industrialized building kept the productive qualities of building activity, but abandoned its social role, Freemasonry abandoned production in order to conserve the sociability. It stands to reason that Freemasonry would model itself after the most autonomous, and most highly respected European building trade guild—that of the masons who worked with the intricately carved stone that was exposed or "free" in the finished building.

Those who have continued their involvement with building design have compensated in other ways. As the process of construction became less social, less meaningful, as well as quicker and more efficient, the process of design became more labor intensive. The socialization of architectural form since the fifteenth century has progressively shifted from occurring during the acts of building and inhabitation to occurring during the professional architect's design process. This helps explain the great emphasis placed upon process drawings in architectural studio criticism, as well as the tradition of requiring students to perform their work within the physical and social confines of the studio, and later to state the reasoning behind their design solutions in public presentations.

The most highly respected designers are today those who best articulate the ideology behind their work (or have others do it for them). They are also frequently architects whose work appears most complex, or at least shows evidence of a complex design methodology. Peter Eisenman's status as a designer owes much to the very visible and seemingly rational processes whereby he generates complex building shapes. Likewise, the notoriety achieved by the California firm Morphosis in the 1980s can be attributed to their superbly crafted design drawings, where conventional orthographic and axonometric views are superimposed amid a blizzard of construction and regulating lines, lending an air of rational inevitability to their work. Finally, the present fame of Frank Gehry can be partially attributed to the credibility he gains by endlessly studying his designs in models. In interviews and articles about his practice, Gehry is often photographed in his studio, surrounded by a myriad of study models.

By piercing the veil of these compensatory practices, I do not intend to suggest that the architectural studio is merely an exercise in nostalgia, or that I can unequivocally claim that the "lies" surrounding the work of the architects just mentioned are not reasonably "good" ones. The studio setting remains the best possible situation where the good lies and difficult truths that constitute the unquantifiable practice of architecture can be learned or produced. The unsteady truce that is the architect's status as a professional is endangered further when it allows the intransitive measuring that takes place within the studio to be gradually usurped by other, less inclusive forms of measurement: licensing exams that test only quantifiable issues, such as technical expertise, surpassing the importance of the architect's traditional studio-based apprenticeship; continuing education and formalized internship requirements reductively over-emphasizing the value of "educational experiences" readily quantified and consumed; professional architects who, aided by a fawning media, conceal their inadequacies as makers behind fictions dedicated to holding us "in awe" of their work.

The studio has proven to be the architect's equivalent of the Island of the Text. It is the last refuge from which architects and students can safely "mobilize their potencies for transformation."[292] It is the place where the necessary analogical relationship between the architect as a clever maker of things and architect as sensitive designer of buildings can remain connected. This island too, is under siege, both from those who would abandon the studio as an inefficient anomaly, and from those too easily seduced by studio-produced professional products. Since the advent of the professional architect, explanatory texts, expert criticism, quantity of effort, geometric perfection, formal complexity, rational-appearing design methods, and endless reiteration have attempted to replace traditional socialization processes as the bases for evaluation of architectural quality.

The need for such substitutes has been accelerated by the speed-sensitive nature of heavily financed capitalist development. As the time spent constructing a building has lessened, there have been fewer opportunities for social interaction among the builders, or between builders and future dwellers. With construction speed, economy, and efficiency crowding out all other concerns, the process of building has indeed become virtually meaningless. Yet, this does not suggest that we can equate the production of a building with the production of any other "text." The printing of a book, for example, is economically inconsequential compared to the production of any reasonably large building. While the production of books has readily lent itself to industrialization and Taylorizing, building construction remains one of the most dangerous and least predictable endeavors one can still pursue in contemporary society. Thus, there remains an element of heroism and pride associated with the making of a building, as was so powerfully demonstrated in Lewis Hines's photographs of the construction of the Empire State Building. The printing of a book only involves similar risks when the text is politically subversive.

Building construction, unlike book production, preserves some opportunities for socialization between the buyer and the producer. While the materiality of the building, or the manner of its making, may stand in direct contradiction to the aesthetic aims or ideological pretensions of its architect (as is often seen in the severe weathering of many modernist buildings), the materiality of a book is much less likely to subvert the intentions of its author. A book is physically a far simpler construction than a building, and it is neither tied to a particular place nor exposed to the elements. Unlike a printed text, the material condition of a building, and therefore what may be read from it, is always changing. An encounter with a work of architecture has as much in common with viewing a live musical performance, or a dance, as it does with reading a printed text. The architectural text is much less predictable, far less stable. As Hugo realized, in the age of the printed text, architecture's substance would be interpreted as a liability, forcing architecture into a subordinate role to the book. Professional architects, sensing this, adopted the text and the projective drawing as their ideals, gradually abandoning their concern for the material and temporal processes of building-dwelling. But still architecture, as "a primitive thing," refuses to become fully "textual."

Avant-gardism, neoclassicism, and other forms of what Manfredo Tafuri called "compositional rigorism" have had limited social significance because they claim total creative freedom for the author-like architect-as-professional, while prescribing absolute submission to builders and occupants conceived as anonymous readers. Such ideologies fail to realize that a time of intransitivity, such as that provided by the unpredictability of materials, the imperfections of builders, or the unforeseeable whims of future building users, is necessary for the forms of socialization we call "building" and "dwelling" to exist. Ideologies cannot replace social and material processes entirely because they offer only direct routes to the commodity they call "architecture," which is in fact a delayed imaginative condition that can only be reached indirectly. In this, they are only the most pronounced instances of the contradictory assumptions underlying the practice of architecture as a profession. Despite recent philosophical alliances between avant-garde architects and poststructuralist literary theorists, these architects, too, imagine only finished forms.[293] These are timeless architectural texts directed at a model reader identical to the architect himself. The architect's much-sought autonomy is today found in the design of his own, or his mother's, house. Much as with the "narrowcast" of many cable television channels, or the Internet chat rooms directed at small audiences with specialized interests, designs that address only an elite of like-minded architects must risk reinforcing social divisions.

As a professional strategy of specialization failing to find universal principles of ideal form, compositional rigorism has usually contented itself with satisfying the tastes of the elite for either novelty or nostalgia. Unlike the early modernists, today's adherents to compositional rigorist ideologies have abandoned interest in the social processes that the production of buildings entails. Aesthetic specialists, they "make architecture (and, of course, themselves) into commodities, which are marketable in a world of vacuous connoisseurship."[294] In this, they are joined by their lower-status professional counterparts, the function specialists. The conventional wisdom separating architects into "idealists" who compose with pure forms and "empiricists" who deal with the realities of building production overlooks the fact that these are merely opposing sides of the same division of labor. The compositional rigorists would be unable to build without the assistance of the production specialists. At the extreme, these architectural technologists place efficiency above all other goals, practicing architecture by emulating engineers. They too, commodify buildings by acceding to market pressures for buildings-as-instruments, while abandoning the effort to provide the necessarily intransitive connections between function and dwelling. Like the supposed opposition between permanence and change, the superficial clashes between "formalists" and "functionalists" belie the large measure of ideological agreement they share.

I have been using Tafuri's term "compositional rigorism" in place of the more common, disparaging designation "formalism," because I believe it more accurately portrays the tendency of professional architects to overvalue visual composition. To describe this situation, the word "formalism" is highly misleading. The mode of architectural practice usually referred to as "formalism" actually trivializes architectural form. Despite my criticism of compositional play, I consider the production of nontrivial form to be a fundamental task of architecture. Given an all-encompassing understanding of architectural form—such as that espoused by Klaus Herdeg in *The Decorated Diagram*,[295] his critique of the reductive design thinking commonly referred to as "formalism"—a fixation with form would be most desirable. My preference for the word "shape" where others might use "form," is a similar attempt to distinguish between a more all-inclusive understanding of form, and the reductive geometric descriptions of shapes.

By the 1980s this emphasis on shapes had taken a new turn, partially substituting a concern for "communication" for that of composition. By reductively treating architectural elements such as arches as disembodied shape-signs, the clerics of postmodernism dissolved the poetic "words" of embodied building into a communication code. Here again, the materiality of the building frequently undermined the aesthetic aspirations of the architect. (Poorly detailed and cheaply constructed postmodern buildings, clad in EIFS stucco, quickly deteriorated, leading, in some cases, to insurance companies refusing to underwrite the use of this building system.[296]) The seemingly different logics of avant-gardism, postmodernism, and neoclassicism are nearly identical in what they agree to ignore, differing only in their area of aesthetic emphasis. Any of these can be effective strategies for a small number of architects and firms who are granted a higher degree of autonomy by clients willing to pay for their ability to produce "symbolic capital," but it could be argued that the role of aesthetic specialist undermines the legitimacy of the profession's claim to be more than stylists. And yet these strategies constitute an understandable response to our current cultural conditions, given that it is only as "artists" that architects are insulated from the competition of other building "professions."

The coincidence of capitalism and architectural practice have continually produced such mixed bags and strange bedfellows. All of these contradictions were preordained at the moment the responsibility for the production of architecture passed from anonymous master and vernacular builders to the professional architect. Avant-gardism was the natural consequence of the building-as-project, while historicism has been a predictable response to the "terror of time." While recognizing that, strictly from the standpoint of social significance, buildings produced by professionals and industrialized builders have tended to be "dead," it would be absurd to ignore the many triumphs that have occurred under this compromised mode of production. Through the fortuitous momentary alignment between the interests of professional architects of great ingenuity and the forces of capitalist development, some startling successes have been achieved. Even if we discount masterpiece individual buildings as wonderful aberrations, we can find entire regions where professionally designed architecture has approached the significance of vernacular building. We may gaze back to sixteenth-century Venice, or to early twentieth-century Barcelona and Santa Barbara, California for evidence that capitalism and architecture have sometimes existed in relative harmony at the scale of the city.

However, we should also note that the more recent the urban success story, the more likely some type of planning controls will have been necessary to temper the tendencies of creative destruction. These bureaucratic controls, so often ineffective and misguided due to their usual reliance on strictly transitive measures, were—in the rare examples of the *Modernisme* buildings of Barcelona's Eixample, and in Manhattan's zoning set-back regulations for tall buildings of the same period—indispensable for reining in both the greed of the developer and the aesthetic autonomy of the architect.[297] The architect and enlightened patron—whether Antonio Gaudí teamed with Eusebi Güell, William Van Alen and the Chrysler Corporation, or an unheralded architect coupled with a forgotten developer—when they have formed a cooperative team, have often succeeded in troping the modern compromised circumstances of building production into inspiring edifices "pervious to every soul." So it is with some justification that Carol Willis refers to the pre-1930s skyscrapers of Manhattan as "capitalist vernacular."[298]

Therefore, to balance this discussion of the problematic professionalization of the architect, I will add that the architecture profession has served the cause of architecture, until recently, *reasonably* well. For additional evidence of professional achievement, I return to Brunelleschi, goldsmith-turned-architect, naming him the starting point of the architectural profession in the West, and then proceed forward in time, until the conclusion of the profession's "golden age" with the death, in 1926, of Antonio Gaudí. I bracket this age on the admittedly specious grounds that these were perhaps the first and the last architects to enjoy the nearly unanimous gratitude of the citizens of their respective cities. Brunelleschi was interred within the *Duomo* he so marvelously completed, having been accorded the full funerary honors of a dignitary. When Gaudí died at seventy-four, a few days after being mortally wounded in an unfortunate encounter with a trolley, his friends and admirers petitioned the Vatican for his sainthood. He too, was entombed in his most famous church, in a chapel crypt of the unfinished Sagrada Familia. Ten thousand people followed his coffin through Barcelona to its burial place.[299]

Despite these professional victories and momentary alliances, the architect has been caught between faith in technological progress—the assumptions underlying the economics of scarcity, and the "terror of time"—on the one side, and the traditional task of architecture to provide not only for the physical, but also the imaginative, human desire for dwelling, on the other. These underlying conflicts undoubtedly fuel much that is written about the supposed "death of architecture." However, a great deal of the pessimism one finds regarding architecture in these writings can also be attributed to the confusion between the practice and the profession with which this essay began. For example, we find Manfredo Tafuri asking, "What [in the late twentieth century] remains of the role played historically by architecture?" and continuing, "Up to what point does architecture's immersion in [capitalist development] render it a pure economic factor?" These questions led Tafuri to the following bleak view:

> Ominously present on the horizon is the worst of evils: the decline of the architect's "professional" status and his introduction into programs where the ideological role of architecture is minimal.
>
> This new professional situation is already a reality in countries of advanced capitalism. The fact that it is feared by architects and warded off with the most neurotic formal and ideological contortions is only an indication of the political backwardness of this group of intellectuals.[300]

There were two separate issues underlying Tafuri's dire predictions. One was the continued commodification of buildings into consumable products. The other was the nostalgic retreat from this reality that architects have made into the realms of pure form and "communication." Aesthetic specialization has had little success in resisting the professional decline of architects because it shares, in fact encourages, the contemporary economic disdain for anything other than the quantifiable exchange value of tangible things. The professional goals of geometric purity or mass communication have combined with the single-minded pursuit of wealth to accelerate the "taking away" of the traditional tasks of the architect. In this respect, architects have often been their own worst enemies. According to Joseph Rykwert, "We have given them weapons to produce buildings more quickly, more efficiently and more cheaply than ever before, without safeguarding those intangible values which even the most obdurate rationalist holds dear," so that the speculators, administrators, and technicians "find now that they can dictate to us, because we have abdicated our responsibility as framers of man's environment."[301]

Rather than directly challenge the dominant modes of commodity production in advanced nations, those who practice architecture in the new millennium will have to pay careful attention to a critical positioning of their work relative to those modes. Following Walter Benjamin, Tafuri identified this as the central question for contemporary criticism. Once this question of position relative to production was asked, Tafuri felt that "many of the so-called masterpieces of modern architecture come to take on secondary or even marginal importance, while a great many of the current debates are

relegated to the status of peripheral considerations."[302] Tafuri
consistently raised a strong voice against the products of "perfidious
enchantment" to come out of the avant-garde's shape-composition
"laboratories" near the end of the twentieth century, even as he refused to
offer any compensatory strategy for architects and architecture, other
than to await the "inevitable" collapse of capitalism.

However, I do not accept the inevitability of Tafuri's, Hugo's, or
any other's warnings of the impending death of architecture. This is not
to understate the profound contradictions that engaging in architectural
practice at present entails. Professional architects may be in jeopardy, but
architecture, although its production has been made difficult, is far more
secure.[303] In such a single-minded age as our own, where so many
human beings are experiencing the "deep solitude of the spirit and
will"[304] foretold by the philosopher Giambattista Vico, authentic
architecture may be in greater need than ever. Architecture may not, as
Le Corbusier once wrote, provide an alternative to revolution, or even
slow our further descent into the single-mindedness Herbert Marcuse
labeled "one-dimensional man."[305] Whether or not the apocalypse is
nearly upon us, we still need places to be at home, places to daydream,
places to celebrate, mourn, and remember. These things have been
constant throughout the entire history of the human race and they have
been provided by architecture. Why should she abandon the
responsibility now?

We have moved from the totally sustainable vernacular
production of architecture, to the largely sustainable production
facilitated by the guilds, and then to the further compromised split
between the architecture profession and the building trades. In each step,
as our societies have become more dependent on the economics of
scarcity, more committed to the unending quest for efficiency, the
production of architecture has become more problematic (if not actually
more difficult). The profession of architecture as we know it may be
nearing the limits of its efficacy. It is possible, however, that the hostile
social conditions have reached a point where, at the dawning of the new
millennium, they have created new opportunities for reconfigured
architectural practices. We can only speculate as to what forms these new
practices might take.

**Seven Strategies for Making Architecture
in the Twenty-First Century**

Scholar/Amateur Builder Henry Mercer's Concrete Castle — Fonthill

In answering the question, "Will the architect survive?" we could say that any
specialisation, and consequently any specialist, is always in danger of becom-
ing outmoded. But it seems to me that architecture is so vague an activity that
it cannot be defined and that which cannot be isolated cannot be eliminated.

Christopher Jones

A commercial, probably for athletic shoes, begins. From above we see a desolate
urban playground. On the basketball court, a lone figure is dribbling a
basketball. The camera zooms in. He is a boy of about ten. The camera moves
closer still, and we begin to hear what the boy is saying. His words are spoken
in the hyperbolic tones of an agitated sports announcer: "Jones has the
ball . . . he crosses mid-court . . . breaks to his left, looking to pass . . . now he
swings back the other way . . . ten seconds left, the Knicks still down by two . . . "
The kid is playing an imaginary basketball game, a big game, probably the
finals of the NBA championship. He, of course, plays the role of the star. We see
him look anxiously at the hoop. He is very far away, in three point range,
"downtown." It does not look like he can even throw the ball to the hoop from
that distance. The seconds tick off, the narrative continues: "five seconds . . .
four . . . Jones pulls up near the top of the key . . . two . . . [another close up of the
kid's determined face] he fakes . . . shoots . . . " We see the ball, in slow motion,
arcing gracefully toward the hoop. Now we see the anxious face of the shooter
intently watching it. Now back to the ball. At last we see it clank off the front of
the rim. He missed. The camera cuts back to the kid's face. For a split second a
look of dejection begins to creep in. But the child's imagination will not be so
easily denied by his lack of strength and skill. The look of disappointment
quickly transforms into one of triumph: "He was fouled! Jones was fouled!
He'll shot two from the line!" screams the announcer . . .

      The little boy playing basketball alone creates an imaginary
situation where success will be determined by his ability to make what,
for him, is a nearly impossible shot. Therein lies the challenge, the thrill,
and the possible glory. His willingness to engage material reality in a
contest of skill lends significance to his actions. Had he chosen the
easiest path to self-gratification, selecting a shot he knew he could make,
his triumph would have been meaningless. The philosopher Gaston
Bachelard measured such challenges on a qualitative scale he called "the
coefficient of adversity." The boy pumps his confidence up, convincing

himself that he can actually make the shot. When he fails, his ability to sustain the role of athletic hero begins to unravel. Until, that is, he imagines an ingenious solution—an outlet—an escape. He cannot erase the miss, for that would cross the ethical line that exists in imaginary boyhood sports fantasies. He is not trying to deny reality, he is trying to frame it in a particular way so that it will make him a hero.

The "truth" of his hero status is not given. In order to be convincing, his truth must be made by his eventually making the winning basket. So his solution cleverly allows the game to continue. He will get another chance to score. The missed shot has been turned, *troped*, into not a triumph—which would have been asking too much—but another chance to triumph. In terms of building suspense, it might prove better that he has delayed victory. Now the game may be headed into overtime and the drama has intensified. There is, of course, a limit to the number of times the boy will be able to get away with this sort of thing. There must always be *some* connection between the believability of the fantasy and his ability to sink a three-pointer. However, the more imaginative he is, the more flexible this tangible but intransitive connection will be.

The mode of imagination the boy employs in the commercial is what Bachelard designated the "material imagination." It is the imagination that takes the body along—it anthropomorphicizes the world. We might also call it—depending on the actions of the body it imagines—the athletic imagination, the erotic imagination, the dynamic, gastronomical, social, or ethical imagination. Architectural practice requires this imaginative ability to transform reality, this power to trope unforeseen situations in a productive way. Thus, a well-developed material imagination is essential for architects. Architects ought to devote time to reading literature and poetry—not to find design inspirations, but because these activities and other creative pursuits will enable them to develop open imaginations.

Buildings are rarely born as architecture; they *become* architecture through imaginative processes that take time. As it was aptly put in Stewart Brand's book *How Buildings Learn,* "A building is not something you finish. A building is something you start."[306] Even the construction contracts used in the United States recognize that a building is never "completed." They refer to a condition known as "substantial completion"—the point at which the building may be occupied for its intended purpose; "final completion" is established primarily by the submission of required paperwork, rather than by any assertion that the building is one-hundred percent complete.

Because "timing" generally trumps "spacing," an undistinguished building can become architecture without assistance from an architect, or without—for that matter—any extensive changes to its shape, appearance, or structure. Conversely, just because a building has been designed by a famous architect, it cannot be guaranteed that it will become architecture, and its failure to do so may be through no fault of the architect. If we allow that the condition "architecture" in its "verb" form is, among other things, a matter of "timing," then it stands to reason that sometimes the timing may be wrong. In other cases, the timing, through sheer accident, may be most advantageous to the condition of architecture. Sir John Summerson, in his collection of essays entitled *Heavenly Mansions*, provided a frontispiece photograph captioned "Saint Faith's Church after damage by a flying bomb, 1944." Summerson, in the text of his essay "The Past in the Future," went on to describe the effects the bomb damage had on this otherwise mediocre building.

> When a flying-bomb destroyed the west end of William Burges' church of St. Faith, Stoke Newingham, a spectacle of incredible grandeur was created out of a church of very moderate artistic stature. It became a torso—the fragment of something infinitely magnificent. The remote apse was patinaed with sunlight sprayed through open rafters; and the west wall had been torn aside sufficiently for the noble and still fresh interior to gain by contrast with its rough-hewn shell. Nothing could have been more moving—and nothing less stable.[307]

What Summerson describes is an example of the serendipitous occurrence of architecture through entirely accidental—but impeccable—timing. It is more accurate to understand architecture as an occurrence than as an object. Its instability makes architecture an event much like a solar eclipse, a Christo wrapping, or the precisely controlled death dance of an abandoned building undergoing explosive demolition. In the unstable condition of ruin, *all* buildings become architecture.

That said, it must be acknowledged that the production of the buildings we require for shelter, if we aspire to dwell in them, cannot simply await a chance flying bomb or the corrosive effects of the centuries. Timing may generally supercede spacing in the production and experience of architecture, but, since the near extinction of vernacular building, the architect has had much greater ability to order space than to orchestrate the events of a building's becoming. Just as authors after the printing press have had to imbue written phrases with an ambiguity reminiscent of the winged words of uttered poetic speech in order to establish literature as a viable social art, so professional architects have had to find ways to instill a similar ambiguous order in their industrially produced constructions.

Marco Frascari has termed this process the "secularization" of construction. Frascari recognized that the mythical foundations of most premodern construction could not be relied upon in our demythologized world. Secularization reverses the imaginative polarity of premodern architectural details, replacing the vernacular builders' traditional methods and their attendant myths with artificial ones, proposed by the architect, which may still trope the realities of contemporary construction into intelligible signs. In contemporary building production it is most often the architect who must coerce the builder into building poetically. Where the vernacular builders' constructions were "natural," like poetic speech, secularized methods of making buildings result in structures that are more like poetic texts. The process of ritualized building was itself a tale—a ceremony, an event, a reenactment of divine creation; authentic details produced by secularized construction methods *tell* tales, which must then be interpreted through a kind of *forensic* reading.[308] While we may literally experience these building parts in the real time of building inhabitation, in our memories and imaginations we simultane- ously look to the past, recreating events back to the building's construc- tion. The tales we read suggest ways of thinking about building and dwelling. Instead of responding to necessity as vernacular builders must, secularized builders must artificially create obstacles, moments of delay, which they then must find ways to ingeniously trope. Much like the boy playing basketball, they intentionally create circumstances where a high enough coefficient of adversity will make their triumphs significant.

However, even the secularized production of nontrivial archi- tecture is made enormously difficult by our current cultural situation. I cannot adequately express my admiration for the architects who have regularly produced such works. By examining how these individuals and firms have positioned their work relative to contemporary modes of building production, I have derived a number of speculative strategies for architectural practice that may still prove useful in the twenty-first century. I will begin with the strategies that are the least disruptive, from the standpoint of the professional architect's job, and proceed to others that redefine this job more radically. The more radical departures from conventional modes of architectural practice, including those that are no longer "professional," shift much of the architect's creative emphasis away from the traditional hardships poetic builders have always faced, and toward the hurdles endemic to the practice of architecture in a late capitalist, technological society. In other words, the most significant obstacles architects now must cleverly overcome are social or cultural, not material.

◇   ◇   ◇

STRATEGY ONE   Collaboration and Conviviality (or Take the Client to Lunch): While it is not possible, in the short term, to replace our current economy with a more convivial alternative, in highly localized situations associated with building production this subversive activity is regularly undertaken, even by the most committed capitalists. This is possible because these practices, which form the basis of my first strategy, are not anti-free market. They seek only to overcome the antisocial effects in disembodied markets of abstractly represented commodities. When construction contractors entertain architects—taking them to lunch or sporting events—they merely reintroduce some measure of sociability into the production of a building. By wining and dining her, the contractor hopes to dissolve some of the architect's fixation with the theoretically perfect building represented in the construction drawings. The contractor attempts to gain the architect's trust through gifts that will not be interpreted as bribes, so that the architect will be made more flexible, more willing to admit that the logic of the building cannot every-where accede to the logic of the projective drawing. Of course, the contractor is also motivated to make a profit, and it is to his economic ad-vantage to cultivate the architect as a cooperative, not hostile, collaborator.

Similarly, the architect hopes to gain the client's respect, if for nothing else so that the client will not be alarmed to find that the perfect building the architect's marketing department promised is not feasible. Most architectural construction drawings contain mistakes, due to the impossibility of the architect's imagining every aspect of a building's construction in advance. They also contain errors because architects, competing for ever-smaller fees, are unable to devote sufficient time to the quality control of the buildings-as-products their clients demand. The drawings and specifications are further flawed because few architects now have the opportunity, or interest, to gain a thorough understanding of material behavior and construction processes. The tendency to produce drawings that contain these sorts of errors is mitigated in practice (not least due to pressure from professional liability insurance underwriters) by a growing conservatism in construction systems and details. Offices tend to recycle proven construction methods as often as they are able. Computer-aided design systems have accelerated this trend by providing data bases of proven techniques, and by facilitating the efficient reuse of these methods from previous to future projects.[309]

By gaining the client's trust, if not friendship, the architect hopes to obtain some leeway in the creation of the building to convince the client that architecture is more than a product. Similarly, the contractor hopes to convert the architect into a helpful source of information. Besides making the construction process more sociable, this would almost inevitably lead to higher quality work. The architect, builder, and client would begin to act more as collaborators, rather than adversaries. Under some circumstances, particularly effective teams might elect to form a semipermanent relationship. Carlo Scarpa's loyal collaboration with Veneto craftsmen is a well-known example. However, on-going collaborations also commonly occur in the construction projects of large corporations or institutions. These clients may employ staff architects of their own, or retain architects and contractors "on call" to perform minor plant modifications that are then paid for on a time and materials basis. This process avoids the extra work that would be required for an architect to produce detailed contract documents, suitable for competitive bidding, for each minor construction job. Such clients presumably realize that the costs entailed in producing a set of working drawings would more than offset any savings that might be realized by competitively pricing the construction. In these instances, as well as in the modification of existing buildings, the cumbersome nature of competitive bidding based on "complete" contract documents becomes obvious.[310]

Similar social bonds could assist in renovation work where it is frequently impossible for the architect to establish the condition of the existing structure before demolition begins. Renovation projects underline the degree to which the timelessness of the working drawing is at odds with the reality of the construction, which is an on-going process of discovery and improvisation. Historic preservation work is often the most difficult in this regard, as some preservationist ideologies deny the "living" nature of buildings, striving instead to turn them into timeless museum pieces. Scarpa's great success in modifying existing structures, such as the Castelvecchio Museum in Verona, was largely made possible by his friendly relationship with the builders, as well as the client's willingness to allow him freedom to modify the building where he saw fit. Much of the animosity that arises between architects, contractors, and clients is directly the result of the conflicting ideologies imposed by an economic system unable to distinguish rewarding social processes from industrial products.

Conventional "lump sum" construction contracts only serve to exacerbate the ideological hostility to change and improvisation. Working under these fixed-price contracts, builders are tempted to exploit any deviation from the contract documents, particularly those required by the architect's errors or the client's changes of mind, in order to recover profit they may have lost due to unanticipated difficulties on other portions of the work. And because time is money, a general contractor may attempt to delay paying subcontractors and suppliers for as long as possible during the project, leading to a further breakdown in the cooperative atmosphere of the jobsite. The heavily financed nature of modern construction means that the speed of completion will also be the owner's primary concern, not the soundness of the construction or the quality of the design. This is a result of the economic misfit between the nature of construction and the way that it is financed and paid for. To the extent these assumptions can be challenged by convivial and professional relations between the parties, the possibility to create authentic constructions begins to improve.

In this, we might learn from contemporary Japanese construction procedures. There are several different methods currently employed by Japanese builders to create a protected space for building-dwelling. One of the most fascinating, although perhaps least useful as one of my strategies, remains the fully ritualized construction of the Shinto Shrines at Ise. The paired temples, which are continually demolished and rebuilt in twenty-year cycles, remain one of the purist examples of "architecture as a verb" in the modern world, and the temple carpenters still follow a tradition very similar to that of the Medieval European guilds.

However, it is not only at this extreme of ritualized Japanese building production that important lessons can be learned. In Japan, the architect's role has always been a collaborative one, requiring cooperation with not only the builder, but also with manufacturers of building components. The Japanese architect's "bidding set" of drawings are, compared to American contract documents, very vague. What we call "design development" occurs, in Japan, *after* the construction cost has been agreed upon. Because architect, builder, and client are culturally conditioned to respect and trust one another, the contractor's bid is treated as an estimate only. Nevertheless, when a contractor prepares a bid for a project whose architect is familiar to him, the bid is likely to be quite accurate. Usually, there will be few written contracts between the parties, and no written specifications. Coordination and design development take place at the job-site, where the architects and engineering consultants have established on-site offices for the project duration. Dana Buntrock describes the activities at such a jobsite.

> The job-site office offers several distinct advantages. Most important, the representatives of each group are in frequent contact and are focused almost exclusively on the project at hand. Office staff (including not only architects and engineers, but also secretaries and even "office ladies" whose role is to keep things neat and serve sweets and tea) tend to arrive on site by 8:00 A.M., and professionals generally do not leave until 10:30 or 11:00 P.M. For a variety of reasons, laborers are encouraged to quit by early evening. This allows the architect . . . to draw and make models in the evening and supervise, or even participate in, construction during the day.[311]

In Japan, the architect's drawings are less idealized than they are in the United States and Europe. Greater attention is directed to the construction process, which is therefore left more open for innovation and improvisation. Influential architects are able to persuade manufacturers to experiment with new materials and custom configurations of building components. The use of full-scale mock-ups is far more common in Japan than in Western construction. Shop drawings, the role of which have been progressively minimized in the United States (at least as regards the architect's willingness to take full responsibility for approving them), play a dominant role in Japanese construction. Buntrock reports that for a 35,000-square-meter building complex, 148 sheets comprised the original bid set of drawings, while 2,105 sheets of shop drawings had been approved by the architects—this when the building was only eighty percent complete. Because shop drawings replace detailed construction documents, and the production of shop drawings is the responsibility of manufacturers, not architects, large buildings in Japan can be designed by smaller offices than would be the case in the United States.

Even though Japanese firms use the same sorts of instrumental drawings as their American counterparts, the social process of building construction prevents the building from becoming conceptualized as a representation of the drawings. Since the builder and component manufacturers are the architect's collaborators, the architect's designs become significant through the interpretive activities of their realization. As even the most avant-garde Japanese buildings are "socialized" in this manner, they are more readily absorbed into the fabric of the society. "Disrupting" building shapes still serve to reinforce the cultural fabric, something American architects have had difficulty comprehending, as they frequently comment on the stylistic "free-for-all" that is displayed in publications of contemporary Japanese building.[312]

Strange as it may seem to Westerners, the high quality of Japanese buildings is owed in part to that society's rejection of the Western ideal of architectural perfection. The close tolerances and precise joints in Japanese construction are readily achieved under their system due to the ability to take exact measurements from actual building parts already in place. This is just one of the many advantages that accrue when construction is not conceptualized as a socially neutral system of commodity production. Of course, the feasibility of all of this is to a degree in the hands of the Japanese government. The willing collaboration among all parties depends on the cultural expectation that all will profit; government protection and subsidizing of the building industry plays a significant role in assuring this expectation will be met. It remains to be seen how long Japan will be able to preserve these protectionist practices in the age of global capitalism.

The techniques I have described so far, both American and Japanese, are attempts to find maneuvering room within what are still primarily capitalist economies. As these practices are conventional, they are not simply isolated exceptions to the dominant economic system, but indications that all economies are to an extent hybrids. The same might be said for the secularization of construction. This mode of building, too, is impure, linking the mimetic faculty with the modern ability to think in terms of texts. Secularization does not always involve procedures as dramatic as those employed by the artist Christo, who specializes in orchestrating large-scale secular ceremonies. Nearly all building construction, even in the present-day United States, retains some ritualized aspects. While the ground-breaking, topping out, and ribbon-cutting ceremonies frequently occurring in American building projects are mostly devoid of their former religious or mythical underpinnings, they are nevertheless rituals that attempt to found the building, however weakly, in our social imaginations. (Not surprisingly, these rituals are taken far more seriously in Japan.)

The parties involved in the construction of a building must do more than simply get along. The imaginative dimension of any fabrication process must be allowed to flower. The socialization of building production is only positive to the extent that it promotes exchanges between creative individuals, so that the sum of values after their efforts is greater than it was before. As both the American and Japanese examples I have cited make evident, partially socialized building production does not imply a socialist national economy. "Socialization" as I have been using it does not refer to state control of economic activity or the elimination of private property; it simply means that economic exchanges are kept personal and tangible enough so that social values may increase, along with whatever profit might be generated.

A somewhat more extensive proposal than my first strategy, one that *did* presuppose structural changes to a national economy, if only in the area of building production, can be found in a 1919 article by Martin Wagner titled "The Socialization of Building Activity."[313] Wagner argued for the socialization of the German building trades, including architects. His article made several claims for the uniqueness of building production, naming qualities that could not easily be eradicated, which thereby naturally insulated construction from the economic abstractions of the global market. Wagner's list of unique attributes included the facts that construction was seasonal, based at a particular work-site, geared to specific local markets, and executed "to order," preventing the stockpiling of excess production. In short, building processes themselves are signs of a heterogeneous world where a winter's day cannot be readily exchanged with a summer's, a column for a beam, or a welder for a mason, thereby forming a "dangerous prohibition"[314] to the universalizing tendencies of advanced technology and global capitalism. The implementation of my first strategy is made easier by the inherently embodied, intransitive nature of construction itself. Along the same lines, Philadelphia architect-educator William Braham has eloquently observed, "Neither the beauty nor the convenience nor even the utility of buildings is bound by the constraints of scarcity, rather they belong to the historically conditioned dictates of necessity, desire, and identity."[315]

Other means of implementing my first strategy include having architect, client, and contractor put forth the effort to meet members of the community where the building is to be situated. Contractors may set aside a number of jobs for persons from the neighborhood. The architect might intentionally select products that are produced in the vicinity of the project site. For the town hall in Nago-City, Okinawa, the loose conglomeration of Japanese architects and craftspersons known as Team Zoo (see my third strategy) commissioned from local workers fifty-six traditional lion figures called "shishi" to decorate the building facade.[316] Such procedures socialize the populace to what might otherwise be purely aesthetic decisions. For a housing project, the future residents might be enlisted to assist in the painting and finishing of their own dwellings. Again, these relationships would be directed towards gaining some breathing space for the project, a space where strictly transitive measures do not usurp all other considerations. When a suitable measure of sociability is restored to the construction process, merely productive labor will have been troped into self-fulfilling work, and the verbness of architecture will have been partially revived.

❖   ❖   ❖

STRATEGY TWO   The Respected Professional and the Troping of Limitations: It would be premature to dismiss the time-honored professional relationship in which the architect gains the respect of the client and the builder. Those architects who are able to maintain this status should enjoy greater creative freedom than their counterparts who are treated as mere service providers. This professional status is different from that of the "star" architect, who may earn the client's respect—but seldom the builder's or community's—through her ability to produce symbolic capital on demand. Unlike the star, the trusted professional is more likely to reject the various Enlightenment-spawned idealizations that I have characterized as haunting architectural practice. Instead of relying on media exposure or the approval of experts, clients are likely to rely on word-of-mouth recommendations to seek out professionals they believe they can trust.

One on-going architectural practice fitting this description is the Arkansas partnership of E. Fay Jones and Maurice Jennings. Jones and Jennings's practice is notable in that, until very recently, it was almost entirely regional. It is also remarkable for somewhat belatedly arriving at an unusual strategy of "specialization"—they design buildings that are fictional forests. Since designing the Thorncrown Chapel in 1980, Jones's office has been primarily occupied with producing variations on the same theme: buildings that metonymically re-present the light-filtering capabilities and lacy structure of a forest canopy in wood or steel. Most of these structures sit in, or next to, actual woods, so a delightful thematic resonance is established between the natural and man-made "roofs."

When Jones visited the site designated to become the Thorncrown Chapel, he determined that heavy construction equipment, if used, would irreparably harm the surrounding woods. By paying suitable attention to the unique qualities of the place, as well as to the means of the building's realization, Jones hit upon the inspiration that would lead to his firm's most widely known design achievements. He decided that Thorncrown's structure should be assembled entirely of light wood framing, utilizing members small and light enough to be carried into the woods by workers on foot. This artificially imposed limit led to the design of a roof structure using closely spaced trusses made of wood chords that were smaller than convention would dictate. The lightness of the individual members was compensated for by their number, producing a roof structure of many interwoven pieces, which began to suggest an analogy with the forest's web of tree branches. Studying this effect in models, Jones and his collaborators sought to enhance it. They included skylights to filter the sun through the trusses; they designed the exterior walls predominantly of glass framed between the vertical wood truss supports. This made the roof appear to float above the ground plane, and as the walls were more transparent than the roof, the tree canopy analogy became stronger still. They then gave the roof a generous sheltering overhang, with the chords protruding beyond the roof edge. Jones had designed a building whose interior was a re-presentation of its exterior, so that the building's occupants were placed at an undecidable boundary between shelter and exposure, artifice and nature.

At some point, the decision was made to extend the crossing wood members beyond their point of intersection, creating the perception that the building frame might be reaching beyond its present limits, attempting to grow, like a living organism. Along the same lines, the intersection between the major truss chords was made, through the use of nearly invisible steel connectors, into an empty space, rather than the solid connection one would anticipate. This detail, too, contributed to the effect of lightness. Jones used local stone for the chapel's base and floor, both to tie the building securely to its site, and as a further contrast to the lightness of the roof. Things continued to fall into place—the ends of the truss chords were cut at an acute angle, lightening them even further, while also suggesting the thorns of the chapel's name. Once in the actual building, all of these architectural gestures going on over visitors' heads invite their gaze upwards. Not since the roof vaults of the Gothic cathedrals had an interior architecture so willfully drawn our imaginations skyward. This was intentional, as Jones acknowledges the small Parisian Sainte Chapelle as an inspiration.[317]

After the chapel opened, word spread quickly of the magnificent little building in the remote hills of northwest Arkansas. As in the social lure of a campfire, the existence of an open and accessible sheltering pavilion, seemingly without walls, set in a tranquil forest offered a nearly irresistible enticement for people to gather. Though Thorncrown was intended to be a wayfarer's chapel, it was soon overwhelmed by requests for wedding ceremonies as well as for traditional church services. This popularity eventually led to the construction of the adjacent Thorncrown Worship Center, a larger, more conventional church, designed by Jones and Jennings utilizing similar themes.

While Jones and Jennings have produced a number of variations of the Thorncrown artificial forest, to their credit they refuse clients' requests to produce near duplicates. The curved and more explicitly Gothic-looking steel structure of the Cooper Chapel required close collaboration with a metal fabricator who had experience forming the curved structural ribs for large holding tanks, suggesting that Jones's practice has already implemented aspects of my first strategy.

There are other positive aspects of Fay Jones's work that make it exemplify this respected professional strategy. First, Jones's practice testifies to the continued viability of the architect-as-professional—at least when the architect has earned sufficient respect in the community to create his own protected sphere of practice. Second, Jones has intentionally kept his practice small, resisting the economic enticements to growth in favor of maintaining (until his fairly recent semi-retirement) direct personal contact with all of the office's projects. His small group of designers sit within a one-room studio, where each is in immediate earshot of the others. Third, the popularity of Thorncrown and its descendents attests to the ability of the public to recognize nontrivial architecture when presented with it. While much of the architectural media in the 1980s was fixated on so-called "deconstructivist" architecture, it was the public who initially "discovered" the more significant architectural achievements, including Thorncrown Chapel and Maya Lin's Vietnam Veterans Memorial. Last, I believe the case can be made that Jones's work, like the basketball fantasy I described earlier, succeeds because of its architect's willingness to playfully engage material reality in a contest of skill. Rather than denying the limitations of material, site, budget, or the builder's skill, or seeking to overcome them with the most expedient techniques available, Jones tropes these adversities into meaningful architectural form.

◇   ◇   ◇

STRATEGY THREE   Unconventional Practices (or the "Day Job"): Due to the decline of the architect's professional status, which Manfredo Tafuri claims is already the reality in countries of advanced capitalism, the professional practice of architecture described in the previous strategy has become extremely difficult to pursue. To deal with this reality, a number of architects have reconfigured their practices into forms that make it possible for them to devote greater attention to building and dwelling. There are many possible forms such practices may take; this is by no means an exhaustive survey.

The first such option is to pursue work, within an existing practice, that does not fit either the economic criteria or the functional building type that normally characterize the office's projects. A firm that specializes in health care facilities might, for example, agree to design a house, even though they realize they will never make a profit by doing so. The house project would serve purposes other than economic gain. It might inspire bored staff to think creatively once again, contribute to the firm's reputation as talented designers, aid in marketing efforts by attracting media attention, etc. The firm's profitable work would be used to fund their unprofitable but more rewarding work; the everyday production of efficient buildings would finance the occasional design of nontrivial architecture. This is really only a slight variation on the struggling musician's "day job" that supports his art. Rather than tending bar or driving a taxicab as an individual artist might do, the architecture firm would partially reconcile itself to the role of mere service provider in order to form its own protected space where economic issues do not override all other concerns. Here, Lewis Hyde explains the rationale behind this "two-faced" artistic strategy:

> First, the artist allows himself to step outside the gift economy that is the primary commerce of his art and make some peace with the market. Like the Jew of the Old Testament who has a law of the altar at home and a law of the gate for dealing with strangers, the artist who wishes neither to lose his gift nor starve his belly reserves a protected gift-sphere in which the work is created, but once the work is made he allows himself some contact with the market. And then—the necessary second phase—if he is successful in the marketplace, he converts market wealth into gift wealth: he contributes his earnings to the support of his art.[318]

Art is erotic property that does not properly belong to the artist or easily conform to the role of commodity. Fitting architectural practice into Hyde's gift-scheme is a bit more complicated than painting or poetry, because not only drawing and designing, but actual construction, would have to be accommodated within the gift-sphere. Yet we need not return to vernacular production for the existence of a limited protected gift-sphere to deliver its benefits—thus the two-part nature of Hyde's strategy. The office that consents to do certain projects at an economic loss is already converting market wealth to the less readily measured feeling bonds that are the signs of gift wealth.

Architects may also volunteer their services to their church or community. University architecture faculty and students are sometimes able to offer *pro bono* design services, without running afoul of the standards of professionalism, to communities who could not otherwise afford professional services. Architect-educator Samuel Mockbee and students enrolled in Auburn University's Rural Studio regularly design and construct houses and other buildings for the poor in Hale County, Alabama. Mockbee's students practice architecture without charging fees; they construct using mostly recycled or inexpensive materials, such as straw bales or old tires, troping these limitations into material constructions of extraordinary ingenuity. Similar services are being offered by the growing number of community design centers (often affiliated with universities) springing up around North America.

These activities should not seem unusual. Part of the rationale for granting professional status has always been the assumption that professionals would place societal interests above individual self-interest. However, the high cost of building, coupled with the small profit margins of architectural practice, combine to place even the most philanthropic architect at a disadvantage when compared to the contributions the developer or contractor might make. Governments, also, can and do play a significant role here. Low- or no-interest community development loans, grants, or other public funding sources can be used to pay for construction costs. More likely to be successful are gifts of service, such as those dispensed by Mockbee's students or by the organization Habitat for Humanity. Also promising is assistance delivered at a smaller, more tangible scale, such as the scattered-site public housing that has been constructed under the direction of Mayor Joe Riley in Charleston, South Carolina. The crucial point is this: in order to preserve some of the imaginative content of the artwork/building/gift, it is only necessary that a portion of the effort and expense of its production be excluded from the entirely transitive measures of the market. The fact that an artist or architect is being paid for her work is not itself reason enough to assume that she has "sold out" to the market.

I can personally attest to the virtues of another method of establishing a limited sphere from within which to produce architecture. This is where the architect becomes a teacher. By obtaining a faculty position within a university, an architect is partially freed from the demands of the market. As market forces have become increasingly pervasive, teaching has become an ever-more desirable refuge for architects. While allowing that there are now more teaching positions to be had, and that most successful architects will usually be recruited for teaching at some point in their careers, it is generally true that in the late twentieth-century a disproportionate percentage of the architects who win competitions and whose works are published have university affiliations. Architecture professors are not necessarily better designers than their peers who only practice in an office setting. However, they have more time to devote to modes of practice, like competitions or theoretical projects, not likely to produce immediate economic rewards. For reasons beyond purely economic considerations (that is, access to libraries and other research materials, inspirational contact with talented and motivated students, proximity to intellectuals in other disciplines, time to travel and conduct individual research) faculty teaching and research positions are the most advantageous day jobs architects are now likely to find. How long this refuge can survive into the twenty-first century remains to be seen. As universities come under increasing pressure to conform to market forces, programs such as architecture, generating little in the way of research dollars or alumni contributions, may face gradual extinction despite their popularity.

Even for those unable or unwilling to teach, Hyde's two-part strategy has merit. Architects may still enter competitions outside of their regular jobs. Sometimes groups of friends, even those employed by different firms, may arrange to enter design competitions jointly. Usually they will gather in the evenings or on weekends to work on these projects. When such groups are comprised of regular members, a kind of informal atelier may be created. The most well-known of these organizations is probably the loosely linked group of Japanese architects and craftspersons known as Team Zoo. As might be expected, Team Zoo originated in the practice of an architect-educator—Takamasa Yoshizaka. Yoshizaka's practice, which was called U-Ken, around 1971 spawned a satellite office to deal with commissions from the Okinawa Islands. This original off-shoot atelier designated itself by the whimsical symbol of a flying elephant. The office grew in response to the demands of larger projects, but because it wished to function in the manner of smaller practices, it split further into additional ateliers, almost all of whom came to be named after various animals. Thus, the original elephant was joined by Atelier Gaii (bull), Atelier Iruka (dolphin), Atelier Wani (crocodile), etc. The various ateliers, presently numbering around a dozen, have different areas of interest and expertise, and they pursue both independent projects and collaborative endeavors with other members of the Zoo. There is little that unites the works of the various teams stylistically. They are joined instead by the desire to work with friends and respected fellow-artists, and to work in a certain fashion. Patrice Goulet describes the Zoo's work this way:

> [It] presents itself as a milieu and not as an object. Then, because it does not
> attempt to deny the fact that it is shaped under the impact of particular

requirements (of setting, of people) which have modeled it, as it were (this is what makes each of their built projects so different) and that it accepts transformation and aging, and what is more encourages it, ... it shows a complete absence of preconceived ideas, of an a priori, of prejudices, a total lack of partisan spirit, a rejection of systems, dogmas, canons that would claim to be the only ones capable of producing good architecture. Finally because it is plural and multi-dimensional and invites a multitude of interpretations.[319]

To a somewhat more limited extent than Team Zoo, Philadelphia architect-educator Wesley Wei follows my third strategy. Wei's office (which has employed a number of my former students) will often fabricate complex building components that would be too expensive if produced by a contractor, or that would be unlikely to be built to his office's standards. One of their first such fabrications was an elaborate metal grill for a lighting showroom. Another was the cabinet-sculptures Wei designed and built as the main spatial ordering elements in a center-city apartment.

Wei has addressed the contemporary conflicts of representation and construction by returning a small portion of his architectural production to the model of the master builder. Wei's office is relatively fixed and conventional in most other respects, while Team Zoo's practice is less predictable than most contemporary practices, more closely resembling the nomadic life of the Medieval tradesman, or even the Gypsies. Perhaps the phrase "Gypsy architecture" provides a suitable emblem for the kinds of flexible and resourceful practices architects will most likely need to survive in the twenty-first century. By choosing to take on uncharacteristic commissions, by establishing informal ateliers, by finding refuge in teaching, or by organizing volunteer designers and builders for community service projects, architects can demonstrate the virtues of unconventional practices.

◇   ◇   ◇

STRATEGY FOUR   The Imaginatively Flawed and the Provocatively Incomplete: When now-famous architect Frank Gehry was beginning his career, he abruptly encountered the realities of contemporary building construction.

> When I started to build buildings, I was shocked by the lack of available craft and by the demoralized individuals that inhabit the construction industry—their lack of pride in what they spend their lives making, their constant bent toward sloppiness and shoddiness, and the total lack of identification with their work. Wham bam, thank you Sam.[320]

Gehry, like most Western architects, was predisposed to see architecture as static. He writes that, at the time, he had "perfection on [his] mind," a result of both his "training and taste." After several years of doing battle with contractors, Gehry started to see the possibility of a better way. Thinking about the work of artists he admired provided the inspiration.

> Jasper Johns made beautiful paintings with broken pieces of wood and metal; Bob Rauschenberg used an old tire. Claes Oldenburg used papier mâché. Ed Kienholz poured plastic over broken dolls. What was beautiful? The workers' lack of craft became more acceptable. I couldn't change the world. They didn't change. I had to work with them. I decided to accept their craft, or lack of it, as a virtue and use it like one uses the tools available. If I couldn't get the craft I wanted, I would accommodate the craft I got. . . . I explored what "finished" was. I designed my own house in Santa Monica, starting with an innocuous gambrelled two-story duplex on a corner next to neighbors' yards filled with camper trucks.

It is significant that Gehry was initially able to carry out his experiments with the "poetics of sloppiness" because he was his own client. Emboldened by the success he achieved in his own house, "finished" in 1978, he began to convince other clients to give low-craft construction a try. The forms of Gehry's buildings at this time—the offices for Mid-Atlantic Toyota, the plans for the Familian and Wagner residences— suggested they would likely be built in a slip-shod manner. This was largely an illusion because, as we shall see, perfection never really stopped being on Gehry's mind, but it was a convincing illusion nonetheless. Its believability was enhanced by Gehry's use of cheap materials: nailed wood studs, chain-link fence, corrugated steel siding, and gypsum board. He left stud walls exposed, tilted them at odd angles, joining and interpenetrating them with all the precision of the typical child's tree house. His work had the lively spontaneous quality he had sought, even though it was produced through the use of exacting construction drawings.

Around the same time, he was experimenting with furniture made of corrugated cardboard and various fish-shaped objects. As with his low-craft buildings, Gehry's furniture had to take into account the materials and methods of its construction. The furniture was true to Gehry's wish for spontaneity, because it was not produced to exacting specifications determined in advance. Inspired by the limits imposed by a flimsy material, he was able to invent articles of great originality. A similar situation exists with Gehry's fish. These also retain his earlier sensitivity to building methods. The "scales" worn by most of Gehry's fish are a highly appropriate solution to the cladding of irregularly shaped surfaces, even if he seldom uses this principle to full advantage in his buildings. An exception is the twisting glazed volume known as "Ginger" (dancing with the more solidly clad "Fred") on the facade of an office building Gehry has designed in Prague. While not strictly a fish, Ginger shares the fish-scale cladding strategy. She is dressed in overlapping sheets of glass, which act as transparent shingles. While the structural frame that supports the glass is presumably an accurate translation of Gehry's models and sketches, the overlapping of the glass shingles suggests that their placement need not have been so precise. Shingles and shakes are a very tolerant method of cladding and sealing building surfaces. The constructive logic of shingles allows them to cover irregular surfaces quickly and easily, using relatively uniform pieces, without the need of frighteningly complex geometric calculations. Shingles used this way produce authentic details, and the shingling method is very close to qualifying as one of Ivan Illich's convivial tools, because it can be readily learned and cheaply executed without need of highly skilled specialists. So, at least from the point of view of his earlier discovery of the virtues of sloppy construction, Ginger is potentially truer to Gehry's initial inspiration than most of his later work.

As Gehry's fame as an architect grew, however, he began to receive commissions for even larger institutional buildings. This new wave of clients were after the novel "look" of a Gehry building, not the unpredictable methods that would most naturally produce them. I suspect both the size of these new commissions and the nature of the clients influenced Gehry to abandon his interest in buildings that were built "sketchily." Turning away from the artistic inspiration he had found in the unstable temporary works of Gordon Matta Clark, Gehry increasingly saw his buildings as static three-dimensional sculptures. He designed primarily in sketches and massing models, abandoning most references, beyond considerations of opacity or transparency, to the method of the building's making. Earlier in his career, the shapes of his buildings had at least *seemed* to spontaneously react to the unavoidable contingencies of construction; now Gehry's shape compositions were derived entirely from the visual tweaking of a three-dimensional diagrammatic model of the building's functional arrangement. In order to translate Gehry's irregular sculptures into working drawings for buildings, his office eventually resorted to a laser mapping system to digitize the final massing models into conventional orthographic CAD drawings. The conflicts of representation and construction—which his earlier inspiration had sought to eliminate, and his working methods had successfully concealed—now emerged into full view.

Gehry's taste for perfection had resurfaced, only this time in the guise of buildings that appear to be about spontaneity and artistic freedom. He finally resorted to employing computer software originally developed in France to model the fuselage of Mirage fighter jets. After his office had translated his sketches and rough models into accurate massing models, and Gehry himself had approved them, they would use a laser pencil "invented for use by neurosurgeons to map the human skull" (otherwise known as a 3D digitizer) to transpose a description of the model's surface into the jet fighter software.[321] From there, it could be electronically transferred to the structural steel fabricator's computer, or to the computer responsible for mapping the stereotomy of the limestone panels that would clad the building. Gehry sees this process as wholly positive, for it restores autonomy to the architect as the sole form-maker, eliminating the errors and some of the economic penalties imposed by a construction industry generally adverse to irregularly shaped buildings. Yet Gehry's computer programs and laser digitizers are only more sophisticated instrumental methods to unambiguously represent shapes. As such, they do not address the intransitive aspects of making buildings. They project Gehry's models and sketches into electronic abstractions of full-size buildings without resolving the conflict of representation/construction that exists between free-form shapes and precise compositions constructed by unthinking automatons.

For these reasons, the representations of the joints in the drawings and computer models of a recent Gehry building can seldom be considered architectural details in Frascari's sense. They are not demonstrations of poetic building, but technical instructions for assembly by robots. Gehry's cleverness in representing his designs has not necessarily resulted in equally clever ways of building them. As Edward Ford points out, the most complex parts of Gehry's buildings are often the invisible crickets, valleys, and flashings necessary to "produce the appearance of straightforward simplicity."[322] Whatever visual delight one derives from viewing the undulating titanium skin of his enormously popular Guggenheim Museum in Bilboa, it is somewhat tempered after seeing photographs of the building's construction. The fantastic twisting and dancing steel armatures that form the building's structure are now almost totally concealed. Within the building they are sheathed not in reflective titanium sheets, but often in mere gypsum wall board. In such situations, construction has been de-ritualized without being secularized; it has not produced the difficult chiasmatic unions between "construction and construing" Frascari claims are necessary for "nontrivial" architecture.

In vernacular building, and most likely in assembling Gehry's early work, the effort to make an artifact was enjoyable work, not mindless economic labor. The first activity is creative, playful, fulfilling, and necessary for living-dwelling, while the latter can be dangerous and disagreeable, leading to the "demoralized individuals that inhabit the construction industry." Unlike his first buildings—which made sense after one understood the logic behind them, regardless of whether one liked their appearance—Gehry's later works can only be judged as (very expensive) aesthetic objects. In buildings such as his American Center in Paris or Vontz Center for Molecular Studies at the University of Cincinnati, the "details" do not tell tales because the making of these buildings is at odds with meanings derived from how they are made. Either one likes Gehry's recent work, or one does not.[323]

Nothing above should be taken as criticism of the *compositional* aspects of Frank Gehry's later buildings (which, to say the least, are original and interesting). My intent here has only been to recall Gehry's initial idea of capturing something of the unfinished quality buildings under construction possess, to show that by adopting this attitude some of the conflict that must inevitably arise between designers with perfection on their minds and profit-motivated contractors can be alleviated, and therefore to suggest this method as one of the ways architecture might still be produced in the twenty-first century. My analysis of Gehry's work has been restricted to questions of its position relative to its production.

We can contrast Gehry, who forsook his earlier inspiration, to Belgian architect Lucien Kroll, who discovered something similar at the start of his career, and remains committed to it. Kroll always considers the way his designs will be produced, and rejects any images that must be realized through means that are "incompatible with or [destroy] the social and cultural context." Here Kroll describes the conservative nature of architects who concentrate strictly on imagery:

> Only appearances change, while the underlying procedures and techniques
> remain the same. The result is visual and aesthetic boredom. They always
> conceive their buildings in isolation according to a private vision, then
> construct them on Taylor's system: their architecture has no connection
> with a living continuum. Imagine how these buildings will be seen in the
> future, twenty-five years later.[324]

Kroll does not totally reject industrial production, but he strives to supplant Taylorism with what he calls the "intelligent organization of work." (Recall that Amish barn-raisings are precisely choreographed and reasonably efficient, proving that vernacular production need not be chaotic.) Kroll uses the computer not to facilitate his absolute aesthetic control, but to produce modular components that will allow for spontaneity on the part of the builder or dweller, thus contributing to the socialization of productive work.

In this strategy, I am not advocating sloppy construction itself, but the possibility of creatively troping situations encountered in the making of a building when the process is approached with the sort of open, improvisational spirit employed by jazz musicians. Under this manner of building a portion of the construction process again becomes a live performance, and the skill of the builder, or his ingenuity in overcoming the lack thereof, becomes valuable once more. The making of a building would then produce social bonds as well as a more imaginative architecture. Because buildings can never be definitively finished, we should not strive to make them inhumanly complete, but rather provocatively incomplete. This might mean producing, like Kroll does, buildings with movable partitions, flexible services, or readily renewed surfaces, or it may involve a less literal approach—making an artifact that invites its users to imaginatively complete it. Such works, like Carlo Scarpa's Brion Cemetery, could be classified as "built ruins." Frascari has described how the distinct physical boundaries of the concrete tombs at Brion are made imaginatively indeterminate through Scarpa's use of the ziggurat motif. Scarpa's corners are "eroded" away through the device of the ziggurat, leading the viewer to reconstruct the "ghost" corners she believes must have been there. The Brion Cemetery does not imitate the appearance of a ruin, so much as recreate the way ruins tend to make us think.

The Vietnam Veterans Memorial in Washington, D.C.—like Scarpa's construction—can only be made complete when it is haunted by human imaginings. Maya Lin's memorial is secularized sacred space so provocatively incomplete that it is the public that has determined how it is used. The National Parks Service may have anticipated the desire of visitors to make rubbings of the names engraved into its stone face, but surely it never expected the vast number of offerings that continue to be left at the wall. In 1982, while the concrete foundation of the wall was being poured, a man is said to have tossed his dead brother's Purple Heart medal into the trench. This unplanned reenactment of an age-old foundation rite foreshadowed what was to come. After the monument was open to the public, so many letters, flags, flowers, and other objects were left there that Park Service workers began to spontaneously collect and catalog them. The collection of these objects forms a kind of shadow to the actual memorial. Or perhaps the collection, and the memories of those that contribute to it, are the true memorial, for which the built artifact is but a scaffolding. In any event, the collection is by now so large that it is stored in a warehouse known, in typically unpoetic bureaucrat-speak, as the "Museum and Archeological Regional Storage Facility," in Lanham, Maryland.[325]

The Vietnam Memorial invites us all to participate in its ongoing construction. While only a handful of visitors at any one time leave objects or make rubbings of the names, the rest of us participate by our presence, our contact with the wall, and our respectful demeanor. As with the convivial constructions produced by premodern societies, our imaginary completion of the wall produces social bonds. It is commonly remarked that the Vietnam Memorial has contributed to "healing the wounds" left in our nation by the Vietnam War. It is also reported that it is the most visited tourist destination in Washington, D.C. The memorial may offer contemporary tourists one of the few encounters with the authentic architecture of an active civic space they are likely to experience. Because of its ability to demonstrate, the memorial instructs its visitors how it may be used; they, in turn, reinterpret and reinvent additional uses and understandings for it. By building what was possible rather than what would be ideal, by producing works open to multiple interpretations and uses, Maya Lin, Lucien Kroll, Carlo Scarpa, and the early Frank Gehry indicate the value of architectural practices structured to produce open works that are provocatively incomplete.

◇   ◇   ◇

STRATEGY FIVE   Build it Yourself (or with Friends): In Doylestown, Pennsylvania, independently wealthy life-long bachelor Henry Mercer from 1909 to 1911 built a strange mansion primarily out of reinforced concrete. One interior wall of the house, known as Fonthill, contains the following message, spelled out in the ceramic tile letters Mercer manu-factured in his tile works, and freely employed throughout his house.

> Here see the names of the men who planned this house, directed its plan,
> executed its construction, adorned its walls, embellished its pavements,
> built with their labor, and the horse who uplifted with its strength . . .

Mercer's message went on to name the principal members of his construction team and their individual responsibilities. Mercer noted that it was he who had "planned" the house. Mercer was never trained as an architect. Although he held a law degree, he was foremost an archeologist, and only an amateur architect-builder. The buildings he built were few, and they were always constructed for his own use. Besides Fonthill, he also constructed the Moravian Pottery and Tile Works on an adjacent site. His largest building was a museum to display his collection of "Tools of the Nation Maker," now known as the Mercer Museum.

The most unusual thing about Mercer's buildings is that they are all predominately constructed of concrete. While reinforced concrete was certainly common when Mercer's projects were being built, it was not customarily used for residential or institutional buildings. Mercer's motivation in selecting concrete as his primary material was a result of his fear that fire might destroy his vast collection of artifacts. In adapting concrete to this novel usage, Mercer was both naive and brilliantly inventive. Unaware that one did not use concrete as a roof surface, to form the mullions of windows, or to make dressers, bureaus, and book shelves, Mercer successfully used it for all of these tasks.

Mercer's buildings share with other eccentric self-built constructions (think of Simon Rodia's Watts Towers) this trait of extraordinary ingenuity coupled with a noticeable lack of restraint. When creative people serve as their own architects and builders they tend not to think about the design of their building conceptually. Most of them lack the ability to draw, and so they proceed from only the most rudimentary sketches. Mercer, as one might expect from a tile manufacturer, chose to explore the design of his house in a rough clay model. If Mercer followed any design principle it was his obsession with a highly complex interweaving of the spaces within his house. As did Jefferson in his design for Monticello, Mercer preferred to keep his options for movement through his house as open as possible. He did not bridge any rooms with his bed, but he did maintain a minimum of two entries into every room, including his bathrooms. Mercer loved stairs, so there are innumerable level changes in Fonthill, and every stair riser provided a surface on which to inscribe cryptic sayings, such as "MORE BEYOND." Mercer's mansion is also unique in that no dining room is found among its forty-four irregular chambers. The bachelor Mercer preferred to dine wherever the light was best, where he happened to be working, or where his particular guest could best be entertained.

Like the more famous designer-collector Sir John Soane, Mercer filled his home with a wide-ranging collection of artifacts—tools, paintings, etchings, decoratively stamped stove plates, and his ornamental tiles—seemingly without regard for whether or not these objects "belonged" together. What united them as a group was simply that Mercer had acquired them and thought highly enough of them to put them on display. Except for the tools that had been used to construct the young American nation (the collection now housed in the Mercer Museum), Mercer's acquisitions were gathered from no particular period, style, or place. His house demonstrates the same lack of regard for conventional notions of consistency. It is a cobbled-together collage of styles, of fragments freely borrowed from places Mercer had been, made barely recognizable after they have been processed through the cement-mixer of Mercer's imagination.

Such an approach to building or collecting frequently infuriates architectural "experts" with perfection on their minds. These believers in abstract categories and building types fail to appreciate the degree to which such abstractions may shackle our material imaginings. Conceptual categories cannot preserve the essential opposition between images of the particular and concepts of the universal. As the philosopher Donald Verene has written, "There are no categories of the imagination because forms of imagination are not determinate judgments." Nor are they, he continues, "a kind of proto or incomplete version of such a judgment." The thinking that produces building types and most art-historical categories "eliminates the opposition between things and makes them into a network of relations."[326] While thinking of this sort may serve a useful cataloging function, it also draws our attention from the tangible and specific immediacy of experience. As supposedly timeless categories, building types and historical periods exclude memory and narrative, those imaginative constructs that allow us to treat oppositions (such as lightness and weight) not as concepts to be reconciled, but as dramatic forces to be lived and dreamt.

Mercer's dedication to the unfolding narrative that was his incomplete understanding of concrete construction naturally led to his making a *monstrous* house. For similar reasons Soane's house contains a monstrous classical column, where the pieces of its dismembered body are stacked together in the wrong order, as if its shoulders were placed on top of its head. Such antics drove Soane's perfection-seeking contemporaries into apoplexy.

> This labyrinth stuffed full of fragments is the most tasteless arrangement that can be seen; it has the same kind of perplexing and oppressive effect on the spectator as if the whole large stock of an old-clothes-dealer had been squeezed into a doll's house.[327]

Soane's critic was unable to appreciate that Soane's sense of order was an entirely original one, an order independent of existing categories. Yet the critic points to both the beauty and the danger of the self-built project. Most of these (usually) amateur constructions, produced by imaginations "unencumbered" by petrifying concepts, are quite naturally monsters. As such, they are often amazing, inventive, and completely novel constructions. Yet their very exuberance, their total lack of concern for established taste, may also make them private, impenetrable to all but the individual who has shaped them.

Here we are at the opposite end of the psychological spectrum from the autonomous intellectual architects who "hold themselves as the only reference for every possible idea on building."[328] At the same time these overly intellectual architects who prefer obsequious clients, or, better still, no client at all, are not so far removed from self-builders like Henry Mercer. There is a kind of escapism in these works, an aggressiveness toward convention that causes me to temper my enthusiasm for them as a strategy for the twenty-first century. The practices I wish to champion challenge the conventional distinctions between architect, client, builder, and financier without escaping into private worlds where anything goes.

I see no reason, for example, why a clever architect and cooperative builder could not design and partially prefabricate a house so that a group of reasonably skilled friends could erect an inhabitable structure over a weekend. Some experimentation in this direction is currently happening; straw-bale, adobe, and rammed-earth construction methods all show promise in this direction. However, I wish to divorce my recommendations from the unbridled nostalgia that often overwhelms these low-tech construction practices. Neither architecture nor conviviality can be guaranteed by simply bringing together a group of well-intentioned people and a stockpile of natural materials at a construction site. Some capacity to imagine architecture, some *talent*, is still necessary. The success of Fonthill as a work of architecture cannot be attributed solely to the fact that Mercer designed and built it himself. Despite his lack of formal training, Mercer proved himself to be a talented architect and skilled builder. Thus, for all the deserved attention that the American architect-builder team known as Jersey Devil has garnered over the past thirty years, one cannot help but notice the uneven quality of its work. Almost diametrically opposed to the latest practices of Frank Gehry, early Jersey Devil projects were marked by their inventive use of materials (such as precast manhole sections for the structural core of a house) combined with a nearly complete lack of compositional success. Despite my appreciation for the building processes that created them, I cannot fathom why anyone would desire to live in Jersey Devil's idiosyncratic Snail House, even more bizarre Sphincter House, or the one-line joke they call Helmut House.[329]

Dissolving the boundaries around the architect-as-professional, which this strategy embraces, is not the same as declaring the obsolescence of the skilled designer of buildings. Mercer's success as an amateur architect-builder stemmed, I believe, not only from his inherent artistic abilities, but also from his willingness to learn from his materials. Rather than simply project a willful compositional idea onto mute building materials (as is Frank Gehry's recent practice), Mercer was able to trope the limitations of his materials into significant constructions. Self-builders who wish to produce architecture in the twenty-first century cannot rely on the illusion of spontaneity (recent Gehry), the fact of self-building (Jersey Devil), or the use of natural materials and earth-friendly methods (straw bale construction) alone. Instead, they will have to utilize a judicious mix of environmental awareness and fiction, conviviality and technical expertise.

A more contemporary, if not better, example than Mercer's Fonthill (which was constructed by a wealthy man) may be found in an unbuilt design by an architect I have already mentioned: Wesley Wei. In a submission to the 1992 New Urban Housing competition, Wei, in collaboration with architect Daniel Magno, proposed a unique solution for low-cost housing on a city slope in Pittsburgh—to stack pre-manufactured modular houses, trailer homes basically, at the street edge of the site. After piling these two high at the street, and wrapping them in facades suitable for their neighborhood, they would append a more "designed" piece, presumably site-built, to their backs. This element, oriented to the light and view instead of the street, would contain the activities we generally associate with a family room. The rear elements were designed and built according to processes that would be normal for an architect-designed house. The difference here was that this particular group of home-buyers would not normally have access to custom design services. Thanks to the efficiency and economy of the modular house core, they would be able to afford one architect-designed room.

On the face of it, this is a relatively modest accomplishment. However, one can also find in Wei and Magno's solution a way of thinking about houses that has wider applicability. Just as Scarpa was able to build a ruin at the Brion Cemetery, Wei and Magno proposed building an addition that is almost simultaneous with the "original" building. Their affordable housing scheme sets in motion a strategy of building that has been largely abandoned in the age of borrowed money. This "pay as you go" attitude implies a greater self-reliance on the part of the home-owner. It suggests an accretion of small improvements, many perhaps owner-built, to a modest but inhabitable beginning. Returning to a proven pattern of urban housing, with a relatively stable street front and a continuously evolving back, Wei and Magno's design is deliberately unfinished. Its provocative incompleteness, coupled with the high design standard of the initial "addition," should serve as an inspiration for future self-building.

This is the essence of my self-building strategy. In order to dwell comfortably, we must all contribute something to the shaping of our environments. While we may lack the ingenuity or the resources of Henry Mercer, we can learn from the materials with which we build, as well as from the examples of talented architects. Building production specialists have largely failed to address what John Connell, the founder of the popular Yestermorrow design/build school, calls our "homing instinct."[330] The conventions of building construction and financing now encourage the direction of resources towards building production "that only deepens societal differences—pushing markets beyond the reach of other social strata and demonstrating possession of means."[331] One of the most effective strategies by which we can challenge this trend is to revive interest in buildings that are partially built by those who intend to use them.

◇   ◇   ◇

STRATEGY SIX   Theoretical Projects: My sixth strategy, which is closely related to the next, has its primary source in the writings of Alberto Perez-Gomez. In an essay that appeared in the *Carlton Book*, Perez-Gomez observed that in 1986 "the external conditions which made . . . traditional architecture possible are generally lacking." He commented that professional architects were no longer truly makers of things, because their erroneous assumption "of the neutrality of projections"—the condition I, following Dalibor Vesely, have been calling the "conflict of representation"—led "by necessity to inauthentic 'architecture' predicated on reductionism." Like Venturi, who advised architects to attend more closely to "their jobs," Perez-Gomez saw the solution to this crisis in a more carefully delimited architectural practice. Perez-Gomez too, wished to limit "their jobs" to what they could fully control, but for him this was not the decorating of functional sheds, but the making of drawings and artifacts that were analogously architectural.

"Embodied making" can occur more readily at the level of drawing or model, under the immediate control of the architect. Projects intended as explorations into the possibility of an architectural order grounded in techné-poesis, in human action itself, even run the risk of avoiding an allusion to "building" altogether, in the conventional sense, as something external to the project. The use of imaginative projections, ambiguities of scale, and modes of perception would obviously impede a conventional reading of plans, sections, elevations, and models as objects, in terms of a projection of our body-image in a Cartesian space. This constitutes in itself a critical dimension, since such "clear reading" has become during the last 200 years the first expectation of architects and laymen alike.[332]

For Perez-Gomez our contemporary cultural situation demands that architecture be "primarily embodied in theoretical projects," presumably "under the immediate control of the architect." While I am uncertain whether I agree that this strategy must be the primary one for architects to follow into the twenty-first century—whether it supercedes restoring conviviality, preserving the beneficial aspects of professionalism, or any of my other proposals—it must be obvious to the reader by now that all of my strategies are essentially the same. A practice founded upon the pursuit of theoretical projects is necessarily an "unconventional practice"; drawings that deny a "clear reading" are most likely "provocatively incomplete," suggesting the need for close collaboration with a skilled builder, therefore the restoration of convivial relations, as well the use of drawings as "demonstrations" of poetic building (my seventh strategy). All of the strategies I am suggesting are directed towards creating a zone of intransitivity, a breathing space, to allow for the poetic taking-measure necessary for architecture. The theoretical project, as Perez-Gomez defines it, creates its own protected space both through the immediate control it grants the architect and through the critical dimension of the project itself, which calls the neutrality of all techniques into question.

To this definition I will append a specification of my own, in order that a theoretical project qualify for this, my sixth strategy: these projects, like the young boy's fantasy basketball game that opened this chapter, must be willing to engage material reality in a contest of skill. Such projects will then be "theoretical" not because they seek to free themselves from all constraints, but because they choose to explore forms of abjection that would otherwise not be available to the architect by way of more conventional projects. These projects test the limits of architecture, as opposed to merely rejecting the limitations of building.

Thus, Giovanni Battista Piranesi's *Carceri* fits my definition of a theoretical project applicable to the twenty-first century, while most of the equally unbuildable projects by Étienne-Louis Boullée do not. Piranesi's fantasy exposes the truthful fiction that all buildings are, at their hearts, tombs. The forced labors of *Carceri's* prisoners are the movements of men already half dead. *Carceri* shows us the hell that would exist if architecture really were nothing but endlessly executed material processes. At this condition of infinite weight we would be chained to our buildings as Prometheus was to his rock, condemned to the unceasing labor of building without the freedom to dwell. This is the "verb" form of architecture taken to its extreme, taken beyond the limits of proportionality. Piranesi does not merely accept the mortality of men and the materiality of architecture, he converts them into tortures. *Carceri* is therefore all too believable as a building, because there is a little of it in all buildings.

In comparison to Piranesi's drawings, which expose the prejudices of projection and critically explore what it might mean to labor as a "prisoner of one's own metabolism,"[333] Boullée's drawings adhere faithfully to the rules of descriptive geometry, and cheerfully abandon the weight of culture and materiality. They extend the heroic stance latent in the building-as-project to the point of megalomania, and so, despite their undeniable power, constitute for us an "inauthentic architecture predicated on reductionism." I qualify my judgment with the phrase "for us" because I wish to emphasize that, despite the power they once had (and to some degree still have), Boullée's projects lack a critical dimension relevant to our present cultural situation. They blithely propose that the total domination of "nature" through human reason is possible. In this they resemble many of the projects that are commonly designated as "theoretical." They dismiss the realities of building without replacing them with other realities suitable to raise their coefficients of adversity to significant levels.[334]

The reductionism characteristic of Boullée's drawings is their obsession with elementary geometric shapes, most notably the sphere. The difficulty with this approach is that an architect's self-imposed restrictions, when they are purely geometrical, do not constitute obstacles with much weight. (They are akin to our young basketball player always selecting shots that looked difficult, but that he was sure he could make.) Unlike the sort of embodied making I envision from Perez-Gomez's description of theoretical projects, Boullée's drawings fail to address the constructed nature of the shapes they propose. Spherical shapes may be among those most readily drawn, and thereby assumed to be elementary, but they are also quite difficult to construct. Yet Boullée clearly drew them as if they were constructed. The awe by which we regard drawings such as those of his monument to Sir Isaac Newton is inspired by imagining the audacious size of the project as a constructed building. If we accept their projective logic, we are left to conclude that these are "realistic" drawings of a possible building, when—financially and socially, if no longer structurally—Newton's cenotaph remains as impossible today as when Boullée first drew it.

Boullée's designs treat the making of architecture as a neutral technique. They share this attribute with many of the escapist fantasies we often call "theoretical" or "conceptual" projects, including the gridded functionalist compositions of J.-N.-L. Durand. In order to discuss the ethical implications of proposals such as Boullée's, we must step outside of the instrumental space in which they are depicted. After so doing, we discover that Boullée's masterful drawings are "realistic" descriptions of a socially impoverished reality. We can imagine what sort of slavery might be required to construct these idealized megastructures. Those who would labor to produce these buildings would be prisoners just as surely as the residents of *Carceri*. Instead of being confined within the walls of a prison, they would be trapped in the mindless execution of a finished ideal form, slaves to unobtainable perfection. Due to their reliance on projective drawing techniques and to their inability to be built, Utopian fantasies such as Boullée's cannot be considered analogously architectural. For these reasons, I do not consider Boullée's projects suitably critical to point the way for architecture in the twenty-first century.

This is a debatable point, for one could also maintain that Boullée's creations served the critical function of revealing what the combined forces of technological positivism and the "terror of time" might make of architecture. In this regard, the unsustainable nature of these fictions may comprise their strongest defense. Under this interpretation we could consider *Carceri* and the Cenotaph to Newton as examples of the polar extremes of architecture: the former demonstrating the terrors of mortification, the latter the frightening implications of instrumental reason run wild. Still, the *Carceri* drawings are much closer to what I wish to propose in this strategy. While describing a more-or-less believable form, and a precise although nightmarish character, they diminish our faith in the neutrality of projective techniques while simultaneously criticizing the supposed perfection of the Renaissance architectural body. No clear reading of the *Carceri* drawings is possible, because the geometric limits of their space are only ambiguously given, and the depicted space itself constitutes an interior with no exterior—a purely negative space that refuses to arrange itself into a "figure."

A more recent example of a theoretical work suitable for this strategy is John Hejduk's Masque projects. In the afterword to a book on Hejduk's Lancaster/Hanover Masques, Wim van den Bergh described these odd imagined constructions.

> In general, Hejduk's Masques are structured like free scenario matrices, with simultaneous sequences of images and texts, "objects" and "subjects." Like a poem, they have a logic of their own. They have neither rational content nor aim, but display a "mysterious sense" which lends them an intense evocative power.[335]

Hejduk spins out various plots along with constructions designed for the peculiar inhabitants of a hypothetical rural farm community. In Hejduk's creations, it is impossible to determine where the character or subject ends and his or her characteristic building begins. Hejduk gives us characters that behave "architecturally," and buildings of both good and bad character. The buildings Hejduk designs are never so precisely defined that we can contemplate them as objects. Instead the buildings are infected with the fears, memories, and personalities of those who inhabit them.

In this they are like the eccentric constructions of Sir John Soane and Henry Mercer: places with an almost disturbing abundance of personality. As Robert Harbison, an aficionado of eccentric spaces, has written, "Places thoroughly lived in become internalized in a series of adjustments till they represent a person to himself, a process the critic can try to follow in reverse, deducing the life from the quarters."[336] Yet Hejduk's thoroughly lived-in creations defy easy deciphering. They resist all efforts to summarize them, losing the would-be cartographer in their labyrinth made of signs. This theoretical project questions the validity of projects themselves.

> In this respect, the Masques contain a fundamental critique—and was
> Momus not the critic of the gods? They are a critique of the practice of
> joining the analytical elements of reality into a structure which assigns
> things and events a fixed place; a critique of the contentedness with
> instrumental logic and therefore also a critique of a culture which considers
> this logic to be of paramount importance.[337]

Since Hejduk's Masques exist only in drawings and writings that have
been collected into books, one might be tempted to call them
"unrealistic." But Hejduk is often quite precise in his specifications for
these buildings. For instance, one of his designs for a hotel is based on a
painting by Edward Hopper. Hejduk fixes it in time (between 1910 and
1936) and in place (America). He then continues to describe the hotel's
awnings and the "little girls with light brown knee socks and black high
shoes" playing in an empty lot near the hotel.[338] Are these specifications
any less realistic than the thousands of construction specifications
produced by professional architects for buildings that, for reasons of
financing or administrative whim, have never been built? Because
Hejduk's works thwart such assumptions—and deny all "clear readings"
while providing a critique of conceptualizations of architecture that
"assign things and events a fixed place"—they are fit to exemplify my
sixth strategy, the theoretical project.

◇   ◇   ◇

STRATEGY SEVEN   Drawings as Demonstrations: I borrow this final
strategy from Marco Frascari's proposal that contemporary architects,
given their inability to control the production of buildings, should
challenge the purely instrumental role of construction drawings, striving
to produce drawings that are demonstrations of poetic building. If the
professional practice of architecture demands that buildings are now
representations of drawings, the only way to insure poetic building is to
make poetic drawings. In order to accomplish this, the poetic "words" of
the building must be demonstrated—must be present—in the drawing.
Details drawn in this manner would not be miniature projected
representations of an imagined building, they would be poetic
constructions themselves, and they would follow the logic of drawings,
not buildings. They would represent the built detail symbolically, in
addition to instrumentally, so that, in Frascari's words, "each angle is an

angel."[339] Frascari explains this aphorism by noting the etymological connection between the two words, and by recalling the navigational procedures used by early Mediterranean sailors, who, while calculating the angles of the stars, thanked the angels who dwelled therein for guiding them safely home. The sailors united the practical and imaginative aspects of representations, much as architects must again learn to do, because "the union of symbolic and instrumental representations in the building [now depends] on their presence and union in the drawing."[340] Drawings of this type would not necessarily look like the finished building. The builder would be required to interpret the architect's drawings, so that there would be an analogical correspondence between what was built and what was drawn.

The union between the two types of representation would be a difficult one, for which no normative prescriptions could be given. Frascari calls these unions "monsters," both because the word designates grotesque bodies comprised of parts that do not necessarily belong together, and because of its etymological roots, connecting it to the Latin and Italian verbs "to show" or "to demonstrate." Frascari's proposal would allow professional architects to concentrate on "their jobs," which would be the production of poetic drawings, without reducing their concerns solely to issues of composition. The architect would ask the builder to produce the same effect in the building as the architect had in her drawings, but the architect would not dictate to the builder exactly how this transformation was to be realized. The architect would presumably, as a professional, impartially judge the results of the contractor's efforts. One advantage of utilizing the partially symbolic drawings-as-demonstrations is that they would permit the architect to draw aspects of an imagined building that are not visible, such as the processes of building and dwelling. Here Frascari explains the nature of the mode of drawing he recommends:

> In his/her drawings, the architect's pursuit in conceiving and constructing architecture is to make visible what is invisible. . . . Architectural drawings are semiotic tools that make tangible what is intangible. In any edifice the substance and the form of the contents and physical expressions are not two separate dimensions, but they are embodied in the built object. Any edifice is a Peircian "dynamic object" that motivates signs: *de-signs* are motivated signs expressed in drawings. In drawings, [a statement by Umberto Eco applies:] "a sign is not only something which stands for something else; it is

also something that can and must be interpreted." An edifice, a nontrivial
building, is the physical result of this process of interpretation.[341]

Another positive attribute, for architects at least, is that these drawings
would not be immediately intelligible to the public. The architect would
have to guide the client and contractor through the drawing's monstrous
maze of technographic images. Through this vital role as guide, some
measure of the architect's past influence over the production of buildings
might then be regained. As a guide, the architect would not prescribe to a
passive client through the authority of ideologies, nor would she simply
present the client with visual compositions from which to select. Instead,
the client and builder would have to be socialized to trust the architect's
judgment—a socialization that would be facilitated by the architect's
ability to tell tales in the form of demonstrative drawings. These
drawings would not be directly translatable to buildings, but would
require the imaginative collaboration of builder, owner, and architect in
order for a "nontrivial edifice" to be erected.

Frascari never explicitly acknowledges the radical nature of the
change he is proposing. Most of the conventions of building production
in First World countries would be overturned if his suggestion were
implemented. There would be no working drawings, hence competitive
bidding would only be possible in a cultural situation similar to Japan's.
The builder's necessarily collaborative role would mean that no two
builders, working with the same design, would be likely to build the
same structure. Building inspectors would be unable to approve designs
in advance, and would therefore be forced to make building safety
determinations only on-site. Lending institutions would not know exactly
what they were financing until the building was occupiable. (Perhaps this
would instigate attempts to develop a "poetic accounting," where the
intransitive "value" of dwelling could be adequately expressed.) Clients
and their bankers would have to trust the architect's judgment to a far
greater extent than is presently the case. This would probably mean that
architects would be selected, once again, primarily on the basis of proven
reputation, not star power or low fees. Because of the necessary close
contact between architect and builder, it would generally behoove
architects to restrict their practices to specific regions, or to specialize by
climate, or building system, or particular theme, rather than strictly by
building function. Scarpa's preference to practice in the Veneto region as
an "architect of spoils," or Fay Jones's practice based on constructing

artificial forests, would be exemplary in this regard. Such sweeping changes would only be possible if living and dwelling well were elevated once more to higher status than the accumulation of capital. Drawings, and from them buildings, would have to become convivial tools again.

◇   ◇   ◇

My seven modest proposals, as I have stated, are intended to create the room necessary for architecture to flower in our present culture. By advocating these forms of practice, I am not implying that a late-capitalist, technologically advanced society must, by its very nature, be hostile to practices such as architecture, which stubbornly preserve their connections to premodern thinking. While the ideology I have described as "modern" is undoubtedly anti-architectural, this ideology has never been wholly adopted, or uniformly accepted, by our culture. No culture is so monolithic. The modern age, while closing off some opportunities for architecture, has opened other possibilities for architectural practice.

But when we assume—because the profession of architecture continues to survive, and architects remain involved in at least a portion of the buildings we construct—that the mode of architectural practice began in the fifteenth century is still appropriate, we place authentic architecture in jeopardy. The superficial resemblance between the products now made by this mode of practice (which has evolved steadily toward a technique for producing buildings as commodities) and architecture is dangerously misleading. Most of the technicians we call "architects" define their practices too narrowly. Such specialists are always in danger of becoming outmoded. We can take heart that the "vague activity," the practices that are truly architectural, can never be isolated and therefore "cannot be eliminated."

The Work of Architecture
in the Age of Efficient Production

Sustaining Cultural Memories Requires, at times, Heroic Effort

It is in the friendship poets have for things, their things, that we can know
these burgeoning instants that give human value to ephemeral actions.

Gaston Bachelard
The Flame of a Candle

One of the most familiar scenes in Mark Twain's *The Adventures of Tom Sawyer* involves Tom painting his Aunt Polly's fence. When young Tom was required to paint a wooden fence around his aunt's yard, he cleverly lured other children in the neighborhood into doing the work for him. He accomplished this deception by pretending that the fence-painting was so enjoyable to him that he preferred it to playing. Tom's ruse was so effective that he ended up charging his friends for the opportunity to do his work. Twain writes that Tom had "discovered a great law of human action," which was the flexible boundary between work and play. Yet Twain's take on this "great law" is, in my opinion, somewhat incomplete. Here is Twain's explanation:

> In order to make a man or a boy covet a thing, it is only necessary to make
> the thing difficult to obtain. . . . Work consists of whatever a body is *obliged* to
> do, and . . . play consists of whatever a body is not obliged to do. . . .
> Constructing artificial flowers or performing on a treadmill is work, while
> rolling ten pins or climbing Mount Everest is only amusement.[342]

Twain, correctly I believe, associates work with necessity. However, he does not explain why some necessary tasks are enjoyable—often as enjoyable as play—while other necessary tasks are simply disagreeable. Twain's selection of fence painting as the activity for his story reveals a nuance of the relationship between work and play that Twain ignored, but that is of particular interest to me: many enjoyable but necessary activities involve what is commonly called "craftwork," and a very high proportion of them concern the making, maintaining, and decorating of architecture.

I concur with Twain's explanation that the degree of difficulty we face in order to obtain a thing has some bearing on whether we find it desirable. For example, we value a perfectly white-painted wood fence in part because it is fairly difficult to have one. But this does not make painting a wood fence around one's property play. Twain implies that Tom's friends found painting the fence enjoyable (playful) because they were not obliged to do it, and because Tom in fact made it difficult for them to do it (by charging them for the privilege). But there is another way to interpret Twain's great law. If it is difficulty that makes us covet a thing, and a lack of obligation that makes an activity enjoyable, we should be able to make a necessary task, like protecting our fences from weathering, more enjoyable by making them *more difficult*. In other words, the logic of Twain's law can be extended to the point that a paradox emerges: the relatively simple boring work of applying a protective coating to a fence becomes more, not less, enjoyable when we add to it the need to evenly apply a pristine coating of white paint. By adding something unnecessary to the coating of the fence, something decorative, some sort of delay, fence painting becomes not play, but enjoyable, fulfilling work. And I believe that this sort of partially necessary, partially cosmetic work that painting a fence involves reveals something fundamental about how architecture is made and preserved.

To understand these architectural practices we as a society will have to re-examine the way we have come to define the word "work." Notice, for example, it is common to find people making and maintaining their buildings with great care, and at the same time deriving intense satisfaction from this effort. Instances where we witness a similar devotion to things—in the care of our houses, gardens, automobiles, etc.—are so frequent as to be unremarkable. What is remarkable is that we, as a culture, lack any convincing explanation for this behavior. Our prevailing economic theories make no distinction between the hostility toward painting initially felt by Tom, and the fulfillment his friends gained from it. Nor, speaking more generally, do these theories have much to say about the difference between those who love the activities by which they earn their livings, and those who despise them. If we are to understand the nature of practices such as building and caring for a house, preparing for a festival, tending a garden, decorating a Christmas tree, or proudly polishing one's automobile, we must restore the distinction between "labor" and "work" that has been lost since the advent of industrialization. We must look more closely at activities such as these, in which we are likely to develop emotional and imaginative attachments to things, and to care for them to a degree that belies either their use or exchange value.

In her book *The Human Condition*, Hannah Arendt addressed
the difference between labor and work. Noting that not even Karl Marx
had granted this subtlety adequate appreciation, she proceeded to
distinguish the two terms etymologically.

> The distinction between labor and work I propose is unusual. The phenom-
> enal evidence in its favor is too striking to be ignored, yet historically it is a
> fact that apart from a few scattered remarks . . . there is hardly anything in
> either the pre-modern tradition of political thought or in the large body of
> modern labor theories to support it. Against this scarcity of historical evi-
> dence, however, stands one very articulate and obstinate testimony, namely,
> the simple fact that every European language, ancient or modern, contains
> two etymologically unrelated words for what we have come to think of as the
> same activity, and retains them in the face of persistent synonymous usage.[343]

Arendt continued, noting that, as opposed to the word "work," "the word
'labor,' understood as a noun, never designates a finished product." That
labor neither designates a product, nor leaves durable objects behind, is
the primary difference around which Arendt's argument was built.

As a laboring animal (*animal laborans*) the human being, according to Arendt, engages in activities immediately tied to the preservation
of both individual life and the life of the species. It is this aspect of
necessity that causes us to assimilate the distress of childbirth and the
bodily pain caused by effort expended to procure food and shelter under
the same term. Arendt also observed that the discomfort associated with
labor turns one's attention inward, so that the laboring body "remains
imprisoned in its metabolism." This self-absorption, this "worldless-
ness," engenders in the laboring man or woman an antisocial mind-set,
and therefore contributes to the loss of a public realm in a society of
laborers. The division of labor in these societies (think of the assembly
line) eliminates the need for cooperation and coordination between
laborers, leaving each person free to concentrate only on his or her job.
In Arendt's thinking, laboring was further distinguished from work in
that "it leaves nothing behind, that the result of its effort is almost as
quickly consumed as the effort is spent."[344]

As opposed to the laborer, the human fabricator (*homo faber*)
works not in response to necessity, but in order to construct a "world." In
other words, the activity of work has not just a practical goal, but also an
imaginative one. Beyond their immediate utility, human artifacts help to
organize and structure our existence. "Their proper use does not cause

them to disappear and they give the human artifice the stability and solidity without which it could not be relied upon to house the unstable and mortal creature which is man."[345] Arendt believed that in order for these artifacts to constitute a "world," the ideals of *homo faber* must be "permanence, stability, and durability."

It is here, as well as in her exclusion of "biological necessity" from the realm of work, that my own thoughts on the matter diverge from Arendt's. For while I agree that the world-making distinction is the fundamental difference between labor and work, it is this imaginary world that must become stable and durable, not necessarily the artifacts that are used to construct it. The results of work must be of lasting significance, but the material durability of products is only one way that this significance can be achieved. For example, neither gardeners nor architects create worlds that are, technically, permanent. However, through her commitment to sustained maintenance, a gardener or architect may create a world that is both durable and significant. If we allow the lack of durability, the perishability, or biological necessity of something we produce to determine that it has been the result of labor instead of work, then the activities of many of our most skillful makers would be mistakenly excluded from the province of work. Anyone who has watched a dedicated chef prepare an exquisite meal can attest to the injustice of drawing the labor/work distinction on this basis.

If permanence cannot be our guide, what then? Arendt proposed several other characteristics to look for in classifying a productive activity. She looked at the movements involved, concluding that the presence of repetitive rhythmic motions was a likely indicator of labor. In part, this was because Arendt believed identical repetitive movements were more suited to machines than human beings. In a footnote to her text, she added that while repetitive laboring was sometimes accompanied by singing, these were, properly speaking, labor songs, not work songs. She maintained that work songs did not exist, because there was no "'natural' rhythm" for work.[346] While this explanation sounds plausible initially, we can also think of instances where cooks, carpenters, or even painters and sculptors hum, sing, or whistle while they work. It is true that they are likely to do these things primarily when engaged in the most repetitive aspects of their work, such as while chopping vegetables or stretching canvases. If we submit these observations to Arendt's logic, we will conclude that all work contains within it periods of labor.

However, the opposite is also true. Like certain unstable chemical elements, labor is a volatile, unsustainable activity. Given the opportunity, we humans will usually seek to convert repetitive and mindless labor into work or play (play being defined as imaginative activity, usually coupled with physical activity, that is deliberately unproductive).[347] The songs sung by laborers, even those sung by African-American slaves while toiling on a plantation, were attempts to reintroduce imaginative activity back into what is basically meaningless and disagreeable bodily exertion. The fact that the slaves' songs were often sung as a group suggests that, through the social activity of singing, the slaves were able to compensate for the antisocial nature of their individual labors. By uniting the slaves in a "world," their singing helped preserve their humanity. (The imaginative activity in African-American slave songs usually centered around the dream of escape. The songs often carried coded messages, including instructions and encouragement to those who might attempt to flee their bondage.[348]) While the slaves' songs often had very little to do with their labors, and only sometimes may have left their mark on the artifacts produced, they are still evidence of our persistent need to imagine while we execute our duties. "Work song" is not such a misnomer if we recognize that such songs are attempts to convert labor into work. Labor, work, and play are neither opposites nor distinct categories, but related activities that shade into one another along a spectrum of imaginative versus productive activity.

In this spectrum of activities, work occupies the middle zone where both production and imagination are optimized. In work, the attributes of labor and play are partially combined; work is playful labor or productive play. While labor itself may produce short periods of very high productivity, its lack of sustainability, as well as the bodily discomfort and/or boredom it creates, make its overall productivity lower than that of work. Work is the only one of our three activities that can be sustained for long periods of time.[349] Play, while highly enjoyable and imaginative, is inherently unsustainable due to its lack of productivity. A worker, who must respond to the requirements of productivity, as well as to natural forces and bodily necessities, is not as free as one who plays. (The freedom in play is not absolute; even playful activities require rules of some sort, to assure that play does not disintegrate into chaos.) However, the uniqueness of work lies in its ability to trope cleverly the necessity of production into an imaginative undertaking that creates a world. Within this world, the imagination of the worker has free rein, so that work, "properly conducted in conditions of human dignity and freedom, blesses those who do it and equally their products."[350]

If this spectrum, where work occupies a keystone position, is basically correct, then fabrication can be argued to be humanity's most characteristic and readily sustained activity. (A corollary to this argument would declare that any discussion of sustainability must include a prominent place for work.) The term *homo faber,* the human fabricator, adequately portrays the nuances of the relationship between imagination and effort only when we recall the ambiguous meaning of the verb "to fabricate." Fabrication encompasses not only making, but also making up. Work and play, which includes play-acting, are the more naturally "human" of the three related activities in my spectrum, because they allow for the making, and making up, of a "world." While Arendt was clear on this point, her understanding of fabrication was also overly influenced by the prejudices of industrialized production. She defined "action" as an activity where there was no separation between knowing and doing, but allowed that fabrication always consisted of two parts: "first perceiving the image or shape of the product-to-be, and then organizing the means and starting the execution."[351] This overly technical concept of fabrication ignores what all craftspeople know: that the design of all works not produced by machines are continually adapted and modified during the fabrication process.

Because labor cannot both make and make up a world, it can be tolerated or justified only by virtue of its outcome—what it physically produces. In comparison to work or play, labor is a strictly literal process. Labor can be measured solely in terms of its output and efficiency. Under extremely controlled situations, human laborers can be restricted from playing (no "goofing off") or from attempting to turn labor into work (no freedom to modify the artifact to suit immediate circumstances, or even whim; no singing, whistling, or conversation permitted). However, these restrictions will result in an inhuman environment that is nearly intolerable for those who labor in it. Any imaginative activity they are able to muster will most often be "let off" as a kind of excess or illicit by-product, such as vandalism, the theft of company property, or—at the extreme—the homicidal outbursts that have become frighteningly common among those who must tediously sort the mail in the United States' postal system.

Laboring under oppressive conditions forms the topic of the film *The Bridge on the River Kwai* (1957), where British prisoners-of-war are forced to construct a bridge. Through their intentional incompetence, the prisoners continually thwart their Japanese captors' attempts to make them into efficient laborers. When the British commander realizes that this resistance to authority is beginning to destroy the military discipline instilled in his men, he agrees to coordinate the building of the bridge. What had been forced servitude at the hands of an enemy is turned into a "British" enterprise, where the soldiers' national pride and engineering acumen are engaged. The British are no longer blindly executing a bridge presented to them as a complete design, but they are now fully involved in the process of designing, as well as building, the span. It should be noted that only after this change occurs do the men begin to whistle while they work. (The tune the soldiers whistle serves as the movie's theme song.) In addition, by eventually pressuring the sick and the wounded to work, the British officer proves to be an even more demanding taskmaster than the Japanese prison commandant had been. Yet so fulfilling is the bridge-building work that the spirits of even these weakened men are lifted, and the British commander loses sight of the fact that the structure his troops are creating will assist the military objectives of his enemy. Here is further evidence that the desirability of work, over labor, cannot be attributed solely to the desirability of its outcomes. In *The Bridge on the River Kwai* the existence of the bridge, to its British makers, is a highly undesirable outcome.

Antagonism between laborers and those who manage them is an unintended but unavoidable result of the concepts—such as the valorization of efficiency and the willingness to acknowledge only those things that can be measured instrumentally—upon which our post-Enlightenment society is founded. In the worldview of a technological society, rational planning is extolled, while the execution of such plans, although recognized as necessary, is conceptualized as a meaningless technique. When the laborer is viewed as merely one component of a production technique, he or she must ultimately be counted expendable, just as any technique is abandoned when a "better" way is discovered. As iconoclastic economist E. F. Schumacher observed, this arrangement often places the employee and employer in a relationship where the goals of one can only be achieved at the expense of the other.

> [The] modern economist has been brought up to consider "labour"... as
> little more than a necessary evil. From the point of view of the employer, it
> is in any case simply an item of cost, to be reduced to a minimum if it
> cannot be eliminated altogether, say, by automation. From the point of view
> of the [laborer], it is a "disutility"; to [labor] is to make a sacrifice of one's
> leisure and comfort, and wages are a kind of compensation for the sacrifice.
> Hence the ideal from the view of the employer is to have output without
> employees, and the ideal from the point of view of the employee is to have
> income without employment.[352]

Schumacher goes on to observe that, under this conceptualization,
anything that reduces labor is a "good thing." The two most well-known
methods for achieving this end, besides automation, are the related
concepts of "division of labor" and "scientific management" championed
by Frederick Taylor and other efficiency experts.

The misconception Schumacher describes, which assumes all
productive effort to be a technique, is the root of the dissatisfaction felt by
modern laborers. Our labor unions have been mostly unsuccessful in
addressing this issue because, as their name implies, they have not
distinguished between work and labor. Labor unions have not challenged
the underlying assumption upon which nearly all economic theories
since the eighteenth century have agreed: that time and human effort
may be accurately portrayed as scarce commodities.

Nineteenth-century labor leaders, although skeptical at first,
eventually accepted Taylor's claim that scientific management would lead
to higher wages (as, initially, it did). Furthermore, they endorsed his
questionable assumption that what the "workmen" most desired were
high wages. More subtle minds than Taylor's might have countered, as
did Simone Weil, that "workers needed poetry more than bread" and
"they need that their life should be a poem."[353] While this may be an
overly dramatic way of describing the worker's need to imagine, it
reminds us that our accepted economic ideologies have neglected this
need in favor of more readily quantified goals, such as high wages.

It is because of this, and the many similar overly reductive
conceptualizations that underlie the triumphs of post-Enlightenment
civilization, that it has been dogged by such familiar phrases as "the death
of the soul," "the loss of aura," "the disenchantment of the world," and the
process whereby "all that is solid melts into air." Any conceptualization,
any social prescription, no matter how benevolent its intentions, when

followed blindly and single-mindedly, must eventually cause us to lose the sense of proportionality that is the basis for ethical behavior. This is why we may have a "work ethic," but no ethic of labor. Committed, willingly or unknowingly, to the single goal of technical efficiency, laborers (unless they step outside of their role as laborers) are not free to consider "indeterminate concepts," to imagine and weigh outcomes, or to exercise the judgment necessary for ethical behavior. This is why sociologist Richard Sennett's recent book on what I call the transformation of workers to laborers is titled *The Corrosion of Character*. A similar case can be made for many of our cherished economic idealizations: once the abolition of private property, the "invisible hand," or free trade become idealized and therefore unassailable, we lose our ability to make ethical judgments about their likely outcomes. In the present global economy it makes no more sense for a laborer to express an allegiance to a particular place, team, job, or employer, than it would for a tree to express a preference for which forest products company should "harvest" it. In a world populated exclusively by laborers, when everything and everyone is seen primarily as a resource, we are all free agents.

◇   ◇   ◇

Do all your work as though you had a thousand years to live, and as you would if you knew you must die tomorrow.

Mother Ann Lee, founder of the American Shakers

Our understanding of time has always been conditioned largely by culture. Premodern cultures most often adopted a cyclical understanding of time, one that mirrored the circular movement of the planets and the cycles of seasonal change. It was not until time lost this mimetic aspect that it came to be thought of as something both linear and scarce. Once declared scarce, time became "our most precious commodity"—a statement that contemporary societies accept as self-evident, yet one that would be incomprehensible to premodern peoples. The flexible, qualitative, or poetic measures of time appropriate to work or play have now been replaced by the uniformity of labor time. The time of labor, lacking involvement of a human imagination, readily permits the transitive measurements of clocks and calendars. Like Cartesian space, the modern time of labor is undifferentiated and homogeneous—time as money.[354] Labor time is universal, uniformly segmented time, effort "by the hour," that pays no heed to natural bodily rhythms (such as the need for a siesta after the mid-day meal), to natural cycles like day and night, or to the changes of the seasons. This is why industrial manufacturing jobs were the first to provide the controlled conditions necessary for labor. Prior to industrialization, even the efforts of slaves were likely to be arranged in harmony with natural agricultural cycles. As opposed to the universal time of labor, work time and play time are "fulfilled" or "autonomous" times.[355] Time spent at these activities cannot be measured by clocks or judged by its production alone, for, in the case of play, there are no tangible products, and, in the case of work, the value attributed to the endeavor must account for both the product and the positive feelings engendered in its making. Because they create a world, work time and play time create their own variable and unpredictable times, fictive times that have only an intransitive relationship with universal clock time.

Persons engaged in enjoyable craftwork often "lose track of (clock) time." Organized play, such as most sport, follows its own temporal pace. Whether it is measured on a game clock (football, basketball) or by some unpredictable unit (a baseball inning), the virtual time of sports only partially parallels clock time. Theoretically speaking, a baseball inning, tennis game, or golf round could last forever. Even though these measures of time are still one directional, they offer an opportunity unavailable in most of the other "kinds" of time we moderns experience: the chance to start each game anew. In this they, and all activities (musical performances, literature, dance, poetry, or our imaginative involvement with works of art) where the passage of time becomes virtual, retain a vestige of cyclical time. The incompatibility between universal clock time and work or play activities is underscored if we attempt to judge a work of art merely by how slowly or quickly it was created. One would not evaluate a baseball game solely on how long it took to play it, or heap high praise on the orchestra that could play a piece of music fastest. Work time and play time are also embodied times, tied to the finite existence of particular, gendered mortals. While *animal laborans*, a sub-species of *homo economicus*, may be neuter, the direct involvement of a worker's body, and the highly corporeal nature of his or her imaginings, will always make work a gendered activity. Men and women may do the same work, but they will dream about it differently.

Workers are always unique; they work at their own pace, and they leave their individual "signature" on all that they produce. It would make no sense to try to eliminate this aspect of work. In fact, variety is one of the attributes of work's products we find most desirable.

Work time also has a more complex relationship with efficiency than uniform labor time. Human beings, aware of their mortality, cannot simply dismiss the need to perform some tasks efficiently. Workers value efficiency, which is the reason that workers sometimes willingly labor, but they value the significance of their activities, the feelings of well-being and fulfillment they may produce, even more. To one who is working efficiency never becomes an end in itself. To those who work in what Weil described as "the light of eternity," efficiency is always a somewhat secondary concern. However, by converting time into money, *homo economicus* has conceptualized our limited time into a scarce resource in which output must be maximized. The technological obsession with efficiency judges the speed of any productive operation to be the most important concern. Since factors like speed and elapsed time are readily measured and easily quantified, because they lend themselves to instrumental representation, while enjoyment and significance do not, our society has tended to overvalue issues like the former and ignore those like the latter. Enjoyable fulfilling time spent working cannot be readily expressed by the instrumental measure of money; it is thus difficult to commodify. For this reason we have replaced the difficult-to-conceptualize activity of work with the more easily represented technique of labor. Obsessed with efficiency, we laborers now must account for every second of our time.

In one section of his amazing exposition on literary themes, *Six Memos for the Next Millennium,* Italo Calvino extolled the virtues of "quickness."[356] The quickness Calvino championed was not, however, the kind a stopwatch could measure. Calvino placed a premium on quick-wittedness, on nimbleness of thought, on the rapidity with which the human imagination can make daring leaps and establish far-reaching connections. Calvino invented a kind of qualitative economy, whereby he judged works of literature by their ability to provide the maximum impact with the minimum of means. Yet, he realized that this minimum of means could never form an absolute measure. In Calvino's economic calculations, it is impossible to discount the value of slowness, of taking one's time, of mulling things over, or of simply avoiding getting down to business. Through the example of Lawrence Sterne's fictional "autobiography," *Tristam Shandy*, a book consisting entirely of digressions of ever-greater ingenuity and absurdity, all directed towards allowing Shandy to indefinitely delay telling his life story, Calvino demonstrated that quickness may sometimes be found in imaginative efforts to outwit time itself. He concluded his discussion on quickness with an economically told tale that is an exemplar for the sort of temporal measurement appropriate to work.

> Among Chuang-tzu's many skills, he was an expert draftsman. The king asked him to draw a crab. Chuang-tzu replied that he needed five years, a country house, and twelve servants. Five years later the drawing was still not begun. "I need another five years," said Chaung-tzu. The king granted them. At the end of these ten years, Chuang-tzu took up his brush and, in an instant, with a single stroke, he drew a crab, the most perfect crab ever seen.[357]

In the tale of Chuang-tzu, it is impossible to say whether we should consider the ten years that proceeded the drawing's creation to have been spent on diligent preparation, or count them as evidence of a brazen scam to defraud the king. As we will see, work time always creates outcomes that defy straightforward quantification.

All of the activities I define as work or play—writing and reading books, drawing, painting, craftwork, dancing, singing—create their own immeasurable "times." These are not the same as leisure time, which is merely the time our society has left over, once we have completed our required number of hours laboring. Leisure time is not, in and of itself, the type of fulfilled virtual time I have been describing. Leisure is a part of the compensation a technological society offers to its laborers. It is the mirror image of labor time: meaningless unproductive time, instead of meaningless productive time. Leisure time does not challenge our modern conceptualization of time as money; leisure time, like labor time, is fleeting time that must be spent.

The work versus labor determination and its connection with how time is imagined and perceived has another dimension. Arendt observed that artists were practically the only true workers left in our society of laborers. We could easily argue that craftspersons, many of the self-employed, scientists, financiers, and the last remaining true professionals (primarily those whose duties have not yet been made certain by technology) still deserve inclusion in the ranks of workers.

Of these, however, artists are most likely to reject the usual compensations offered by an economic system that rewards laboring more than work, in favor of less measurable returns. We should also recognize that one of the attributes of art, one "blessing" bestowed on the products of the artist's work, is also the ability to create "worlds." In this way the work of art mirrors the work on art that produces it. Each of them—the fulfilling productive activity and the product with which we actively engage to find fulfillment—have the ability to create worlds where time deviates from universal clock time. This kind of temporal disruption (which is similar to that of the festival) can therefore be utilized to identify the presence of art. Once we have recognized this fact, we can begin to employ it as a means of art criticism.

Umberto Eco proposed a similar method to distinguish dramatic films that happen to feature sexually explicit scenes from pornography. As an improvement over the vague "community standards" test favored in the United States, we could use Eco's "infallible rule of time" to separate art from smut.

> When trying to assess a film that contains sexually explicit scenes, you should check to see whether, when a character gets into an elevator or a car, the discourse time coincides with the story time. Flaubert may take one line to say that Frédéric traveled for a long time, and in normal films a character who gets on a plane at Logan Airport in Boston will, in the next scene, land in San Francisco. But in a pornographic film if someone gets in a car to go ten blocks, the car will journey those ten blocks in real time. If someone opens a fridge and pours out a Sprite that he's going to drink in the armchair after switching on the TV, the action takes precisely the time it would take if you were doing the same thing at home.[358]

Eco reasoned that pornographic-film makers would not expend the effort necessary to turn these "filler" scenes into authentic fiction, because their customers were interested in sex, not drama. Therefore, the filler scenes are shot in "real time"; they exist simply to kill time between the sex scenes.

The passage I quote is from Eco's book *Six Walks in the Fictional Woods*. In his six walks, Eco demonstrates the myriad ways fiction distends time and space. Temporal distortions are the tracks left by all imaginative activity. This is why Marcel Duchamp proposed to designate his artworks not as paintings but as "delays." It is also why philosopher Gianni Vattimo claims that many of the "epoch-making" literary works of the twentieth century, such as Marcel Proust's *Remembrance of Things Past* or James Joyce's *Ulysses*, "concentrate, even at the level of content itself, on the problem of time and on ways of experiencing temporality outside of its supposedly natural linearity."[359] Eco shows us the inanity that occurs when transitive measures of time are imposed upon the work of even the most talented artists. He quotes at length a passage from Alexandre Dumas's *The Three Musketeers* where Dumas, because he was paid by the line for the novel (which was published in installments), needlessly stretches out the dialog between two characters. Eco's criticism is that this type of lingering serves no purpose within the work; it does not contribute appreciably, for example, to the heightening of tension within the story. It served only to increase Dumas's income, and so it was similar to the "deceleration" Eco identified within pornographic films.

A similar level of absurdity follows whenever we attempt to treat activities that are properly work as labor. When artists and musicians are paid by the hour, brush stroke, or note, when novelists or poets are compensated by the line or word, we witness the corruption that occurs whenever fulfilling activities are portrayed as commodities. (This corruption cuts two ways, as Adolf Loos recognized, as he railed against postindustrial Europe's irrational awe of the quantity of work needed to produce a highly ornamented building, in his essay "Building Materials.") Only the products of work, not work itself, can be bought and sold. Artists that are paid for the products of their work have not necessarily "sold out." However, any artist or worker who allows her efforts to be minutely quantified, either by measuring her time or some other aspect of her output, will be tempted to distort her work to fit the particular quantification method. The rule here seems to be that the smaller the unit of transitive measure applied, the greater the distortion. That is, being paid by the word is more injurious to the writer than being paid by the page, because it is far easier to conceal a few surplus words within a story than it is to slip in unnecessary whole pages. The degree to which art is corrupted, if at all, by the incursions of the market is, once again, primarily a matter of proportionality.

Because the work on art does not readily subscribe to the logic of technique, or our conventional economic assumptions, artworks are very difficult to price. Dave Hickey, a contemporary critic of art and culture, explains this by stating that "art and money never touch.... Money does nothing to art but facilitate its dissemination and buy the occasional bowl of Wheaties for an artist or art dealer."[360] Art always gives us more than is literally "there," leading Lewis Hyde to maintain that all works of art ought to be considered gifts. According to Hyde's analysis, three kinds of gifts must accrue in order to create art. First, a "gifted" artist or artists, who could not otherwise acquire the talents with which they have been blessed, engage in work. Thus, they create an artifact that exceeds the value of the effort (transitively measured) that went into making it. This increase, which is not paid for, is the second gift. Lastly, this artifact, although it may be purchased by an individual, is "offered to the world in general"—the third gift.[361]

◇   ◇   ◇

A civilization based upon the spirituality of work would give to man the very strongest possible roots in the wide universe, and would consequently be the opposite of that state in which we find ourselves now, characterized by almost total uprootedness. Such a civilization is, therefore, by its very nature, the object to which we should aspire as the antidote to our sufferings.

Simone Weil
The Need for Roots

While perhaps only gifted workers may produce art, all work produces an imaginative product, a world that exceeds the literal value of what is objectively present in the object that has been made. The products of work are all, at least partially, gifts. The products of labor are exclusively commodities (unless, of course, they are given away). Work and its results are underappreciated in a society of laborers—a society with a limited capacity to utilize gifts. It is, economically speaking, a disadvantage to love your work in a laboring society, because your attachment will prevent you from bargaining the highest price for it. Again we think of the impoverished condition of many artists, or the ballplayer who must settle for below-market value in order to remain with the home team. As Hyde observes, art and similar fulfilling work "cannot be undertaken on a pure cost-benefit basis" because they do not produce commodities or "things we easily price or willingly alienate." Those who are fully committed to their work "automatically inhibit their ability to 'sell themselves' at the moment they answer their calling." Fulfilling work requires an emotional commitment "that precludes its own marketing."[362]

Since we cannot judge the results of work without accounting for the increase—that "something extra" that is an artifact's imaginative content, its gift—and since the nature of this gift, like all works of the imagination, will not be entirely predictable, we will never be able to know in advance whether the products of work will be successful. Work always involves taking risks. (Recalling the Calvino story quoted earlier, one wonders at the risks Chuang-tzu took, should his drawing of the crab have failed.) To be sure, this is another reason why work is ill fitted to a technological society. When time is money, a society cannot afford mistakes.

In his book *The Nature and Art of Workmanship*, David Pye cleverly avoids some of the overly simplistic assumptions that have bedeviled other critics of industrialization. What I have been calling simply "work," Pye designates by the more specific phrase "the workmanship of risk." My "labor" is his "workmanship of certainty." Pye sidesteps the mistaken assumption that the mere presence of machines in a production process is enough to indicate that it must include laboring. Instead of focusing on the degree of mechanization, or how advanced the technology, Pye concentrates on this question of risk versus certainty. When the outcome of a process has been made certain, any humans involved will be reduced to automatons, whether or not actual machines are involved. As Pye notes, "To distinguish between two ways of carrying out an operation by classifying them as hand- or machine-work is . . . all but meaningless." Pye cites the example of a dentist using a drill to dispel the notion that the use of advanced machinery alone can indicate that an operation involves less skill or risk than a similar task done by hand. As Pye puts it, "The distinction between the two kinds of workmanship is clear and turns on the question: 'is the result predetermined and unalterable once production begins?'"[363] Neither work nor play, as opposed to labor, strive to make their outcomes predictable.

We also need to recognize that processes done by hand, where the movements are repetitive and the risks are low (but still present), such as the hand-sharpening of tools or the hand-planing of a board, while they may appear mindless and therefore laborious, may have the purpose of training one's imagination for more challenging work. Apprentices to skilled crafts have traditionally begun their training by learning how to care for the tools of the trade. Beginning carpenters' apprentices were often expected to sharpen saw blades and hone the edges of planes and chisels. Japanese temple carpenters' apprentices could spend several years learning how to properly plane and saw boards. These tasks would always be partially ritualized, and they would be accompanied by indoctrination into the work myths of the trade.

This rather inefficient training system can be justified only if we consider that the years spent at relatively simple tasks might serve to "weed out" apprentices who lacked the imagination to trope their repetitive labors into more satisfying work. These persons would inevitably grow bored with their duties, the quality of their production would as a consequence decline, proving them too impatient to become masters of their craft. However, the more imaginative apprentices would likely invent ways to turn labor into work. They would begin to accept the life-narrative that gives structure and purpose to the members of their trade. Besides singing or humming while they worked, they might begin to attribute human characteristics to their tools, and to the materials with which they worked. In so doing they would develop an emotional attachment to their work. Mute substances would, for them, come alive. The famed Japanese-American furniture maker, George Nakashima, spoke of the need to see into "the soul" of a tree; architect Louis Kahn "talked" to bricks.

Attractions of this sort, which the philosopher Gaston Bachelard called a "friendship for things," typify the creative worker's attitude toward her tools and raw materials. When we become friends with inanimate things, we begin to lose the ability to treat them impersonally as commodities or resources. Just as with the work we love, the things we love cannot be easily priced or willingly alienated. Children often exhibit this tendency, choosing a special toy that, to them, becomes priceless. Artists and craftspersons show similar signs, as they lavish care and attention onto their works beyond that which mere utility, or market value, would justify.

In our care of our homes and our gardens, we typically exceed the degree of effort that can be economically justified. In a society where all productive effort is counted as labor, our homes and gardens should incorporate the latest labor-saving features; we should wish them to be "maintenance free." Most economists would tell us that it is irrational for a highly paid corporate CEO to cut his own grass, tend his flower beds, or paint the trim on his house. From the standpoint of a philosophy that fails to distinguish labor from work, the economist is correct. However, by participating in these activities, these types of work, the executive obtains something he could not otherwise have—the opportunity to dwell.

Dwelling is an activity much like work in that it unites the physical and the imaginative. Dwelling is work and requires work. Like the word "work," "dwelling" can be used to designate a process as well as its result. The work of dwelling primarily involves what we call "building," although it also includes cleaning, mowing, painting, and other forms of maintenance. While much of this work is fairly mindless, like the duties of the beginning building trade apprentice, those who accept it and continue it are apt to develop the most imaginative relations with their houses: they become friends with them. The condition we call "home" is largely an imaginative relationship with a familiar and friendly place. Persons who contract out for all the maintenance of their houses— hiring lawn care specialists, cleaning services, interior decorators and house painters—are much less likely to develop deep emotional attachments to the place where they live. Certainly, there are other factors involved in making a place one's home—its physical configuration, the presence of loved ones within it, the memories of past events it contains. But all of these are amplified when we do the work of dwelling. The shape of the house becomes not merely a compositional strategy dictated by an architect, but something we have helped to determine, or at least sustain. Joining family members and friends in the common tasks of building and caring for a home strengthens the social bonds between us, and the sum total of all the additions and alterations we have made over the years are spatial and temporal landmarks for our memories.

Nonsensical terms such as "homebuyer," "home builder," "townhome," and "home seller" are the results of intense efforts by realtors and others in the "home" industries to obscure the reality that dwelling is a delayed imaginative condition that cannot be purchased as if it were a commodity. A home is a condition that can only be fabricated. While these efforts to confuse the meaning of the word "home" with that of "house" are willfully misleading, they are fully in concert with our economic assumptions, which consider a home simply to be a desirable building. Many of the most popular "home plans" sold today are those that incorporate complicated roof layouts, with multiple intersecting gables, and complex footprints, all to simulate the sort of incremental expansion once common when families continually added to and modified their homes over many decades. This design strategy is generally combined with another that is equally popular, but, to the imagination at least, totally incompatible with it: a rapidly assembled building, made of no-maintenance materials, is given the appearance of a house that has been, and will need to be, worked on for a long time. While these buildings may look like homes, they will prove to be difficult to dwell within since they offer their owners few opportunities to do the work of building and dwelling.

In our age of specialization we would expect that the typical homeowner's lack of skill in the building trades would inhibit her from attempting difficult building or repair tasks. While this is partially true, it must also be noted that the risks involved when the corporate executive serves as her own plumber make the successful completion of a repair all the more satisfying. Undoubtedly, the homeowner's repair will take longer to complete than would an expert's. Surprisingly, this type of delay is, imaginatively speaking, often beneficial. Another connotation of the word "dwell" is to go slowly. The initially slow-going, but rewarding, work of building-dwelling engages all of our mental faculties, making its learning curve quite steep. Imagination and memory go together, so the imaginative, embodied engagement with one's house that is the work of building-dwelling makes acquired skills relatively unforgettable. The transition from beginner to reasonably competent novice takes a remarkably short time. This rapid learning can also continue indefinitely, allowing the do-it-yourselfer to continually attempt ever more complex tasks. Other than the lack of time or motivation, there is nothing to stop a corporate executive, or an assembly line laborer, from becoming a master woodworker, stonemason, or metal smith.

This open-endedness of skill acquisition is another thing that makes work more challenging, and more rewarding, than labor. Workers may constantly improve their skills, and the traditional categories of skilled workers—apprentice, journeyman, master—reflect this advancement, whereas laborers are often expected to perform the same task, the same way, indefinitely. Apprenticeship, training "on-the-job," is perhaps the most effective way of learning for workers, while its intertwining of learning and productivity, which benefits both the worker and his employer, confounds our contemporary preference to compart-mentalize these activities into the mutually exclusive commodities we call "education" and "labor." (Continuing education requirements for professionals exist not because there is a demonstrable lack of continued learning among these individuals, but primarily because on-the-job learning cannot be readily quantified, and therefore attributed the certainty of a number.)

The work of building construction can never be transformed into a totally predictable, risk-free labor operation because the dangers of making buildings are built into their substance and size. The immensity of buildings means that they will always pose a threat to those who work on them, and the imperfections of materials will always introduce novel, potentially health-threatening, conditions. For these reasons, building is often heroic, and it is always a partially alchemic operation.[364] Unlike a technique, it is characterized by an incomplete control and a continual need to make adjustments to compensate for unforeseen circumstances. The skillful builder, like the alchemist, knows that he cannot simply order matter to execute his commands. Both workers must patiently educate materials, coercing them to accomplish the desired task. This process, which is similar to teaching or coaching, Georg Simmel described as "the most sublime victory of the spirit over nature." The alchemy of meaningful building, instead of reducing materials to neutral "resources," anthropomorphicizes them, guides them, just as a student or apprentice might be guided to realize "our will through his own." In this process, "The very tendency of his own nature is made to execute our plan."[365] Both the alchemist and builder are striving to "elevate" matter: one into gold, the other into architecture. Like all workers, they run the risk of botching the job, but they also gain the possibility (and this may be work's greatest blessing) of creating something better than they had originally imagined. All masterpieces are to some extent happy accidents, gifts, where creative workers have troped unanticipated circumstances into works of startling ingenuity.

While it is currently fashionable to speak of "sustainable architecture," this term is most often applied to buildings built in ways that minimize negative effects on the planet's ecosystem. A truly sustainable architecture would add to these concerns the requirement that the building be predominantly a product of work, not labor, and that its making and maintenance serve to increase its, and therefore our, human dignity. Only a poetic force as powerful as the friendship for things—our incessant desire to trope labor into work—can counter behaviors ingrained in an advanced technological society that has adopted the rule of the universal Cartesian clock, the time of labor. When the assumption that time is money goes unquestioned, work is marginalized, risk is deemed inefficient, and a commitment to endless economic expansion is institutionalized. While it is possible in such societies to distinguish between more and less environmentally destructive means and to strive to replace the former with the latter, this version of "sustainability" accepts a reductive understanding of "the environment." If we include in our definition of a suitable environment our social interaction with others, our need to dwell as opposed to being "housed," and the need for our imaginations to be engaged by the productive activities we do so that they become fulfilling, we must then recognize that the destruction of human nature may be as serious a problem as the ravaging of a rain forest.

The friendship for things points to a more encompassing version of sustainability, one that includes both our need to refrain from poisoning the earth and our longing to find significance in all that we do. This friendship stands in direct opposition to the ideal of ever-increasing consumption and planned obsolescence, as well as to the doctrine that places efficiency above all other concerns. It also calls into question economic ideologies that would have us abolish all private ownership. It tells us that the "stability and solidity" Arendt rightly sought to organize our existence may often be found in our most mundane activities, among our most cherished, if not economically valuable, belongings. Through the making and then maintaining of our human artifacts, we can assure that proper use will not cause them to disappear.

◇   ◇   ◇

Furthermore, it is quite easy to establish that the eurhythmy *of an active rubbing motion, on the condition that it be sufficiently gentle and prolonged, brings about a* euphoria. *One has only to wait until the violent acceleration has settled down, until the different rhythms are coordinated, to see the smile and the look of peace return to the face of the worker. This joy cannot be explained objectively. It is the indication of a specific affective power.*

Gaston Bachelard
The Psychoanalysis of Fire

Due to its unpredictability, building is always new work. Maintenance tasks, on the other hand, involve less risk, but greater familiarity. Much of the work we do to maintain our homes is actually unnecessary. An

ornamental garden not only serves no practical function, it takes up time
that could almost certainly be spent at more profitable pursuits. So it is
with polishing one's furniture or one's car. We strive to produce the
shine for creative, not practical reasons. Bachelard explains,

> The minute we apply a glimmer of consciousness to a mechanical gesture,
> or practice phenomenology while polishing a piece of old furniture, we
> sense new impressions come into being beneath this familiar domestic
> duty. For consciousness rejuvenates everything, giving a quality of
> beginning to the most everyday actions. It even dominates memory. How
> wonderful it is to really become once more the inventor of a mechanical
> action! And so, when a poet rubs a piece of furniture—even vicariously—
> when he puts a little fragrant wax on his table with the woolen cloth that
> lends warmth to everything it touches, he creates a new object; he increases
> the object's human dignity; he registers this object officially as a member of
> the human household.[366]

The type of care Bachelard describes is re-creative and restorative. It
re-creates not primarily the object to which it is devoted (which in many
cases could survive perfectly well without this attention) but the world,
the "human household," to which the object belongs. While Arendt
thought the worlds of *homo faber* depended on the stability and durability
of objects, Bachelard shows that sustained care can maintain a world by
continually re-creating it. Bachelard's position has the advantage of being
founded on something that is both possible and commonplace, rather
than on the vain wish for material permanence.[367] Even if it were
possible to construct a permanent house, its predictability and perfection
would preclude us from working on it. Its condition would always be
certain. We could not increase such an object's dignity or become friends
with it. In it, time would pass uniformly and we would be unable to
dwell. Bachelard declared that such a house could lead only to serious,
sad thoughts, "not to dreams."[368]

When we do "useless" work on the things we possess, we are
replacing a practical maintenance with an imaginative one. But in the
mind of *homo faber* it is impossible to divorce completely the practical
from the useless. We fabricators always hold some hope that the effects
of work that *homo economicus* would dismiss as merely cosmetic will have
greater impact. This dream is partially in response to our powerlessness,
to the incomplete control we will always have over material things. When
a teen-aged driver lovingly polishes his old jalopy, his effort is, in part,

compensation for his inability to afford a better car, or to pay for needed mechanical repairs. By treating his car like a friend, he is hoping it will respond in kind. The attention Venetians have historically paid to the appearance of their slowly eroding, imperceptibly sinking buildings is another instance of this tendency. Since nothing can be done about the effects of water on their buildings' foundations, Venetian building owners have focused on what they can affect. In a strategy as irrational as it is familiar, Venetians apply the finest building materials to the light, screenlike facades of their *palazzi*, re-stucco their exteriors with a frequency unwarranted by practical concerns, and lavish expense and care onto them, all in hope of forestalling the inevitable. Donald Kunze characterizes this sort of thinking, "where the concerns of one kind are written in the language of another," as the "logic of displacement."[369]

Polishing can serve as an emblem of all such useless, wishful work. The value of polishing has only a little to do with the physical needs of the artifacts we subject to it. Polishing is work that we moderns have assumed to be labor, and labor we have assumed to be unnecessary, and therefore we have sought to eliminate the need for polishing, given that our irrational attraction to shininess persists, by inventing products with permanent shines. As these shiny objects have proliferated, one of the fundamental ways we have expressed our friendship for things has become nearly extinct, leaving us only rare access to the "displaced" world of the proud polisher.

I have chosen to elaborate on polishing as an example of work because its "specific affective power" has remained, over the centuries, inextricably linked to its corporeality. It is an instance of what Weil calls "time entering the body," where, through work, "man turns himself into matter."[370] As we elevate the status of the objects we polish, so, through the logic of displacement, do we elevate ourselves. I have also chosen this example to dispel the impression that the worlds one creates while working might be entirely arbitrary, or that the risks one encounters in working are indistinguishable from the uncertainties faced by laborers in an advanced capitalist economy. The life-narratives workers create are inextricably (and intransitively) linked to the substances with which they work. This gives to their imaginings a weight that distinguishes them from the uncertainties one faces as a free agent in the global economy. Workers never achieve perfection; however, they do gain a deep understanding of what they do.

In the case of polishing it is the rarity of shininess in nature—causing us to attribute a special status to the sun, moon, stars, and other things that glow—that forms a context, a natural order of shininess, against which we must measure our attraction to shiny things. These attractions, such as our tendency to associate the only truly reflective parts of the human body, the eyes, with fire—as in the "spark of life," the "fire in the eyes" of one who is angry, or the "smoldering gaze" of sexual arousal—are not arbitrary displacements. The affective powers of things that glitter are as natural and inevitable as gravity. The relationship between the tangible world and the significance we attribute to shiny things is a substantial one. That is, while it cannot be reduced to a concept, it is not simply a subjective whim or a matter of social convention. It follows from our tendency to intermingle dreams of one kind, say of the youthful vitality of "bright-eyed" children or the heat and passion in a lover's gaze, with dreams of another, such as the orderliness of a world of objects neatly polished or the friendships we establish with things we treat with great care.

These relationships, which we moderns find the most difficult to comprehend, are the result of what we may call the material or corporeal imagination. Bachelard (who preferred the first term) maintained that our material imaginings were most likely to occur in moments of reverie. These daydreams, unlike our nocturnal dreams, have the added benefit that they can readily occur while we are working. You will recall from the times you have spent polishing things that this type of work actually promotes daydreaming. And this is another reason why polishing is among the most fundamental expressions of our affection for things.

In the corporeal imaginings of our reveries, our friendships with things are not always innocent affairs. A physical relationship involving constant manual rubbing must often cross into the area of erotic attraction. Like the myth of the sculptor's love for his beautiful statue, an artist's or craftsman's "love of his work" is not just an empty metaphor. In craftwork polishing is often the last operation necessary to "finish" a piece. By then, the creator and creation are intimately acquainted, and polishing may be difficult to distinguish from a lover's caress. More intense rubbing will produce heat between hand and object, giving us another substantial reason to associate polishing with sexual love.

In primitive societies, fires were often started through friction. Here Bachelard describes the typical mindset of the fire-maker. You will see its close relationship to that of one who polishes, and also how a potentially boring and exhausting repetitive activity can be imaginatively troped into rewarding work.

> The warm sense of well-being arising from physical love must have been transferred into many primitive experiences. To set fire to a stick by sliding it up and down in the groove of a piece of dry wood takes time and patience. But this work must have been very agreeable to an individual whose reverie was wholly sexual. It was perhaps while engaged in this gentle task that man learned to sing. In any case it is an obviously rhythmic kind of task, a task which answers to the rhythm of the worker, which brings him lovely, multiple resonances: the arm that rubs, the pieces of wood that strike together, the voice that sings, are all united in the same harmony and the same rhythmic increase in energy; everything converges on the one hope, on to an objective whose value is known.[371]

Our willingness to attribute life to inanimate things, as opposed to our conceptualizing them as neutral resources, opens the possibility of such friendships or love affairs.

By virtue of both its rarity and its ability to "catch our eyes," the shine that results from our affectionate care calls positive attention to itself. We associate shininess with the benevolent qualities of light: life-giving illumination, light as knowledge, light that reveals the truth. We use words describing reflectivity to indicate excitement. Starting with the modest "lustrous," we build in intensity through "shimmering," to "sparkling," then to "glittering" and "glistening," onward to "dazzling," and "resplendent." We call famous persons "stars" and "luminaries," our most promising the "best and brightest." Any great idea or performance is apt to be described as "brilliant." Against these positive associations we have the family of dull words: the dim, the faint, the corroded, the unclean.

Even in the most "corrupted" of modern languages, words reveal our tendency to displace one thing into another, giving "human value to our ephemeral actions." As Arendt demonstrated in her comparison between labor and work, words retain memories of their past. "Polish," like many of the words associated with work where process and product are too integrally connected to be clearly distinguished, can serve as a verb or a noun. Such words remind us that the separation of the making from the thing made is a relatively recent phenomena. The adjective "polished" can be used to describe both a state of high accomplishment or a condition of great refinement. Polishing is a way of ordering the

264 THE EMERALD CITY

material world that requires work and that brings us satisfaction. Its connection with order is further revealed when we consider the other words that share its Latin root *Politus*: polite, police, politics. If we are tempted to dismiss polishing as an activity dedicated to a merely cosmetic result, we should also recall that "cosmetic" shares a kinship with "cosmos." Some degree of cosmetic attention will always be present when we engage in the world-making of work.

Still, polishing is *almost* useless. With many of the things we say we polish, we are in fact polishing another substance—an oil, wax, or lacquer—that has been applied to the surface of the object. Most often it is this coating that protects the substrate material, and the coating could perform its task quite well without having been buffed to a high gloss. The wax coating, not the shine, protects our shoes. This truth is somewhat obfuscated, perhaps intentionally so, by our tendency to name these coatings "polishes," as in "shoe polish" or "chrome polish." Much as with the Venetians' illogical attention to the appearance of their buildings, our desire for shininess is rationally indefensible. Automobile finishes make this point nicely. The best protection for steel automotive bodies would be afforded by a thick and resilient paint, like most enamels. This is the finish we apply whenever protection is our primary goal: on steel handrails, steel tools, on construction equipment and industrial machinery. On our cars, however, we apply a thin, brittle coating of lacquer. Much harder than enamel, lacquer can be more highly polished. We can add tiny flakes of metal to the translucent lacquer to provide still more glitter. Of course, since the lacquer is hard and thin, it can be easily scratched or chipped. Once this happens the coating's protective value is lost and rusting begins. Automobile manufacturers do not apply durable finishes to car bodies, they apply the types their customers want, those that brilliantly shine.

Why do we persist in such nonsense? A polished thing is at its best. It is showing off. The polished object tangibly demonstrates the care that has been lavished onto it. Our cars are usually at their shiniest for special occasions, such as weddings or proms. That fire engines are kept highly polished assures us that they are always in a fine state of repair and readiness. Thanks to the logic of displacement, we are willing to assume that a gleaming fire engine is in peak operating condition. That it is nearly impossible to conceive of a fire company's taking advantage of this tendency, keeping up only the appearance of readiness by polishing trucks that are mechanically flawed, shows us that there are some limits to our willingness to displace concerns of one kind into another. The imaginative connections I have been describing between something that is made and the meanings that are thereby made up always proceed on good faith. That is, they are not disingenuous or intentionally deceiving. They are good lies that create plausible (though possibly fantastic) worlds, and through these worlds they serve to establish and strengthen social bonds. When the young car owner with limited funds polishes his car, he is not perpetrating a scam. Out of necessity, he sincerely hopes that his effort will have benefits beyond the mere protection of his car's paint. In addition, through the shine he has created he demonstrates his affection for his car to others.

This is different from the unscrupulous used-car dealer who polishes a mechanically inferior car before placing it on his lot, in order to defraud his customers. The act of polishing, for this swindler, does not create a world, nor does it displace one sort of concern into the realm of another. Polishing in this case is strictly labor, strictly a technique of deception. The identical activity, depending on whether or not one's imagination is actively engaged in good faith, can be for one person labor, and for another work. We regularly see this principle played out in any residential neighborhood, where some residents devote great care and attention to their properties, deriving sincere pleasure from their work, while other neighbors seek to minimize these maintenance labors, either by neglecting them or by hiring them out.

Notice that the used-car dealer's aim is to minimize the costs, in time and money, needed to place an appealing car in his lot, thereby maximizing his profit once it is sold. Since it is presumably easier to wax and polish a used car than to repair its mechanical defects, the car dealer is using polishing as a labor-saving technique. In other words, he has inverted the logic of polishing, exploiting that which is generally a demonstration of great care and affection for a thing, debasing it into a code—a conventional sign—that he knows to be disconnected from material reality. In the shine on the defective car, much as with the phony arches employed on postmodern buildings, the logic of displacement has been supplanted with the logic of technique. The shifty car dealer and the postmodern architect have discovered more efficient ways to have the appearance of a sound automobile or an ingenious masonry construction without the effort, the work, that should be required to have them.

266 THE EMERALD CITY

While the lovingly polished automobile or the well-crafted masonry arch may say something significant, they cannot be reduced to instruments of communication. The meaning of a polished object cannot be made certain. The shine may give testimony to the care that has been lavished on the article but, as Jacques Derrida has stated, there can be no objective proof, no certainty, about a testimony.[372] It has been presumably offered, and we must interpret it, in good faith. We also see this ambiguity in the similarity between meaningful work, such as skillful building or careful polishing, and other highly artificial forms of behavior in which we testify to something, most notably rituals and ceremonies. Consider again the endlessly repeated cycles of building that occur in the famed Shinto shrines at Ise, Japan. Instead of efficiently building their shrines "once and for all," the temple carpenters at Ise blur the distinction between building and ritual. By refusing to complete their tasks, making building into ceremony, they outwit time. Just as the imagination will usually convert labor into work when it is allowed to run free, when normal purposeful movement incorporates a deliberate delay, time will be disrupted, imaginative displacements may occur, and a ceremony will result. Dwell, for a moment, on the astounding ingenuity of this displacement: the logic of technique seeks to respond directly to our limited time by institutionalizing impatience, by asking us to speed up everything we do; the logic of the ceremony makes our limited time more meaningful, more memorable, by coercing us to slow down.

Speed, as Milan Kundera writes in his novel *Slowness*, is the enemy of memory.

> There is a secret bond between slowness and memory, between speed and forgetting. Consider this utterly commonplace situation: a man is walking down the street. At a certain moment he tries to recall something, but the recollection escapes him. Automatically, he slows down. Meanwhile, a person who wants to forget a disagreeable incident he has just lived through starts unconsciously to speed up his pace, as if he were trying to distance himself from a thing still too close to him in time.[373]

By building an arch or a shrine slowly, by polishing a car by hand, these activities become vividly lodged in our memories. The memorable times we spend carefully building remain always available to us; they can be recalled to consciousness at any instant, so that, through memory and imagination, we circumvent linear time.

Such "unnaturally" slow productive behaviors have complex relationships with material reality. Like polishing, or endlessly rebuilding a temple, tending an ornamental garden is an unnatural activity intimately dependent on nature. The spotless gleaming car, the perfectly trimmed hedge, the repeatedly constructed shrine, the weedless flower bed—all are (like the memories they inspire) forms of extreme artifice. These are instances of an imagined and humanized nature, a nature that has been anthropomorphicized. The great effort required to achieve these unnatural and unavoidably temporary conditions strikes the economist and technologist alike as useless toil. Having forgotten their childhood reveries in the company of friendly things, these persons plot to eradicate such time-wasting activities from our lives. They assume that we can remove the delay and yet retain the ceremony. Or that we can derive fulfillment from maintenance-free gardens and objects that permanently shine.

The metaphysical impatience that is at the heart of late modernity's single-minded pursuit of saving time leads to the harried existence we know as the "rat race." This impatience is based upon a simplistic and unimaginative response to our mortality. When we obsess over saving time, we begin to lose our ability to proffer, displace, and outwit it. When we find shininess desirable, and yet construe polishing as labor, we are led to believe that we should find more efficient ways to polish things. Ideally, this reasoning goes, we should eliminate the need for polishing altogether, creating objects that are permanently shiny. Of course, if after we had learned to make shoes forever shiny, everyone always wore shiny shoes, shoes would no longer give any sort of testimony about the person who wore them. While these shoes could indicate, according to a conventional code, they could not demonstrate.

This is a lesson for those who wish to create architecture or any meaningful construction. The authentic building and dwelling that produce architecture are predominantly work, not labor. More precisely, while these practices may include periods of labor, these must be in a suitable proportion to the amount of work. The exact proportional limits between labor and work for architecture cannot be stated, because they can only be discovered through the time-intensive work of building a particular piece of architecture. There can be no theory of practice, of work, that makes the outcome of practice certain. Such a theory would only destroy that which it seeks to explain with certainty. Therefore, we may discuss productively the spatial and temporal characteristics of a work of architecture in qualitative proportions and poetic measures, but not in mere mathematical ratios.

◇   ◇   ◇

It is a commonplace that modern identities are more fluid than the categorical divisions of people in the class-bound societies of the past. "Fluid" can also mean adaptable. But in another train of associations fluid also implies ease; fluid motion requires that there be no impediments. When things are made easy for us . . . we become weak; our engagement with work becomes superficial, since we lack understanding of what we are doing.

Richard Sennett
The Corrosion of Character

In another portion of the text cited above, Sennett refers to "a terrible paradox" regarding the productive activities of human beings.[374] The paradox is this: as the things we do become easier, they tend to mean less to us. Sennett's paradox is not so far removed from one aspect of the great law proposed by Mark Twain: "In order to make a man or boy covet a thing, it is only necessary to make the thing difficult to obtain." Both Sennett's paradox and Twain's law point to the self-limiting character of technology. As far as architecture is concerned, this self-limiting principle suggests that we cannot produce architecture by means that are entirely efficient. Neither can we make architecture from no-maintenance materials, permanently shiny substances, or components that require no work on the part of their owner in order to sustain them.

Architecture is a practice involving work. A work of architecture is the result—can only be the result—of work *on* architecture. This places architecture, as well as all arts and crafts, in a peculiar position in the age of efficient production. If construction managers, value engineers, efficiency experts, real-estate agents, and developers succeed in their desire to produce buildings with the same certainty and efficiency as other industrially produced commodities, they will have eliminated architecture from our society. I have no fear that this is likely or even possible. Our human desire to dwell is too persistent, our tendency to make friends with things too prevalent, our illogical genius to displace the difficult into the significant too ingrained in our natures. However, those who have adopted this agenda assume that things are far easier, far simpler than is in fact the case. They lack an understanding of what they are doing. As one who loves to practice architecture, I thought I should point this out to them.

The Impact of the Computer
on Architectural Practice

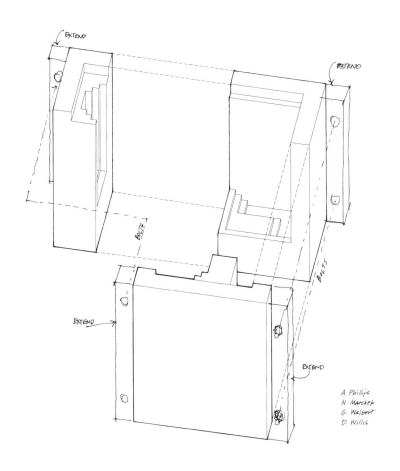

EXTEND

EXTEND

BOLTS

BOLTS

EXTEND

EXTEND

EXTEND

A. Phillips
N. Marchek
G. Walbert
D. Willis

Concrete form-work design drawing, using 'Form Z'
(with suggested modifications hand-drawn)

The enormous saving of time and therefore increase in the output which it is
possible to effect through eliminating unnecessary motions for the men
working in any of our trades can be fully realized only after one has personally
seen the improvement which results from a thorough motion and time study,
made by a competent man.

Frederick Winslow Taylor
The Principles of Scientific Management

Frederick Taylor, the author of the preceding citation, was not wrong. His "scientific" quest to recast all work practices as efficient techniques delivered, at least initially, what he had promised: increased productivity, higher wages for employees, and larger profits for employers. Taylor simply popularized the technical logic, applied to human productive activities, that had already proven its effectiveness in other areas, such as in the design of machines. Taylor's thinking contained a number of oversimplifications, of course. He assumed what the "workman" cherished most was high wages, when I would agree with Simone Weil that what anyone most wants is to lead a happy and fulfilling life. That these two conditions, material wealth and happiness, are not necessarily synonymous is often remarked upon in modern culture. Taylor also failed to recognize that the never-ending quest for efficiency must eventually begin producing adverse social and cultural effects.[375] He was unaware that certain meaningful endeavors, such as ceremonies, derive their impact from just the fact that they are deliberately inefficient. Work can often be considered a "blessing" in that it always contains a trace of ceremony, and therefore produces a gift, an increase, an aura— something significant, that cannot be predicted with certainty or made entirely efficient.

It is tempting to counter the over-simplifications of Taylor and the innumerable technocrats who followed his lead with a single-mindedness of our own, by rejecting outright the logic of technique when applied to architecture or other significant practices. This type of direct opposition is not, however, a properly critical response. While architecture is a practice necessarily involving work, not a technique, architecture has always utilized techniques freely (although warily). However, it has never become a part of technical logic. Unlike the technocrat who believes that one set of criteria for judgment, one manner of reasoning, one "best" way, is applicable to all times and places, the architect produces out of the sort of wisdom that selectively chooses among various ways of engaging reality. One very useful way of engaging reality for those who wish to fabricate significant "worlds" is to utilize labor-saving techniques. This is why architects and builders need not reject the use of the latest technical innovations in their practices.

That said, we must also acknowledge that the logic of technique, the never-ending quest for greater efficiency, has a tendency to override all other concerns. Architects and builders who wish to produce architecture must guard against applying technical logic disproportionately to their endeavors. Like the ceremony, architectural practice cannot be made efficient beyond a certain point or ever become totally predictable or fully cost-effective. The degree to which the practice of architecture can absorb periods of efficient labor, tolerate the incursions of the market, the control of the state, or the demands for greater speed of production is a matter of proportionality.[376] The lack of a suitable verb form to the words "architect" and "architecture" alerts us to the impossibility of architecture existing solely as a technique. As a philosopher friend eloquently put it, "The nature of architecture's defining activity is open to constant debate and interpretation. . . . The absence of a governing verb reminds us that architecture is not an enterprise of technical expertise so much as it is a craft or art."[377]

Those who practice architecture must therefore proceed cautiously with regard to techniques designed solely to increase the efficiency of building production. I would like to continue the analogy of sailing presented in the introduction to this book to illustrate the sort of wary alliance architecture must maintain with technology in order to preserve its status as a culturally significant practice. Anyone who has watched television coverage of recent Americas Cup sailing competitions or has personally witnessed a competitive sailing event is aware that sophisticated technologies—such as satellite navigation, computer-aided design (CAD), composite materials, and advanced aerodynamics and hydrodynamics—are routinely employed by the competing teams. A distinct technical advantage, no matter how slight, can and often does determine the winner. Yet despite the great importance placed on technical superiority, there are artificial limits placed upon the types of innovations that will be permitted in sailing races. The most obvious is that the quest for higher speed and greater efficiency cannot lead to the use of propulsive means other than the wind. To allow gasoline engines, steam turbines, or solar-powered electric motors on the boats would destroy the practice of sailing. The governing bodies that sanction sailing competitions must therefore carefully legislate the legality of technical improvements designed to enhance the sailboat's performance. Beside outlawing engines, they sort racing boats into well-defined classes. Exacting criteria are used to handicap the different types of boats that may compete; some boat classes require racers to maintain fully equipped galleys and heads (thus indirectly controlling the boat's weight) and nearly all specify the number of crew, permitted materials of construction, hull length, and allowable sail area.

To some extent, the same sort of performance limitations are necessary in nearly every competitive endeavor or sport. Lately, there has been much discussion as to whether technical improvements to golf equipment risk making the game "too easy." Not long ago the National Football League moved the spot of a kick-off further from the opponent's goal line, in recognition that improved kicking techniques and strength training had made it too likely that the kick-off would sail deep into the end zone. Some college baseball teams are beginning to reconsider their use of aluminum bats. Many collegiate coaches feel that metal bats are adversely altering the nature of collegiate baseball. While any of these examples might have sufficed, sailing has some further characteristics that make it the most suitable metaphor for architectural practice. Unlike sailing or architecture, golf, football, and baseball are games. As such, they were never intended as purposeful activities. Sailing, like architecture, is a practice with ancient origins, and it was once the primary means of ocean-going transportation. Sailing and architecture both respond to practical needs, yet they do so in a manner that is unlike that of a pure technique.

Sailing and architecture combine the purposeful with the pleasurable. Because these practices are pleasurable (a trait they share with games) we would not want to make them so efficient as to eliminate the practice itself. Sailing is not simply an answer to the problem of transportation over water, because sailing is in itself enjoyable. In sailing, as in making architecture, getting there is at least half of the fun. More efficient means of navigation, or of producing buildings, are not as rewarding because they are too easy to make their achievements significant. This, I believe is the nature of all practices: they thrive on engaging adversity. Thus, as sailors gain skill they often venture into more hostile waters, attempt longer trips, or begin to enter racing competitions. Techniques such as Taylor's "scientific management" are, on the contrary, dedicated to eliminating uncertainty and inefficiency. At some point they become victims of their own success. With uncertainty banished, life becomes boring and predictable.

Sailing and architecture are also alike in that they reveal the virtue of approaching a goal indirectly. Regardless of the level of technology they employ, sailors cannot control the speed or direction of the wind. This means that sailing vessels are forced to negotiate with nature, often "going out of their way" to accommodate both their desire to reach a particular destination and the limitations imposed by the sometimes fickle winds. In a similar manner, architecture is charged with making the spaces in which we live out our lives meaningful, yet architecture has no direct control over these spaces. While our intention may be to affect what is contained (our lives), architectural practices may only manipulate the container (our buildings). When the naval architects who design sailing vessels and the architects who concern themselves with our need to dwell on land do their jobs well, the forms of their structures and activities will often demonstrate their clever redirection of natural forces. One could say that the billowing of a sailboat's sails, or the graceful curve of a masonry vault, frame natural forces in a way that is significant, while a boat powered by an engine, or a span overcome by a simple beam, do not. Sailing and architecture make qualities of nature, which might be otherwise invisible to us, visible through their demonstrative actions. The sailboat lets the wind be itself; it accepts the wind in all its glorious unpredictability. The arch lets stones be stones, hard and heavy, lacking in tensile strength. In neither case are the wind or the stones reduced to the status of resources, and their natures are not defined as obstacles to be overcome. This is the essence of the difference between a practice and a technique.

> In a sailboat there is a dependency of the boat upon the wind and water, and one is always aware of this dependency. A sailboat is a thing of the water. By contrast, a motor boat is a machine used to overcome the water through the power of its engines. The currents and winds around a body of water also enter into motorboating, but do so as obstacles to be surmounted. In motorboating one attempts to dominate the river, and can gain the illusion that such domination is possible. No such illusion is possible in sailboating. It is precisely such an illusion of domination that lies at the core of scientific technology.[378]

In sailing, one is always aware of the dependency on the wind; in architecture, one is always aware of the dependency on the qualities of building materials, and on the skill of builders. Sailors may utilize many sophisticated techniques as long as they do not lead to the illusion of domination over the wind and water. Architects and builders may adopt high-tech solutions intended to make their practices more efficient, providing they do not succumb to the illusion that these techniques grant them domination over substances, spaces, and lives.

According to present Western convention, architectural practices have been split into three related activities: the designing of buildings and environments (the profession of architecture), the building of these (the building trades), and the care and maintenance of the "finished" building (the responsibility of the owner, dweller, or the professional facilities manager). For the remainder of this essay, I will focus on the first area, and consider the impact of the introduction of a single, although multi-faceted, technical innovation—the computer—into the contemporary architecture firm.

◇   ◇   ◇

Today, most of the applications to which computers are devoted in architectural offices aim to make the production of architectural drawings more efficient. These computer applications were marketed to architects initially with the claim that the more efficient production of working drawings would allow the architect to spend more time designing. This is the promise that has always been used to promote labor-saving techniques; it is identical to the claim that improved manufacturing techniques would save enough time to allow laborers greater amounts of leisure. This promise rests on another questionable Taylorist assumption: that the production of architectural drawings is meaningless—a purely instrumental operation. It also assumes that designing, that is conceptualizing architectural forms, is the only meaningful activity for the architect. You will recognize in this ideology similarities to the mind/body, management/labor split that is the hallmark of industrialization.

Earlier in this volume, I have questioned both the desirability and the seeming inevitability of this division of labor. Here, I wish to challenge the veracity of the claim that computerization would allow architectural firms more time to design. In my experience, precisely the opposite has occurred. Economic pressures for greater speed of production have been exacerbated by client expectations, fueled by the marketing of architects themselves, that computerized drawings of a building of photographic realism can be generated virtually overnight. The increased production speed that the computer has facilitated[379] has only resulted in a demand for even quicker production. These demands, as well as an ever-increasing amount of time occupied by the necessity of marketing (which all purveyors of commodities must face) have been accommodated through an ever-shrinking amount of time devoted to designing.[380]

The computer has been marketed simply as a tool to make the architect's production of drawings more efficient. However, its presence on the architect's desk is also a symptom of the architect's growing dedication to "saving time" and increasing "output." The computer, through its supposed necessity, contributes to this sense of urgency. Just as cyberspace defines virtual "reality" that is predominately Cartesian and visual, CAD redefines "design" as an instrumental technique for the efficient production of visually stimulating buildings. Architectural design, for most of the twentieth century, was a time-intensive process requiring constant interaction with the client. Much of the architect's design effort now occurs during the marketing phase of a project, when the architect is trying to win the commission. Many clients are seduced by the provocative imagery architects may produce in the scant few weeks that they are often given to respond to a request for services, to the extent that they fail to consider that this imagery has been produced without their in-depth input. Prospective clients now routinely ask architecture firms to produce extensive proposals that, thanks to desk-top publishing capabilities, often rival the graphic quality of the best professional journals from only a decade ago. Public speaking skills, written eloquence, graphic design talent, the ability to compose stunning photographs, and computer modeling capabilities are rapidly replacing the thorough command of all aspects of design and building as the most desirable attributes for architects. What we mean by "design" is today almost wholly visual, more directed toward making an initial impact, more closely resembling fashion or product design than what we meant by it three decades ago.

Once again, the computer is not simply a cause of these trends, but neither is it, as some try to maintain, neutral in its effects on them.

The more powerful the technique, the more powerfully it reinforces technical logic as a whole, and therefore the more pronounced its effect on practices that exist for other than primarily technical reasons. The most powerful techniques are also those whose unanticipated and unintended effects are likely to be the most troublesome (for example, the "Y2K" problem faced by many computer networks). Just as computer manufacturers never intended to accelerate the redefinition of architectural design, neither did they foresee their substantial role in transforming the staff within the architecture office from workers to laborers. Architectural drafting, which for most of its practitioners was once craftwork (where the ability to letter beautifully was once a reliable way to identify an architect), is now approaching the efficient certainty of labor. CAD drafters arrange standard details, prefabricated assemblies, predetermined building systems, layers of engineering drawings, and building shapes dictated by "design architects" (as well as letter fonts that imitate the appearance of hand-lettering) in order to assemble the professional products clients demand.

Yet, just as with sailing, there is a limit to the extent that the activity of making buildings—and this includes the full range of practices from designing to construction to dwelling—can be made efficient before it begins to lose all significance for us. It is not possible to practice architecture solely as a laborer or human resource under the dominion of the Cartesian clock. In order to dwell in the buildings and landscapes we create, we must be willing, at times, to slow down. In response to a client's demand, "How long will it take to create this work of architecture?" the only truthful response an architect could give would be, "I don't know" or, at least, "I am not sure." Bruno Zevi tells a tale of Carlo Scarpa's work for the design of the Italian pavilion that was to be a part of Expo '67 in Montreal. An early planning meeting with the Italian officials was proceeding splendidly until Scarpa was asked, "How long will it take?"

> Scarpa hums and haws. "Don't know. Perhaps I'll get an idea tomorrow, perhaps in a year, perhaps never." The officials gape and I have to intervene to stop them from stripping him of the commission. He proves perfectly efficient.[381]

Scarpa, who was certainly exaggerating the amount of uncertainty involved in architectural practice, appears to have been putting his clients on notice that some unpredictability would always remain about his work. Perhaps Scarpa was testing the limits of his client's patience in an attempt to secure the greatest amount of time possible. Scarpa wanted his clients to know that architecture takes time. Yet it returns this time to us, with interest—not literally, but by slowing our experiences of it, by making the duration of our days meaningful and fulfilling.

Just as the "best" sailboat is not that which is the slowest or most difficult to sail, it would be absurd to claim that the "best" architecture is that which takes the greatest amount of time to create. Here we would, once again, be countering the single-minded desire to save time with an equally misguided single-mindedness of our own. The ethic that determines the proper balance between the meaningful delay and the efficient technique in any practice is not readily conceptualized into such generalizations. The nostalgic wish for labor-intensive slowness errs by considering only transitive measures of time. Scarpa was eventually able to perform "efficiently" because he was a gifted architect, and because his clients allowed him adequate time to practice his skills. Had Scarpa employed computers in his office, it is doubtful that they would have altered his dedication to somewhat uncertain and inefficient practices.

The professional practice of architecture is founded on the client's willingness to trust that good work takes time, and that the architect will not simply "waste" time. For much of the twentieth century the time necessary for an architect to design a building (approximately nine months to a year for most buildings) and the cost of these services (about ten percent of the cost of the building's construction) were simply a given. While zealous advocates of free trade would be correct to note that these conventions resulted, in part, from the profession's efforts to stifle competition, they were defensible in a number of ways. For one thing, most clients were satisfied with the level of service they received from their architects. The nearly year-long design duration allowed the architect to explore a number of design options, to endure a few missteps, and to make significant design revisions whenever the client had a change of heart or mind. For another, while most architects were able to make a comfortable living pursuing their profession, few ever became truly wealthy from practicing architecture. The modest monetary compensation architects received was balanced by their love for, and dedication to, their work.

Now, forced to do things more quickly, for lower fees, architects seldom have the luxury of studying a "design problem" as thoroughly as they once had. At the end of the twentieth century, most architecture firms have elected to computerize, not out of the desire to explore areas of architecture that only computers can facilitate, but merely to execute their duties more rapidly. A growing percentage of architectural drawings are being produced by CAD operators who, because of their lack of an accredited architectural degree, have no hope of ever becoming architects.[382] Meanwhile clients, and their lawyers, are demanding ever-greater certainty and predictability about the products architects produce. These changes suggest that the logic of technique has assumed a disproportionate control over the activities of professional architects. It also suggests that we may have reached a point where it is necessary to radically reconfigure our understanding of suitable architectural practices.[383]

◇   ◇   ◇

If all techniques produce unintended effects, as is entertainingly demonstrated by Edward Tenner in his book *Why Things Bite Back*, we should by now be able to discern a few more specific consequences of the computerized production of architectural drawings. I begin by returning to the two primary uses of computers in architectural firms, beyond the word-processing and accounting applications that are common to nearly all businesses: the production of working drawings and the generation of "realistic" building images.

The ability to quickly produce dazzling perspectival views of buildings has, much like architectural photography decades earlier, unintentionally increased the importance of visual composition to those who judge the design of buildings. Stunning sculptural compositions—or, depending on the audience, "classical," "vernacular," or "contextual" appearances—are now the "products" architects are expected to produce. There are several ways the computer, when used unwarily as "a tool just like a pencil," exacerbates the conversion of architecture from a practice to an aesthetic commodity. We can start with the lack of connection between the digital image of a building and the materials and methods by which an actual building must be realized. Now this aspect of CAD drawings is only slightly more pronounced than in instrumental building representations produced by hand. Manually drafted working drawings differ from CAD drawings not in the instrumental logic they share, but in the speed by which they are produced and the degree of tactility that remains in the drafting operation. Manual draftsmen pressed harder with their pencil leads to emphasize certain lines, joints, or corners. They drew their ruling pens more slowly across the linen to create the most significant lines on the sheet. Now CAD operators using their mouse cannot vary the "weight" of a line as it approaches its end point; no longer does the sureness or tentativeness with which they draw leave its trace on the page. This ability to vary drawing speed and pressure was one of the ways that the manually drafted drawing (weakly) mirrored the building operations it depicted. Louis Kahn attempted to make this analogous fit more explicit through his recommendation that the architect's pencil pause for an instant at the significant joints in the construction.

Unlike the "dreaming" ink of a poet or the contemplative graphite of Kahn, the building shapes one manipulates on a computer are by definition disembodied abstractions. The construction of a virtual building on a computer is only rarely in any way analogous to the construction of a real building.[384] Therefore the joints one sees in a virtual building have only been placed out of adherence to convention, or the desire to imitate the look of something else.

The software used for applying the look of building materials to the geometric polygons the computer generates treats wood or brick as weightless, depthless, surface patterns. There is typically no attempt by the software developer to coordinate the module of the bricks and the proportions of the openings in the virtual brick wall. This very necessary (assuming the building is intended to be built or regarded as if it could be built) coordination must be added, as an additional concern and several extra steps, by the computer operator. Thus the logic of construction with bricks is exactly reversed. Whereas when building with bricks it is always easier to construct objects sized with the brick module in mind, on the computer it requires more work to respect this module. The computer finds one-fiftieth of a brick as plausible as a whole brick, and the brick pattern can just as easily be applied to a ceiling as a wall. Bricks represented this way lose not only their actual but also their imaginative weight—they lose their brickness. This attitude toward building materials turns them into mere resources. The thinking behind this type of computer use is single-minded. It simultaneously rejects or ignores the burdens of building in the world while remaining oblivious to its own limitations, secure in the illusion that the domination of nature is possible, and that a computer is a neutral tool.

Even the more sophisticated CAD programs, those that allow the architect to create wall "assemblies" that represent both the depth and individual layers of the wall's construction, are only more thorough in their ability to model a wall three-dimensionally. Temporal issues, such as construction sequences, and problems related to the ergonomics of building, such as the inability of the mason's trowel to perform properly in too small a cavity, have never been easy to anticipate in orthographic drawings. Since the institution of the working drawing as a supposedly complete description of the building assembly, and therefore as a contract document to be faithfully followed by the builder, it has been the responsibility of the architect to attempt to anticipate, and allow for, the necessary processes of construction. The relatively slow pace of the hand-drafted working drawing afforded the architect or draftsperson who was knowledgeable of building practices ample time to imagine the steps that would be involved to build the building. And, as I have already mentioned, the manual draftsperson could vary the pressure with which she made her lines or retrace certain lines for emphasis in an effort to understand or emulate the operations of the builder.

Unlike the pencil, however, the ease with which the computer can be relied upon to translate the composition of the wall assembly from one view to the next can lead to an unthinking overreliance, similar to that I have developed to the spell-check feature of my word-processing program. The greatest risk of error in the hand-drafted drawing centered around omissions—something vital was simply left off the drawings. With the widespread computerized production of working drawings, it is more likely that inapplicable details or assemblies will be erroneously imported into a project's drawings where they do not belong. Like spell-check programs, CAD dimensioning systems make mathematical errors in dimensions nearly impossible. However, they cannot prevent the inclusion of dimensions that are technically correct but to inappropriate tolerances. Nor can they tell the novice draftsperson *which* dimensions are critical to the construction.

Such tendencies are even more visible in the way architects now "write" construction specifications. Using a computerized master specification, spec-writers simply delete all sections that do not apply to a particular project. Since spec-writers are not infallible, their specifications usually contain sections or products not actually required to construct the building. Most of the architects with whom I have raised this issue agree that computer-generated sets of construction documents tend to contain more drawings than their hand-drafted counterparts, just as specifications generated from a "master spec" are bloated compared to their written-from-scratch, or manually cut-and-paste, predecessors.

The computer's ability to rapidly copy from one part of a drawing to another, or to appropriate details and assemblies wholesale from past projects, has also contributed to a conventionalizing of construction details. When details become entirely conventionalized, without the possibility of improvisational responses to highly specific conditions, they become imaginatively dead, just as do building shapes that respond to convention alone, or to wholly conventional languages.[385] This tendency toward conservative details and assemblies is one of the hidden propensities of computer-aided drafting. These limitations or tendencies are a result of both those tasks the computer does not do well and its amazing virtuosity in the narrow area for which it is suited, and they are several orders of magnitude more pronounced in their effects than the limitations of the pencil.

While CAD influences architects to be less adventurous with building methods, it has the corresponding effect of freeing them to experiment with a greater variety of building shapes. Recently, well-known architects, most notably Frank Gehry, have creatively employed sophisticated CAD software to rid themselves of architecture's 500-year-old dependence on the orthogonal. It is now feasible for architects to design shapes that, due to their irregularity and complexity, would have been nearly impossible to draw just a few decades ago. The computer has been widely hailed for granting us this new freedom. However, is the ability to create an ever-wider variety of novel shapes as valuable as the architectural media and CAD marketing hype would have us believe? In the past, the pencil and parallel rule undoubtedly burdened the architect with the tendency to overemphasize rectilinear building shapes. (These drafting techniques, as I have noted, also had their unforeseen ramifications.) Was this tendency simply the arbitrary consequence of the limitations of these now antiquated drafting tools? Has the rectilinear building been an albatross around the neck of the architect's imagination?

With regard to the vertical extension of a building, a thoughtful examination of building methods reveals that more than arbitrary conventions and limitations were at work. Thousands of years of plumb walls and columns cannot be attributed simply to a lack of imagination or drawing ability on the part of their architects and builders. The practice of building vertically, perpendicular to the level surface of the earth, primarily stems from the inescapable limit-condition that is gravity, not from an inflexible manner of drawing. In their poetic praise of the right angle, Amédée Ozenfant and Le Corbusier noted that the "vertical and the horizontal are among the sensitive manifestations of the phenomena of nature, constant verifications of one of its most directly apparent laws." They went on to claim that "the human being works according to the right angle (just look around you)."[386] Our desire to build upright buildings that mirror our own vertical standing, and abide by the principles of structural stability, is not merely a matter of arbitrary fancy. This is also true in the horizontal plane, where many of our most popular building methods—those that produce frame structures, particularly of wood and steel—are inherently easier to execute for rectilinear plan configurations. The evidence suggests that the orthogonal proclivities of the pencil and parallel rule have not been weighing down the imaginations of architects since the Renaissance, because these limitations are generally analogous to the ways we build and stand, and to the vertical axes of our dreams.

This should give us pause before we uncritically extol our newfound computer-aided ability to draw, and therefore construct, novel shapes with little or no connection to either the ways we build, stand, or dream. In praising the right angle, Ozenfant and Le Corbusier suggested an interdependence between architecture and gravity that is akin to the sailboat's dependence on the wind. If we thoughtlessly abandon this dependence, simply because a new tool has made doing so suddenly efficient, we may be perpetrating the equivalent of bringing an engine onto a sailboat. Should the computer grant us the ability to finally sever the tenuous thread of analogy that still remained between the professional architect's hand-drafted working drawings and the constructed building, it will only have succeeded in eliminating our professional ability to produce authentic details. We may have a proliferation of unusually shaped buildings, but this technique will not produce architecture.

Throughout architectural history novel shapes and departures from the orthogonal have always required novel ways of building, always necessitated new and clever details, such as those needed to construct the fabulous masonry structure of Gaudí's Güell Crypt outside Barcelona.[387] Yet many of the most formally inventive buildings today are also among the most conservative, most conventional in their construction. The University of Cincinnati's DAAP Building, by Peter Eisenman, shares its construction methods (steel frame, light gauge steel wall framing, interior gypsum drywall, and EIFS exterior cladding) with nearly every low-budget speculative office building and retail store built in the 1990s.

For much of history, the material of a building's construction was simply given for a particular region, climate, and culture. A building's shape was always conceived in negotiation with the tendencies of the dominant building method. Now, particularly with the assistance of CAD, architects can conceive novel compositions without regard for the method of their construction, leaving it to engineers, "production architects," and other technicians to project these shapes onto mute substances. There is seldom anything cunning or clever about these assemblies, and their connections are usually kept hidden, so as not to interfere with the purity of the sculptural composition. The tilted wall has been disembodied into a shape-sign unconnected to the manner of its construction, and the freedom granted by the computer to compose with unconventional shapes has helped to accelerate the extinction of authentic details.

The homogenizing effect in the output of products designed and drafted on the computer is a tendency seemingly shared whenever practices are replaced by techniques.[388] The solution to this dilemma is not, as most of those who manufacture computer software believe, an even more thorough attempt to simulate reality. Computer simulations can never be made into exact replicas of real buildings. The rules of construction practices are always changing in response to new innovations and novel conditions; no software designer could ever keep up. Computerized design and production techniques can never be made fully transparent. This is no reason for despair. Except for the ability to dazzle clients with photo-realistic graphics, the close simulation of reality offers little that is useful to architects. Unlike the pilots who train on flight simulators, architects risk no physical harm when they ply their trade in the real world. Instead of attempting to make our virtual buildings more real, *we should be attempting to put their unreality to more imaginative use.* Authentic virtual constructions are no doubt possible to produce using computers, but they must begin by rejecting the instrumental assumptions, the supposed neutrality of projective geometries, on which the currently popular simulations are always based.

As Italo Calvino might say, we should be training our computers to look indirectly and to accept their particular burden, which is to be governed by nearly weightless bits. For example, consider how the frustratingly mechanical manner of thinking that one is forced to adopt when interacting with a computer (the ultimate reduction of everything finally to a "yes" or "no" response) tends to deaden one's ability to imagine, or even tolerate, ambiguity. This quality is no mere glitch; it is intrinsic to the algorithmic nature of computer software. Computer software will always offer us choices that are not really choices (such as the improper command messages that require the operator to acknowledge "OK" before the computer will proceed—a miniature version of the sort of coerced confessions that oppressive regimes always extract from nonconformists) and force us to make irrevocable commitments before we can thoughtfully do so.

Yet, for all its single-minded inflexibility, the process of navigating through a computer program also has an intriguing unintended similarity to a most fascinating architectural situation: that of being trapped in a labyrinth. The frequent associations computer users make with being trapped, lost, or held prisoner are not arbitrary metaphors. Hollywood has already given us numerous films where persons are captive in virtual reality, or where prisoners escape their virtual restraints to wreak havoc in the "real world." Does not the language of computers abound in talk of nets and webs where we must obtain the services of a "navigator" to find our way? The point is that computers, too, have bodies—or perhaps anti-bodies—where their own unyielding conceptual structure begins to be felt as a kind of oppressive weight. The place where we are most aware of the computer's single-minded limits, where the supposedly liberating tool of our creation frustrates and constrains our movements the most, is the hidden location of its opacity and materiality. Computers do not liberate us. They weigh us down with their single-minded way of making us think. They force us to carry them with us, and burden us with useless information. Only when we begin to feel this weight can we start to see its analogous relationship to Daedalus's labyrinth, Borges's infinite library, to Piranesi's prison, and Poe's horrific House of Usher. If we are to find a suitable use for the computer in architecture, I think we must begin here.

The sublime inflexibility of the computer is far more fascinating than its so-called "virtual reality." Where the structure of the computer, however accidentally, mirrors certain architectural situations, this is where the fragment of a body that can and does imitate will allow us to move beyond always pointing the same way, to the realm of demonstrations and authentic constructions. We must find ways to use the computer as a substance, a medium, rather than as a neutral technique. This will not be possible until we free our computer-aided drafters from the obsession with efficiency. As long as architects use computers solely in the instrumental mode for which they are intended, the computer's basis in conventional algorithms will allow it to "express only a small part of what can be thought"[389]; words, or in this case lines and polygons, will be turned to stone and architecture will be distorted into a lifeless simulation of itself.

The most successful computer-generated drawings make positive use of the computer's ability to readily deform shapes, producing drawings that incorporate transparency, anamorphosis, collage, and multiple layers implying a temporal depth. These drawings challenge the assumption that architecture can be evaluated from quick initial readings, that one can deem compositions as pleasing or shocking at a glance. Instead of treating the output of the computer as something pristine and untouchable, as artifacts that would only be profaned by the touch of a human hand, some of my students manually draw over their color laser-printed drawings, or cut them apart and reassemble them into collages that, in addition to effectively portraying spatial experiences, also serve to question the supposed near reality of the computerized image.

Despite the best efforts of brilliant engineers and scientists, there remain risks associated with making drawings on a computer. Computers crash; programs have glitches and unpredictable limitations. While Frederick Taylor (or Bill Gates) would likely be exasperated by the continued existence of these inefficiencies, I find in them further reason for optimism. As long as the computer never attains absolute transparency in its operations, the possibility of using it poetically remains. To date, only a few intrepid explorers have begun to discover ways to turn the computer's corporeality to their advantage. Those persons who are able to practice using computers today are those whose computer use is confined to the far edge of what is possible to do with a computer. If we are not to limit computers to minor role-players in architectural practices, we must continue searching for ways to imbue our computerized creations with the fertile substance of uncertainty. We must face the sublime burden of the computer with the resolve to turn it to our advantage, with the agile leaps of imagination and the refusal to look directly that are the only services that architects—the prototypical navigators—have ever provided to the world.

Notes

Introduction: Heavy, Not Dead

1 I borrow this term from my friend Donald Kunze.

2 Karsten Harries, "Building and the Terror of Time," *Perspecta: The Yale Architectural Journal* 19 (1982): 59.

3 Richard Sennett, *The Corrosion of Character* (New York: W. W. Norton, 1998), 72.

Architecture as Medicine

4 Michael Taussig, *Mimesis and Alterity: A Particular History of the Senses* (London: Routledge, 1993), 57.

5 Quoted in Robert Hughes, *Barcelona* (New York: Alfred A. Knopf, 1992), 403.

6 Hughes, *Barcelona*, 403.

7 Taussig, *Mimesis and Alterity*, 86.

8 Alfred W. Crosby, *The Measure of Reality: Quantification and Western Society 1250–1600* (Cambridge: Cambridge University Press, 1997), 85.

9 Ivan Illich, *In the Mirror of the Past: Lectures and Addresses 1978–1990* (New York: Marion Boyers, 1992), 220.

10 Andrew Weil, *Spontaneous Healing* (New York: Alfred A. Knopf, 1995), 5.

11 Ibid., 14.

12 Dalibor Vesely, "Architecture and the Conflict of Representation," *AA Files* 8 (1988): 21.

13 Ibid., 26.

14 Dr. Richard Selzer, quoted in Jenny E. Young, "The Role of Architecture in Promoting Healing Environments in the Design of Small, Rural Hospitals," *The Proceedings of the ACSA 84th Annual Meeting* (Washington, D.C.: Association of Collegiate Schools of Architecture, 1996), 571.

15 Theodor W. Adorno, "Functionalism Today," in Neil Leach, ed., *Rethinking Architecture* (London: Routledge, 1997), 10. Adorno's essay persuasively argues that the reductionist logic of functionalism "does not coincide with the question of practical function."

16 Ivan Illich, *Medical Nemesis* (New York: Pantheon, 1976; reprint, New York: Bantham, 1977), 25.

17 Quoted in Stephen Jay Gould, *The Mismeasure of Man* (New York: W. W. Norton, 1981), 151, my emphasis.

18 Gould, *Mismeasure of Man*, 262.

19 The conventional assumption is that the types of measures we "moderns" employ to evaluate things are neutral; they objectively record facts without distortion. When we look at this matter carefully, however, we notice that the range of usefulness for this manner of measuring is fairly narrow. Love, beauty, justice, friendship, happiness—all refuse to be measured in this way. Yet the aggressive ideology behind these instrumental measures conceals its own limitations by doubting the existence of anything that cannot be measured with certainty. While a more thorough accounting of the benefits of architecture, such as that advocated for all business ventures in Paul Hawken's *The Ecology of Commerce* (New York: Harper Business, 1993), can and does help us argue in favor of it, such an accounting cannot negate the disadvantage architecture and all other "immeasurables" face in an age that worships the certainty of numbers. My only disagreement with Mr. Hawken's thesis is that he seems to believe accounting practices can, if we *will* them to, be made neutral, so they will not favor certain types of investments over others.

20 Ivan Illich, *Tools for Conviviality* (Berkeley: Heyday Books, 1973), 89.

21 Richard Sennett, *The Fall of Public Man* (New York: Alfred A. Knopf, 1974; reprint, New York: W. W. Norton, 1992), 328–9.

22 Ignasi de Solà-Morales, *Fin de Siècle Architecture in Barcelona* (Barcelona: Gustavo Gili, 1992), 39.

23 Ibid., 16.

24 Ibid., 42.

25 Ibid., 48.

26 David Mackey, *Modern Architecture in Barcelona: 1854–1939* (New York: Rizzoli, 1989), 38.

27 Langdon Winner, "Artifact/Ideas and Political Culture," *Whole Earth Review* (Winter 1991): 24.

28 By making this observation I do not deny that such a skill is a reasonably good indicator of one's likely success in technical or business pursuits.

Architecture as Medicine (contd.)

29 Quoted in Young, "Role of Architecture," 569.

30 The "IDP," as the Intern Development Program is known, is designed to assure that intern architects receive sufficiently broad experience, that they do not, for example, spend their three-year apprenticeship in the office print room. However, what NCARB defines as broad experience focuses almost exclusively on what I might call "skill areas" within the conventional model of architectural practice (such as "code research," "document checking and coordination," and "building cost analysis"). There is some attempt (for which NCARB should be applauded) to recognize the value of, and therefore permit internship credit for, such things as teaching, research, and community service. Still, if we compare the IDP to the Vitruvian ideal, or any notion of a well-rounded generalist, the IDP falls short. To broaden the scope of the IDP, it might give credit for the publication of articles in professional journals regardless of whether this occurred under the auspices of a "NAAB (National Architecture Accreditation Board) -accredited professional degree program," for exhibits of theoretical work, for competitions entered outside of the office practice, for research that leads to patents for the creation of new building systems, for continuing education in the form of acquiring craft skills in making wrought iron, cabinetwork, stained glass, etc. The IDP could also strongly encourage the intern to read widely, to travel, to learn a second language, to become knowledgeable about other arts, sciences, and politics. All of this would help to dispel the images of the "narrow-minded aesthete" and the equally "narrow-minded technician" that presently polarize the profession.

31 Robert Fielden (President of NCARB), "The Evolution of Architectural Practice: National Certification and Reciprocity," in William S. Saunders, ed., *Reflections on Architectural Practice in the Nineties* (New York: Princeton Architectural Press, 1996), 101.

32 Continuing education requirements and similar programs, at least as far as the professional practice of architecture is concerned, provide a short-term solution to the architect's declining professional prestige. In a society that does not recognize talent, ability, or wisdom unless they can be quantified in some way, it is reasonable for the AIA to propose a numerical measure of competence. However, in the long term, the reliance on such measures only serves to further restrict the definition of "architecture" to issues that can be readily expressed in numbers.

33 Manfredo Tafuri, *Architecture and Utopia*, trans. Barbara Luigia La Penta (Cambridge, MA: MIT Press, 1976), 176.

34 Quoted in Marco Frascari, "The Tell-the-Tale Detail," *Via* 7 (Philadelphia: Graduate School of Fine Arts, University of Pennsylvania and MIT Press, 1984), 32.

35 David Michael Levin, *The Opening of Vision: Nihilism and the Postmodern Situation* (New York: Routledge, 1988), 102.

36 Quoted in Young, "Role of Architecture," 571.

The Valor of Iron

37 David Pye, *The Nature and Art of Workmanship* (London: Studio Vista Limited, 1968), 40.

38 Ivan Illich, *H_2O and the Waters of Forgetfulness* (Berkeley: Heyday Books, 1985), 3.

39 Quoted in Susan and Michael Southworth, *Ornamental Ironwork* (Boston: David R. Godine, 1978), 95–6.

40 Mircea Eliade, *The Forge and the Crucible* (Chicago: University of Chicago Press, 1978), 65–70.

41 Giambattista Vico, *New Science*, trans. Thomas Goddard Bergin and Max Harold Fisch (Ithaca, NY: Cornell University Press, 1948; reprint, 1984), 70.

42 Gaston Bachelard, "The Cosmos of Iron," *The Right to Dream*, trans. J. A. Underwood (Dallas: Dallas Institute, 1988), 39.

43 Adolf Loos, *Spoken Into the Void: Collected Essays 1897–1900*, trans. Jane O. Newman & John H. Smith (Cambridge, MA: MIT Press, 1982), 81–2.

44 For the distinction between "representation" and "re-presentation," see the essay "The Weight of Architecture" in this collection.

45 Octavio Paz, "Use and Contemplation," introductory essay to *In Praise of Hands: Contemporary Crafts of the World* (Greenwich, CT: New York Graphic Society, 1974), 19.

46 Gaston Bachelard, *Water and Dreams*, trans. Edith R. Farrell (Dallas: Dallas Institute, 1983), 13.

47 Henri Focillon, *The Life of Forms in Art* (New York: Zone Books, 1992), 166.

48 Georg Simmel, "The Ruin," in Kurt H. Wolff, ed., *Essays on Sociology, Philosophy and Aesthetics* (New York: Harper Torchbooks, 1959), 264.

49 Paz, "Use and Contemplation," 21.

50 Pye, *Nature and Art.*

51 Bachelard, "Cosmos of Iron."

52 Paul S. Hurd, *Metallic Materials: An Introduction to Metallurgy* (New York: Holt, Rinehart, Winston, 1968), 6.

53 Eliade, *Forge and Crucible*, 27–33.

54 Ibid., 67.

55 Richard F. Burton, *The Book of the Sword* (New York: Dover, 1987), xv.

56 Eliade, *Forge and Crucible*, 63.

57 Burton, *Book of Sword*, xv–xvi.

58 Gaston Bachelard, *The Flame of a Candle*, trans.

Joni Caldwell (Dallas: Dallas Institute of Humanities and Culture, 1988), 4.

59 Marco Frascari, *Monsters of Architecture* (Savage, MD: Rowman & Littlefield, 1991), 35.

60 Gaston Bachelard, *Lautréamont*, trans. Robert S. Dupree (Dallas: Dallas Institute Publications, 1986), 30.

61 John Ruskin, *The Queen of the Air* (1872), in John D. Rosenberg, ed., *The Genius of John Ruskin: Selections From His Writings* (London: Routledge & Kegan Paul, 1979), 359.

62 Bachelard, "Cosmos of Iron," 40.

63 Octavio Paz, "Chillida: From Iron to Light," in Pittsburgh International Series, The Carnegie Institute, *Chillida* (Paris: Maeght éditeur, 1979), 12–3.

64 Bachelard, "Cosmos of Iron," 42.

65 See, for example, the iron and steel tendrils characteristic of the metal work of Albert Paley.

66 "Interview with Richard Serra," *Richard Serra: Torqued Ellipses* (New York: Dia Center, 1997), 17.

67 Ibid.

68 Hannah Arendt, *The Human Condition* (Chicago: University of Chicago Press, 1958), 139.

69 Hans-Georg Gadamer, *The Relevance of the Beautiful and Other Essays*, ed. Robert Bernasconi, trans. Nicholas Walker (Cambridge: Cambridge University Press, 1986), 78–9.

70 If the diversity Pye champions were deemed sufficiently desirable (that is, profitable) by the manufacturers of iron products, they would seek to simulate it, much as computer programs (such as "Squiggle") are presently used to make CAD drawings simulate a hand-drawn sketch.

71 Walter Benjamin, "The Work of Art in the Age of Mechanical Reproduction," *Illuminations*, trans. Harry Zohn (New York: Schocken Books, 1969), 217–51.

72 Illich, *H₂O and Waters*, 7.

73 Bachelard's two volumes on "earth and the reveries of will" and "earth and the reveries of repose" are as yet not translated.

74 Paz, "Chillida," 15.

75 Truly delicate plant stems, petals, and other fragile constructions in wrought iron would be other examples of the nature of a material being revealed through the image of its opposite.

The Weight of Architecture

76 Milan Kundera, *The Unbearable Lightness of Being*, trans. Michael Henry Heim (New York: Harper & Row, 1984), 5.

77 Vesely, "Architecture and Conflict," 22.

78 This summary is certainly a glib and truncated assessment of complex historical events, but I believe it to be essentially accurate for the present purposes. For a more detailed treatment see Joseph Rykwert, *The First Moderns* (Cambridge, MA: MIT Press, 1980) and Alberto Perez-Gomez, *Architecture and the Crisis of Modern Science* (Cambridge, MA: MIT Press, 1983).

79 See, for example, the description of the Australian aborigines' *waninga* in Joseph Rykwert, *On Adam's House in Paradise* (Cambridge, MA: MIT Press, 1981), 183–92.

80 I have, largely for rhetorical reasons, rejected the distinction some authors make between "significance" and "meaning." I do not dismiss the value of their distinction; however, I felt it an unnecessary complication for the present essay, particularly because it is not followed by many of the sources I cite.

81 Genesis 11: 7–9.

82 See the essay "Active Architecture from Christo to Christmas Trees" in this collection.

83 Genesis 11:6.

84 Ernst Cassirer, *Language*, trans. Ralph Mannheim, vol. 1 of *The Philosophy of Symbolic Forms* (New Haven: Yale University Press, 1955), 158.

85 See, for example, the essay "Deconstructivist Architecture" in the Museum of Modern Art exhibit catalog by the same name (Boston: Little, Brown and Company, 1988), 10–20. In it author Mark Wigley presents dubious assertions such as "the form is distorting itself," and claims that buildings whose visual appearance suggests aggressive fragmentation must produce feelings "of unease, of disquiet, because [they challenge] the sense of stable coherent identity that we associate with pure form"(17). Even more suspect is Wigley's statement "architecture is a conservative discipline that produces pure form and protects it from contamination"(10).

86 British mathematician G. Spencer-Brown has made an ingenious attempt to establish a universal system of signification that not only tolerates but is capable of embracing ambiguity. This new "calculus," introduced in the volume *Laws of Form* (New York: E. P. Dutton, 1972), amazingly proceeds from a most basic gesture of indication. Spencer-Brown's calculus contains only two terms: "marked" and "unmarked." Because the act of marking (or "calling") is an ambiguous gesture, Spencer-Brown's system could be said to proceed from a more fundamental state of language than that of meanings assigned on the basis of abstract convention. Unlike the binary opposites that are the basis for computer languages, Spencer-Brown's alternative states can preserve imaginative, as opposed to strictly rational, distinctions (such as, from my Tower of Babel example, the distinction between sacred and profane). Representing distinctions is, in fact, all

The Valor of Iron (contd.)

Spencer-Brown's system does; it attempts to produce a system of notation without a point of view. What knowledge I do possess of *Laws of Form* I owe to my Penn State colleagues Donald Kunze and James Martin, who conducted a *Laws of Form* seminar in the Department of Architecture during the summer of 1995.

87 Donald Kunze, "From Either/Or to Both/And," *Journal of Architecture & Planning Research* 8 (1991): 92–6.

88 Frascari, *Monsters of Architecture*, 106.

89 Gaston Bachelard, *The Poetics of Space*, trans. Maria Jolas (Orion Press, 1964; reprint, Boston: Beacon Press, 1969), xi–xii.

90 Robin Evans, "Not to be Used for Wrapping Purposes," *AA Files* 10 (1985): 72.

91 Ibid.

92 Hellmut and Richard Wilhelm, *Understanding the I Ching*, trans. Cary F. Baynes and Irene Eber (Princeton, NJ: Princeton University Press, 1995), 25–6, my emphasis.

93 Galileo Galilei, *"Dialago sopra i due massimi sistimi, giornata I,"* quoted in Italo Calvino, *Time and the Hunter*, trans. William Weaver (London: Picador, 1993), 58.

94 Charles Darwin, *The Autobiography of Charles Darwin*, appendix and notes by Nora Barlow (London: Collins, 1958), 138–9.

95 Gaston Bachelard, *Air and Dreams*, translation of *L'Air et les songes, essai sur l'imagination du movement* (1943), trans. Edith R. and Frederick Farrell (Dallas: Dallas Institute Publications, 1988), 7.

96 Gaston Bachelard, *The Poetics of Reverie*, translation of *La Poétique de la Rêverie* (1960), trans. Daniel Russell (Boston: Beacon Press, 1969), 5.

97 Bachelard, *Air and Dreams*, 2.

98 Frank Lloyd Wright, "In the Cause of Architecture: Composition as a Method of Creation" (1928), in Bruce Pfeiffer, ed., *Frank Lloyd Wright: Collected Writings*, vol. 1 (New York: Rizzoli, 1992), 259.

99 Erwin Panofsky, *Meaning in the Visual Arts* (New York: Doubleday Anchor Books, 1955), 1.

100 Walter Benjamin, "On Language as Such and on the Language of Man," *Reflections*, trans. Edmund Jephcott (New York: Schocken Books, 1986), 314.

101 Joseph Rykwert, *The Necessity of Artifice* (New York: Rizzoli, 1982), 23.

102 Cassirer, *Language*, 180.

103 Maurice Merleau-Ponty, *Phenomenology of Perception*, trans. Colin Smith (London: Routledge & Kegan Paul, 1962), 189.

104 Italo Calvino, *Six Memos for the Next Millennium* (Cambridge, MA: Harvard University Press, 1988), 5.

105 Ibid., 12.

106 Italo Calvino, *Invisible Cities*, trans. William Weaver (New York: Harcourt Brace Jovanovich, 1974).

107 Calvino, *Six Memos*, 8.

108 Ibid., 3.

109 "Ambiguity" is not used here to mean vague, equivocal, or indistinct—although I recognize common usage allows for these interpretations. I use "ambiguous" to refer only to the condition where two or more meanings coexist My familiarity with this practice and this distinction I owe to Donald Kunze.

110 Merleau-Ponty, *Phenomenology of Perception*, 188.

111 Joseph Rykwert, *The Dancing Column: On Order in Architecture* (Cambridge, MA: MIT Press, 1996).

112 Cassirer, *Language*, 181.

113 Donald Philip Verene, *Vico's Science of Imagination* (Ithaca, NY: Cornell University Press, 1981), 211.

114 Cassirer, *Language*, 183.

115 Verene, *Vico's Science*, 210.

116 Cassirer, *Language*, 182.

117 Marco Frascari establishes the connection between Vico's thought and demonstrations in his *Monsters of Architecture*.

118 Maurice Merleau-Ponty, *The Visible and the Invisible*, ed. Claude Lefort, trans. Alphonso Lingus (Evanston, IL: Northwestern University Press, 1968), 155.

119 Marco Frascari, lecture to the Pennsylvania State University Department of Architecture, 20 April 1992.

120 George Lakoff and Mark Johnson, *Metaphors We Live By* (Chicago: University of Chicago Press, 1980), 3.

121 Mark Johnson, *The Body in the Mind* (Chicago: University of Chicago Press, 1987), xv.

122 See Paul Ricoeur, *Hermeneutics and the Human Sciences*, trans. John B. Thompson (Cambridge: Cambridge University Press, 1981), 170.

123 Lakoff and Johnson provide several examples of metonymy in everyday speech, including (with the metonymical phrase italicized): "The *ham sandwich* is waiting for his check," "The *Times* hasn't arrived at the press conference yet," and "I've got a new *set of wheels.*"

124 Edgar Allan Poe, "The Coliseum," *The Complete Poetry and Selected Criticism of Edgar Allan Poe*, ed. Allen Tate (New York: New American Library, 1968), 79.

125 Donald Kunze, "Thin Architecture, Thick Banquets," lecture to the Pennsylvania State University Department of Architecture, 3 March 1993.

126 My colleague Katsuhiko Muramoto is fond of saying—and I am sure he is loosely quoting a source that I cannot identify—"the first poet to compare a woman's cheek to the petal of a rose may have been a creative genius, but all those who have repeated the comparison are unimaginative idiots."

127 Moshen Mostafavi and David Leatherbarrow, *On Weathering: The Life of Buildings in Time* (Cambridge, MA: MIT Press, 1993), 47.

128 Frascari, *Monsters of Architecture*, 7.

129 Marco Frascari, "A New Corporeality of Architecture," *Journal of Architectural Education*, vol. 40/no. 2 (Washington, DC: Association of Collegiate Schools of Architecture, 1987), 22.

130 Donald Kunze, "The Thickness of the Past: The Metonymy of Possession," *Intersight* 3 (1995).

131 Frascari, *Monsters of Architecture*, 111.

132 Tafuri, *Architecture and Utopia*, 176.

133 Frascari, *Monsters of Architecture*, 11.

134 I disassociate myself from any "typological" theories of architecture. I use the term "archetype" in the sense of something that appears to be fundamental, much as human birth and death are fundamental. The act of piling one layer of stones upon another, creating a construction that narrows as it rises, is as close to an archetypal building activity as I can imagine.

135 This statement does not apply to flat roofs having gardens on them, or those providing space for sleeping in the cool evening air, as the roofs of traditional houses in Baghdad often have. Gideon Golany, *Babylonian Jewry: Culture, Neighborhood, and Home* (unpublished manuscript).

136 Douglas Baglin & Yvonne Austin, *Galvo Country* (Sydney: Ure Smith, 1979), 5.

137 Cited in Edward R. Ford, *The Details of Modern Architecture*, vol. 2, *1928 to 1988* (Cambridge, MA: MIT Press, 1996), 359.

138 Bachelard, *Air and Dreams*, 15.

139 Ibid.

140 Calvino, *Invisible Cities*, 82.

141 Bachelard, *Water and Dreams*, 13.

142 Ibid., 2.

The Emerald City

143 L. Frank Baum, *The Wonderful Wizard of Oz* (1900; reprint, New York: Scholastic Books, 1958).

144 I realize this may have been because Baum was attempting to *satirize* rather than fantasize.

145 Mayor Giuliani offered this opinion (in jest) on "The David Letterman Show."

146 Joseph Rykwert, *The Idea of a Town* (Princeton, NJ: Princeton University Press, 1976; reprint, Cambridge, MA: MIT Press, 1988).

147 Taussig, *Mimesis and Alterity*, 86.

148 This observation was offered by Donald Kunze in a graduate seminar he offered at Penn State University in Fall 1996, where I presented an earlier version of this paper.

Active Architecture from Christo to Christmas Trees

149 Francesca Rogier, "Growing Pains: From the Opening of the Wall to the Wrapping of the Reichstag," *Assemblage* 29 (April 1996): 66.

150 Ibid.

151 Quoted in Jacob Baal-Teschuva, *Christo & Jean-Claude* (Cologne: Benedikt Taschen, 1995), 85.

152 Quoted in Baal-Teschuva, *Christo & Jean-Claude*, 9, my emphasis.

153 Rogier, "Growing Pains," 66.

154 Suzi Gablik, *Has Modernism Failed?* (New York: Thames and Hudson, 1988), 34.

155 Quoted in Rogier, "Growing Pains," 86.

156 Walt Whitman, "A Song for Occupations," *Walt Whitman: Selected Poems* (New York: Gramercy Books, 1992), 95.

157 Calvino, *Invisible Cities*, 82.

158 Rykwert, *Dancing Column*, 391.

159 Illich, *Tools for Conviviality*.

160 See the following essay, "Vernacular Architecture and the Economics of Dwelling," for an initial sketch of this theory.

161 Lewis Hyde, *The Gift: Imagination and the Erotic Life of Property* (New York: Vintage Books, 1983).

162 Whitman, "Song for Occupations," 88.

163 See George Hersey, *The Lost Meaning of Classical Architecture* (Cambridge, MA: MIT Press, 1988), 4.

164 Ibid., 1–45.

165 Taussig, *Mimesis and Alterity*.

166 Any work is open to multiple interpretations, whether its creator wishes it to be or not. This is not what I am calling an "open work." The difference is that the truly open work may offer multiple readings, but these do not necessarily undermine or substitute for the preferred reading of the author. Instead, the author's intentions constitute one possible meaning, which other equally plausible readings do not refute. An open work allows us to simultaneously entertain multiple interpretations of a work.

167 This succinct statement, as well as the time machine idea, were suggested to me by Penn State professor of philosophy Daniel Conway.

168 Bachelard, *Air and Dreams*, 2.

Vernacular Architecture and the Economics of Dwelling

169 The claim that the object created, the barn, is roughly equal in importance to the event of its creation may at first seem debatable. However, the most notable feature of the Amish barns—the reason that they are known to most of us—concerns the way they are constructed, not any particular aspect of the barns themselves.

Vernacular Architecture and Economics (contd.)

170 "Modernity," as I will use it for the purposes of this essay, is not so much a historical period as a set of assumptions about the world. While I can define a set of assumptions as characteristically "modern," I cannot identify a historical period or geographic area where these assumptions are ever adopted totally, or without question.

171 Edward Tenner, *Why Things Bite Back* (New York: Vintage Books, 1997), 33–4. Tenner attributes this phrase to Aaron Wildavsky.

172 Since I will often be using the terms "conviviality" and "sustainability," the following distinction needs to be made: while I will use the two words interchangeably, I consider "conviviality" to be the broader term. Sustainability (conventionally understood to refer to sustainable environments) is, to me, a function of conviviality. Conviviality connotes a "friendly" relationship with both nature and one's fellow human beings.

173 Illich, *Tools for Conviviality*, 89.

174 Victor Hugo, *The Hunchback of Notre-Dame*, English translation of *Notre-Dame de Paris* (1830; reprint, Philadelphia: Running Press, 1995), 154, my emphasis.

175 In a "pure" society of vernacular builders, there might not be even an opportunity cost associated with "vernacular labor," as the close match between a task and the time "proper" for it ("a time for every purpose under heaven") would preclude any alternative productive activity. The quotation marks around "vernacular labor" indicate that this is, according to my point of view, a contradiction in terms, since vernacular production involves work, not labor. For more on the distinction between work and labor see the essay "The Work of Architecture in the Age of Efficient Production" in this collection.

176 Quoted in Taussig, *Mimesis and Alterity*, 92–3.

177 Ibid., 74–5.

178 Giambattista Vico, *New Science*, trans. Thomas Goddard Bergin and Max Harold Fisch (Ithaca, NY: Cornell University Press, 1948; reprint, 1984), 75.

179 Taussig, *Mimesis and Alterity*, 93.

180 Ibid., 94.

181 Hyde, *Gift*.

182 Illich, *Tools for Conviviality*, 11, my emphasis.

183 Jan Yoors, quoted in Isabel Fonseca, *Bury Me Standing: The Gypsies and Their Journey* (New York: Vintage Books, 1995), 53.

184 See for example Lisa Jardin, *Worldly Goods* (New York: Nan A. Talese/Doubleday, 1996).

185 Alfred W. Crosby, *The Measure of Reality: Quantification and Western Society, 1250–1600* (Cambridge: Cambridge University Press, 1997), 52.

186 Hugo, *Notre-Dame*, 241.

187 Fonseca, *Bury Me Standing*, 30.

188 Ibid., 29.

189 Illich, H_2O *and Waters*, 10.

190 Jerzy Ficowski, quoted in Fonseca, *Bury Me Standing*, 231.

191 Adolf Loos, "The Poor Little Rich Man," *Spoken Into the Void: Collected Essays 1897–1900*, trans. Jane O. Newman and John H. Smith (Cambridge, MA: MIT Press, 1982), 127.

192 Illich, *Tools for Conviviality*, 40.

193 Martin Heidegger, "Building Dwelling Thinking," *Poetry, Language, Thought*, trans. Albert Hofstader (New York: Harper & Row, 1971), 145–61.

194 Illich, *H2O and Waters*, 8.

195 Stephen Parcell, "The World in Front of the Work," *Journal of Architectural Education*, vol. 46, no. 4 (May 1993): 257.

196 Bachelard, *The Poetics of Space*, 61.

197 Hugo, *Notre-Dame*, 252.

198 Ibid., 249–50.

199 Ibid., 203.

200 Ibid., 121.

201 Norman O. Brown, *Hermes the Thief: The Evolution of a Myth* (University of Wisconsin Press, 1947; reprint, Great Barrington, MA: Lindisfarne Press, 1990), 41.

202 Ibid.

203 Georg Simmel, "Exchange," in Donald N. Levine, ed., *On Individuality and Social Forms* (Chicago: University of Chicago Press, 1971), 44.

204 Bernard Rudofsky, *Architecture Without Architects* (New York: Museum of Modern Art, 1965).

205 Bachelard, *Water and Dreams*, 6–7.

206 Jacques Ellul, *The Technological Bluff*, trans. Geoffrey W. Bromiley (Grand Rapids, MI: William B. Eerdmans, 1990), 7.

207 Lisa Heschong, *Thermal Delight in Architecture* (Cambridge, MA: MIT Press, 1979), 16.

208 Kenneth Frampton, "Towards a Critical Regionalism: Six Points for an Architecture of Resistance," in Hal Foster, ed., *The Anti-Aesthetic: Essays on Postmodern Culture* (Port Townsend, WA: Bay Press, 1983), 27.

209 The sole exception to this are the very highly skilled specialists, such as the French *Les Compagnons*, who work on the highest profile, and highest cost, restorations of monuments or historic buildings.

210 George B. Johnston, "Value Engineering or Architecture in the Pursuit of Happiness," *The Proceedings of the 85th Annual Meeting and Technology Conference* (Washington DC: American Collegiate Schools of Architecture, 1998), 539.

211 Joseph Rykwert, "Meaning and Building" (1957), in *The Necessity of Artifice* (London: Academy Editions for Rizzoli International, 1982), 16.

212 Ibid.

213 Christina Rouvalis, "Shopping by Design," *Pittsburgh Post-Gazette*, 23 March 1997, D-4.

214 Jacques Ellul, *The Technological Society*, trans. John Wilkinson (New York: Alfred A. Knopf, 1964; reprint, New York: Vintage Books, 1964), 219.

215 This question of size was the driving principle behind E. F. Schumacher's well-known piece of economic heresy, *Small is Beautiful: Economics as if People Mattered* (London: Blond & Briggs, 1973; reprint, New York: Harper & Row, 1989).

216 Bachelard, *Poetics of Space*, 51.

Gendered Words, Neutered Spaces

217 See "Vernacular Architecture and the Economics of Dwelling" and "The Work of Architecture in the Age of Efficient Production" in this volume for the arguments to support this claim.

218 The connection between authority and the standardization of language is explicitly evident in the efforts of Spanish grammarian Elio Antonio de Nebrija to convince Queen Isabella, in 1492, to adopt and officially impose his Castilian grammar on the populace of Spain. His argument was that by eliminating vernacular variations in speech, the queen's authority would be both consolidated and made systematic. The attack on the vernacular would "give the monarch's power increased range and duration." See Ivan Illich and Barry Sanders, *ABC: The Alphabetization of the Popular Mind* (New York: Vintage Books, 1989), 65–70. The phrase "the King's English" suggests another connection between authority and standardized language.

219 Illich, *Tools for Conviviality*, 89–90.

220 Fonseca, *Bury Me Standing*, 58.

221 Gaston Bachelard, *The Poetics of Reverie*, trans. Daniel Russel (Grossman Publishers, 1969; reprint, Boston: Beacon Press, 1971), 29.

222 Gabriel García Márquez, *Love in the Time of Cholera*, trans. Edith Grossman (New York: Penguin Books, 1988), 167, my emphasis.

223 Ellul, *Technological Society*, 219.

224 He might have added poverty. The only book Poe ever published to make it beyond a first edition was an elementary school science text on seashells, for which he received $50—and he actually wrote only the introduction. In 1845, he earned $8 from his publisher for one of the most famous poems ever written in English, *The Raven*.

225 Saul Bellow, *Humboldt's Gift*, quoted in Hyde, *Gift*, 240–1.

226 Despite its etymological connection to the *corpus*, the modern corporation is, by contrast, a legal entity invented to *avoid* just this sort of personal accountability, as is signaled by the once-popular corporate designation "Ltd.," for "limited," as in "limited liability."

227 Illich, *In the Mirror of the Past* (New York: Marion Boyars, 1992), 172–4.

228 Crosby, *Measure of Reality*, 124.

229 Hugo, *Notre-Dame*, 249.

230 Cited in Rykwert, *Dancing Column*, 93.

231 David Leatherbarrow, *The Roots of Architectural Invention: Site, Enclosure, Materials* (Cambridge: Cambridge University Press, 1993), 107.

232 Gaston Bachelard, *The Poetics of Space*, trans. Maria Jolas (Orion Press, 1964; reprint, Boston: Beacon Press, 1969).

233 Gaston Bachelard, *Gaston Bachelard: Subversive Humanist*, translation of *L'Intuition de l'instant* (Paris: Stock, 1932), trans. and comp. Mary McAllester Jones (Madison, WI: University of Wisconsin Press, 1991), 35.

234 Bachelard, *Poetics of Reverie*, 6.

235 Bachelard, *Air and Dreams*, 266.

236 George Simmel, "The Metropolis and Mental Life," *On Individuality and Social Forms*, ed. Donald N. Levine (Chicago: University of Chicago Press, 1971), 325.

237 Gaston Bachelard, *La Terre at les rêveries de la volonté* (Paris: Corti, 1943), 80–1, cited in Richard Kearney, *The Poetics of Imagining* (London: Harper Collins Academic, 1991), 93.

238 Kearney, *Poetics of Imagining*, 93.

239 Illich, *Mirror of the Past*, 181. Illich uses the term, "Island of the Alphabet." I have substituted "text" for "alphabet" because this terminology aligns more closely those of my other sources.

240 Bachelard, *Water and Dreams*, 2.

241 Bachelard, *Poetics of Reverie*, 60.

242 Cited in Bachelard, *Poetics of Space*, 45.

243 Manuela Antoniu, "The Walled-Up Bride," in Debra Coleman, Elizabeth Danze, and Carol Henderson, eds., *Architecture and Feminism* (New York: Princeton Architectural Press, 1996), 109–29.

244 Claudio Scarbi, "The Architect's Belly," in Nadir Lahiji and D. S. Friedman, eds., *Plumbing: Sounding Modern Architecture* (New York: Princeton Architectural Press, 1997), 185.

245 These connections, between architecture and building processes/building materials, and between the social construct gender and male and female bodies, are "corporeal," but not *direct*. They are not simple *transitive* or *projective* relationships. (More on transitivity soon, in this essay.)

Gendered Words, Neutered Spaces (contd.)

246 Ivan Illich, *Gender* (Berkeley: Heyday Books, 1982), 122.

247 This is not to claim that the strict gender roles in traditional societies were "equal." A comparison between modern attempts to promote "gender equity" and traditional gender roles forces us, just as when comparing technological to pretechnological societies, to evaluate situations lacking a common point of reference. Modern women may have gained nearly full status as members of *homo economicus*, but may have lost their ability to dwell comfortably in their own bodies; women in traditional societies suffered no such disorientation, but they were trapped in social roles that often strike our contemporary consciousness as cruelly oppressive. In *Gender*, Illich tried to show that the form of gender equity that results from transforming men and women to the neuter *homo economicus* would not necessarily lead to a humane form of equality.

248 Illich, *Gender*, 81.

249 Donald Kunze, "Poché," in Nadir Lahiji and D. S. Friedman, eds., *Plumbing: Sounding Modern Architecture* (New York: Princeton Architectural Press, 1997), 137–62.

250 Ken Kesey, *One Flew Over the Cuckoo's Nest* (New York: Signet Books, 1962), 11.

251 Paul Walker Clarke, "Dwelling, Housing, and Gentrification," *Proceedings of the 81st Annual Meeting* (Washington, DC: Association of Collegiate Schools of Architecture, 1993), 393.

252 David Cayley, *Ivan Illich in Conversation* (Concord, Ontario: House of Anasi Press, 1992), 31.

253 Andres Duany, "Urban or Suburban," *Harvard Design Magazine* (Winter/Spring 1997): 48.

254 Because I agree with some, but not all, of the goals underlying the new urbanist movement, it is tempting to distinguish these from the techniques or devices (like codes) designed to achieve them. However, as Duany's zealous enthusiasm for codes suggests, there is not a simple cause-and-effect relationship between goals and techniques. The technique of a code is not neutral. Like all techniques, codes tend to change the way we look at the sphere in which the technique operates. The "goals" the new urbanists pursue are influenced by their assumptions regarding the techniques they believe they can employ. Since these assumptions do not include, for example, the distinction between gifts and commodities, or the double sense of the word "fabrication," their goals pay little attention to the conditions under which buildings and towns are *made*. Even when codes are structured as performance specifications, as opposed to rigid prescriptive rules, the criteria for evaluating performances they contain will generally rely on quantitative measures. The only way out of this trap is to propose performance criteria that are ambiguous signs that must be interpreted, much as is done in the traditional Chinese practice of *feng shui*. See the essay "The Weight of Architecture" in this collection for a brief discussion of why this is so.

255 I was tempted here to borrow Kenneth Frampton's term, the "trans-avant garde," to distinguish architects who may boldly experiment with building shapes, but who accept the conventions of contemporary building production as given, from more authentic revolutionaries. I refer here to the former meaning.

256 Bachelard, *Poetics of Space*, 235.

257 David Harvey, "The New Urbanism and the Communitarian Trap," *Harvard Design Magazine* (Winter/Spring 1997): 68, 69.

258 Russ Rymer, "Back to the Future: Disney Reinvents the Company Town," *Harper's* (October 1996): 65–78.

259 Lucien Kroll, *An Architecture of Complexity*, trans. Peter Blundell Jones (Cambridge, MA: MIT Press, 1987), 25.

260 Martin Heidegger, " . . . Poetically Man Dwells . . . ," in Neil Leach, ed., *Rethinking Architecture* (London: Routledge, 1997), 114.

261 Frascari, *Monsters of Architecture*, 106.

262 Heidegger, " . . . Poetically Man Dwells . . . ," 117.

263 The "truth to materials" argument errs by presuming there can be a purely projective, transitive relationship between building and dwelling. For an in-depth discussion, see the essay "The Valor of Iron" in this volume.

264 Charles Moore, Gerald Allen, and Donlyn Lyndon, *The Place of Houses* (New York: Holt, Rinehart and Winston, 1974), 20.

265 Harvey, "New Urbanism," 69.

266 Sennett, *Fall of Public Man*, 295–6.

267 Bruce Krajewski, *Traveling with Hermes* (Amherst, MA: University of Massachusetts Press, 1992), 47.

268 Vittorio Gregotti, *Inside Architecture* (Cambridge, MA: MIT Press, 1996), 24.

269 Scarbi, "Architect's Belly," 197.

The Contradictions Underlying the Profession

270 Kenneth Frampton, "Reflections on the Autonomy of Architecture," in Diane Ghirardo, ed., *Out of Site: A Social Criticism of Architecture* (Seattle: Bay Press, 1991), 17.

271 Joseph Rykwert, *The First Moderns* (Cambridge, MA: MIT Press, 1983), 15.

272 Vesely, "Architecture and Conflict," 21–38.

273 Robert Venturi, Denise Scott Brown, and Steven Izenour, *Learning from Las Vegas* (Cambridge, MA: MIT Press, 1977), 93.

274 Marco Frascari, "A New Angel/Angle in Architectural Research: The Ideas of Demonstration," *Journal of Architectural Education*, vol. 44 no. 1 (November 1990): 11–9.

275 Edward R. Ford describes the construction that would be required by Coop Himmelblau's unbuilt "Open House," a project that began with a sketch drawn with closed eyes: "While the inner floor is parallel to the ground and the walls are perpendicular to it, the outer walls, soffit, and roof are not. This necessitates two sets of joists and studs in some locations. The irregular corners of the steel frame were [intended to be] shop-welded for greater strength and accuracy, necessitating bolted field splices of the resulting L-shaped pieces, and the wood framing is rarely at right angles to the steel, making a complex arrangement of blocking and double joists necessary." From *Details of Modern Architecture*, 405.

276 Harries, "Building and Terror," 59–69.

277 Roy Sheldon and Egmont Arens, *Consumer Engineering* (New York, 1932), 61, quoted in Stuart Ewen, *All Consuming Images* (New York: Basic Books, 1988), 51.

278 Henry-Russell Hitchcock and Philip Johnson, *The International Style* (New York: W. W. Norton & Company, 1932; reprint, 1966), 50–5.

279 Jean-Louis Bourgeois, *Spectacular Vernacular: The Adobe Tradition* (New York: Aperture Foundation, 1996), 166–74.

280 Cited in Roland L. Schachel, "Ornament kein verbrechen," *Arkitekt* (September 1994): 499–502.

281 Mostafavi and Leatherbarrow, *On Weathering*, 86.

282 Umberto Eco, *Six Walks in the Fictional Woods* (Cambridge, MA: Harvard University Press, 1994), 8.

283 Kenneth S. Lynn, ed., *The Professions in America* (Boston: Beacon Press, 1967), 9.

284 Margaret Crawford, "Can Architects Be Socially Responsible?" in Diane Ghirardo, ed., *Out of Site: A Social Criticism of Architecture* (Seattle: Bay Press, 1991), 28.

285 Ivan Illich, et. al., *Disabling Professions* (London: Marion Boyers, 1977), 11–39.

286 James S. Russell, "Nine Months of Research and Development Yield Stone Fabrication Innovation," *Architectural Record* 185 (November 1997): 102–3.

287 Robert Venturi, *Complexity and Contradiction* (New York: Museum of Modern Art, 1966), 20–1.

288 Crawford, "Can Architects Be," 29.

289 Hugo, *Notre-Dame*, 249–50.

290 Marco Frascari, "The Tell-The-Tale Detail," *VIA* 7 (1984): 23.

291 Adolf Loos, "Building Materials," *Spoken Into the Void: Collected Essays 1897–1900*, trans. Jane O. Newman & John H. Smith (Cambridge, MA: MIT Press, 1982), 63.

292 Kearney, *Poetics of Imagining*, 93.

293 For architecture to be an "open work," it must share with an open literary work not only a sort of textual ambiguity but also an ability to embrace (that is, trope) the inevitable effects of material and social change. In literature the abstraction we call "text" remains stable, while the context (or world in front of the work) is always changing; in architecture *both* the text and the context are always changing. (The timeless abstraction "the text" does not actually exist, just as the ideal drawings of a building do not exist, although texts that appear on the Internet, or CAD-drawing files, approximate these ideal conditions. As my editor, Clare Jacobson, has helpfully pointed out, there is a materiality to all published books. We react differently to a rare antique book than we do to a newly printed volume.) In order for a work of architecture to permanently produce the same reading, it would have to continually change in response to its shifting context. The most successful compositional rigorist works, such as Peter Eisenman's Wexner Center in Columbus Ohio, benefit from needing to satisfy functional programs requiring them to accommodate change. In the case of the Wexner, this is the need to house a range (albeit a fairly narrow range) of temporary artistic exhibits. In this instance, the poor little rich man is allowed to bring new paintings into his house.

294 Peter Davey, "The Erosion of Public and Personal Spaces," in William S. Saunders, ed. *Reflections on Architectural Practice in the Nineties* (New York: Princeton Architectural Press, 1996), 115.

295 Klaus Herdeg, *The Decorated Diagram: Harvard Architecture and the Failure of the Bauhaus Legacy* (Cambridge, MA: MIT Press, 1983).

296 "A Major Insurer No Longer Underwrites Synthetic Stucco," *Fine Homebuilding* (January 1997): 40.

297 I suspect the success of the 1916 New York Zoning Ordinance, requiring tall buildings to decrease in size as they increased in height, in order to stay within the confines of the "zoning envelope," owes much to the fact that the law imposed on architects the necessity to configure the building in a more-or-less pyramidal shape. Hugh Ferriss was perhaps the first to realize the poetic potential of this restriction. Ferriss's drawings revealed that the zoning law had restored the need for buildings to taper as they rose upward; this phenomenon, which masonry construction naturally

The Contradictions Underlying the Profession (contd.)
necessitated, but which had been made obsolete by the
steel frame, had always permitted masonry towers to re-
present the process of their own becoming, as well as to
demonstrate the effects of gravity and wind on a tall
structure in a manner that was "pervious to every soul."
That is, the stepped masonry tower, the ziggurat, is an
artificial re-presentation, a metonymical trope, of a
mountain. Because these archetypal structures elicit
connotations of a heroic struggle skyward, Ferriss's renderings illustrated how well fitted the ziggurat was to
construe the power and promise of corporate capitalism. And even though it was not technically necessary
for the steel-framed towers to adopt the wide base/nar-
row top shape, it did provide *some* benefit, mostly in
terms of resistance to lateral forces, as the unclad skele-
ton of the Eiffel Tower shows. Therefore, the ziggurat
towers were not merely representations of an outmoded
construction system; they were, at least partially, authentic architectural tropes—good lies—in their own right.

298 Carol Willis, *Form Follows Finance* (New York:
Princeton Architectural Press, 1995).

299 Robert Hughes, *Barcelona* (New York: Alfred A.
Knopf, 1992), 464–581.

300 Tafuri, *Architecture and Utopia*, 177–8.

301 Rykwert, "Meaning and Building," 12.

302 Manfredo Tafuri, *The Sphere and the Labyrinth*,
trans. Pellegrino d'Acierno and Robert Connolly
(Cambridge, MA: MIT Press, 1990), 288–9.

303 As I write, thanks to the late-nineties economic
boom, architectural services are in great demand, and
architects are being well compensated for their labors.
However, this economic prosperity has masked the
continual dissolving of the terms of our professional
truce: institutions that solicit the services of architects
now routinely refer to these parties as "bidders"; architect's fees as a percentage of construction cost continue
to shrink, as does the time allotted for design investiga-
tion in most firms; and marketing takes up an ever
larger portion of the typical firm's budget.

304 Vico, *New Science*, 424.

305 Herbert Marcuse, *One-Dimensional Man* (New
York: Beacon Press, 1964).

Seven Strategies for Making Architecture

306 Stewart Brand, *How Buildings Learn* (New York:
Penguin Books, 1995), 188. This otherwise superb
book is marred only by the author's overly functionalis-
tic definition of "architecture."

307 Sir John Summerson, *Heavenly Mansions* (New
York: W. W. Norton & Company, 1963), 238.

308 The term comes from the writings and teaching
of Donald Kunze.

309 See "The Impact of the Computer on Architectural Practice" in this volume.

310 In large-scale construction projects in the U.S.,
the trend is for the owner to engage a construction
manager, who uses a partial set of construction documents, usually about eighty or ninety percent complete,
in order to offer the owner a guaranteed maximum
price. This price, the "GMP," often contains a number
of "allowances" to accommodate areas of work that
remain uncertain.

311 Dana Buntrock, "Collaborative Production:
Building Opportunities in Japan," *Journal of
Architectural Education* vol. 50 no. 4 (May 1997): 222.

312 I owe my awareness of this fact to my colleague,
Katsuhiko Muramoto.

313 Martin Wagner, "The Socialization of Building
Activity," in Manfredo Tafuri, *The Sphere and the
Labyrinth* (Cambridge, MA: MIT Press, 1987; reprint,
1990), 234–63.

314 Bernard Tschumi, *Architecture and Disjunction*
(Cambridge, MA: MIT Press, 1994), 123.

315 William W. Braham, "Correalism and
Equipoise: Kiesler and Giedion on the Sustainable," in
R. Cambell-Howe and B. Wilkins-Crowder, eds.,
Proceedings of the 22nd National Passive Solar Conference,
vol. 22 (Washington, DC: American Solar Energy
Society and the American Institute of Architects
Committee on the Environment, 1997), 163.

316 Patrice Goulet, "Wild and Uncertain Times:
Team Zoo's Savoir-Faire," in Manfred Speidel, ed.,
Team Zoo: Buildings and Projects 1971–1990 (New York:
Rizzoli, 1991), 23.

317 Cited in Robert Adams Ivy, Jr., *Fay Jones*
(Washington, D.C.: American Institute of Architects
Press, 1992), 35.

318 Hyde, *Gift*, 274–5.

319 Goulet, "Wild and Uncertain," 23.

320 Frank Gehry, "Detailing," *Terrazzo* 2 (1989): 60.

321 Owen Edwards, "Curvilinear Crusader," *Forbes
ASAP*, 4 December 1995, p. 94.

322 Ford, *Details of Modern Architecture*, 407–11.

323 I mention expense in connection with the construction of Gehry's buildings because Gehry's recent
design methodology all but insures that his work will
be affordable to only the wealthiest clients. While we
could easily imagine a "Usonian" version (after Frank
Lloyd Wright's small middle-class house designs by the
same name) of Gehry's early houses, perhaps fur-
nished with his cardboard chairs, no such affordable
versions of Gehry's latest designs are possible.

324 Lucien Kroll, *Architecture of Complexity*, 31.

325 Thomas B. Allen, *Offerings at the Wall:
Artifacts from the Vietnam Veterans Memorial Collection*,

(Atlanta: Turner Publishing, 1995).

326 Verene, *Vico's Science*, 216.

327 Adolf Michaelis, quoted in Summerson, *Heavenly Mansions*, 95.

328 Scarbi, "Architect's Belly," 188.

329 I believe Jersey Devil's built works tend toward kitsch, while Mercer's do not, because—despite the fact that Jersey Devil builds its own designs—they do not seem to learn and improvise from their materials. Works such as their Helmut House seem to be conceived from the outset as finished forms. The specific circumstances of their construction do not seem to modify or trope the initial concept to the degree necessary for them to become demonstrations (see strategy seven) of poetic building.

330 John Connell, *Homing Instinct: Using Your Lifestyle to Design and Build Your Home* (New York: Warner Books, 1993).

331 Giuseppe Zambonini, "Notes for a Theory of Making in a Time of Necessity," *Perspecta: The Yale Architectural Journal* 24 (1988): 23.

332 Perez-Gomez, *Architecture and Crisis*, 191.

333 Hannah Arendt, *The Human Condition* (Chicago: University of Chicago Press, 1958), 102–9.

334 For example, in John Hejduk's "masque" projects, the weight of building is replaced by weight of another sort, such as the burden of guilt borne by those who must dwell with the memory of the Holocaust.

335 Wim van den Bergh, "Icarus' Amazement, or the Matrix of Crossed Destinies," in John Hejduk, *The Lancaster/Hanover Masque* (London: Architectural Association, 1992), 83–4.

336 Robert Harbison, *Eccentric Spaces* (New York: Knopf, 1977; reprint, New York: David R. Godine, 1988), 22.

337 van den Bergh, "Icarus' Amazement," 87–8.

338 Hejduk, *Lancaster/Hanover Masque*, 22.

339 Frascari, "New Angel/Angle," 12.

340 Frascari, *Monsters of Architecture*, 109.

341 Ibid., 92.

Work of Architecture in the Age of Efficient Production

342 Mark Twain, *The Adventures of Tom Sawyer* (New York: Random House Value Publishing, 1989), 14.

343 Arendt, *Human Condition*, 80.

344 Ibid., 87.

345 Ibid., 136.

346 Ibid., 145.

347 It is interesting that Arendt barely mentions play in *The Human Condition*, since it would seem to fit neatly into her category of "action." When it appears (127), it is used to argue against defining any activity that is not labor as "play." Arendt is protesting an over-simplification very similar to the conventional contemporary practice of subsuming everything that is not labor under the category of "leisure."

348 I am not claiming that the slaves were entirely successful in their efforts to turn labor into work, or that they might have actually enjoyed what they were forced to do, only that their singing, coupled with their dreams of escape, helped to make their situation bearable. It is also true, as Arendt maintained, that we must be careful not to mistake all such coordinated social activity as a sign of imaginative freedom, and therefore of at least the attempt to turn labor into fulfilling work. Under some oppressive conditions, people may perform in concert, even singing or marching together, but this will be a mindless activity of unimaginative sameness, where all sense of individual autonomy has been lost. The effort to make everyone the same, and therefore interchangeable, is often an effort to forestall the emergence of leaders, or to discourage political activity in general. This helps explain why prisoners are generally required to wear uniforms.

349 From the existence of both the Sabbath and the sabbatical we might assume that, at its uppermost limit, human work and labor would together consume about six-sevenths of our waking hours.

350 Schumacher, *Small is Beautiful*, 59.

351 Arendt, *Human Condition*, 225.

352 Schumacher, *Small is Beautiful*, 57. I have changed Schumacher's terminology to agree with the work/labor distinction to which I adhere in this essay.

353 Simone Weil, *Gravity and Grace*, trans. Arthur Wills (New York: Putnam, 1952; reprint, Lincoln: University of Nebraska Press, 1997), 235.

354 The disembodied uniform time of labor is a child of Cartesian doubt. Therefore, it assumes the same dominant position in all the major modern political and economic systems. In his biography of Frederick Taylor, Robert Kanigel reports that Taylor's ideas were eventually received with enthusiasm by both Mussolini and Lenin. (Robert Kanigel, *The One Best Way* [New York: Viking Penguin, 1997], 523–5.) The time of labor is not an exclusively capitalist phenomenon.

355 Gadamer, *Relevance of Beautiful*.

356 Calvino, *Six Memos*, 31–54.

357 Ibid., 54.

358 Eco, *Six Walks*, 61.

359 Gianni Vattimo, "The Structure of Artistic Revolutions," in *The End of Modernity*, trans. Jon R. Snyder (Baltimore: Johns Hopkins University Press, 1988), 107.

360 Dave Hickey, *Air Guitar: Essays on Art and Democracy* (Los Angeles: Art Issues Press, 1997), 109.

Work of Architecture in the Age of Efficient (contd.)

361 Hyde, *Gift*, 190–1. Hyde, by the way, also comments on the difference between work and labor in his book, but he reverses the terms, applying a definition very close to what I have been calling "work" to "labor."

362 Ibid., 107.

363 Pye, *Nature and Art*, 8.

364 Alchemy might be defined as "ceremonial chemistry." In alchemy, spirituality and speculative philosophy remain integral to the alchemist's efforts to study matter, and to transmute base substances into precious ones.

365 Georg Simmel, "The Ruin," in Kurt H. Wolff, ed., *Essays on Sociology, Philosophy, and Aesthetics* (New York: Harper Torchbooks, 1959), 259.

366 Bachelard, *Poetics of Space*, 67.

367 Like so many other practices I have been describing, it is possible, in caring for one's things, to lose one's sense of proportionality. We have all perhaps known a neighbor who was obsessive in his care for his property. Bachelard mentions that too much cleanliness can become, morally speaking, a kind of uncleanness.

368 Bachelard, *Poetics of Space*, 61.

369 Donald Kunze, "Architecture as the Site of Reception, Part I: Cuisine, Frontality, and the Infra-Thin," in Alberto Perez-Gomez and Stephen Parcell, eds., *Chora* 1 (Montreal: McGill-Queen's University Press, 1994), 84.

370 Weil, *Gravity and Grace*, 235.

371 Gaston Bachelard, *The Psychoanalysis of Fire*, trans. Alan C. M. Ross (Boston: Beacon Press, 1968), 28.

372 Jacques Derrida, "Politics and Poetics in the Self-Unsealing Text," lecture at the Pennsylvania State University, 1 April 1998. Briefly put: if we are absolutely certain of something, there is no need for anyone to testify to it; testimonies are always sought in the absence of certainty.

373 Milan Kundera, *Slowness*, trans. Linda Asher (New York: HarperCollins, 1996; reprint, New York: HarperPerennial, 1997), 39.

374 Sennett, *Corrosion of Character*, 72.

The Impact of the Computer on Architectural Practice

375 See the essay "The Work of Architecture in the Age of Efficient Production" in this volume.

376 I have adopted the use of this term from Ivan Illich. See, for example, *Papers on Proportionality*, Working papers no. 8 (University Park, PA: Penn State University Science, Technology, and Society Studies).

377 Daniel Conway, in written comments to an earlier version of this manuscript.

378 Harold Alterman, "Heidegger's Critique of Science and Technology," in Michael Murray, ed. *Heidegger & Modern Philosophy* (New Haven: Yale University Press, 1978), 49.

379 For working drawings of small, non-standard buildings, such as private residences, there is little efficiency gained through computerized drawing production. In the production of drawings for larger buildings, the productivity gains realized through computerization remain the subject of much debate.

380 In the twenty plus years I have been practicing architecture professionally, the gap between the way design is taught in architectural schools and the way it is practiced in the typical office has widened greatly. In the academic studio, no design is ever "good enough." Students are encouraged to study multiple approaches to a project before committing to a single way. Then they are coached to endlessly explore modifications to their design in study models, drawings, collages, paintings, analogous constructions, and—lately—computer simulations. Students almost always begin a project by building a physical model of a site and its context. In most professional offices, the "design" of a project begins by an analysis of the project schedule and fee. From this, the number of staff hours allotted to the design are determined. If the marketing effort to secure the project has been particularly expensive, or if the client's schedule is "aggressive," the amount of time or fee available will likely prohibit exhaustive exploration. No context model will be built, and the design will tend to be conservative—a sure thing. Most savvy firms will mask this conservatism in the building design and construction method by providing enough compositional delight (often presented through slick visuals, from perspective renderings to meaningless computer-animated walk-throughs) to convince their clients that they have been "creative."

381 Bruno Zevi, "Beneath or Beyond Architecture," in Francesco Dal Co and Giuseppe Mazzariol, eds., *Carlo Scarpa: The Complete Works* (New York: Electa/Rizzoli, 1985), 271.

382 In the earlier part of this century, the tradition in most offices had been that the bulk of the drafting was done by persons who were apprentices. While these members of the architect's staff might never become professionally licensed, the opportunity for them to do so did exist. Greater prestige and responsibility was available within the practice for all who might seek it. The recent restriction of architectural licensing to those with university degrees has created a two-tier hierarchy within architectural offices, reinforcing the perception that creativity only takes place at the rarefied level of the "design" architect.

383 See "Seven Strategies for Making Architecture in the Twenty-First Century" in this volume.

384 I have so far discovered two drawing tasks for which computerized drawing more closely resembles the making of the "actual" building component than hand drafting does. One is drawing complex assemblies that are made of identical parts, such as a screen, scaffolding, trellis, or framework. In these instances, the drafter creates an object or figure on the computer, one that is the basic element of the structure, and then merely replicates as many of these as necessary. This more closely approximates how such structures are built than hand drafting, where the drafter usually breaks the structure up into a series of vertical and horizontal lines. Another task is drawing formwork for casting complex shapes in concrete, such as the ziggurats in Carlo Scarpa's Brion Cemetery. The computer modeling program formZ has proven itself quite valuable at this task. Once one has visualized the object one wishes to create, it is often very difficult to imagine its negative—the shape necessary to mold it. This difficulty has little to do with the actual way of making forms for concrete. The program formZ makes it easy to draw the negative of any solid, thereby helping to overcome the "mental block" that seems to strike most designers when they try to imagine the negative of a complex shape.

385 See "The Weight of Architecture" in this volume.

386 Quoted in Lahiji and Friedman, *Plumbing*, 28.

387 Gaudí's extraordinary funicular model of these vaults has now been recreated and is on display in the crypt of the Sagrada Familia.

388 Much of what I have stated about the computer also holds for manual drafting methods that produce only instrumental representations. It is the domineering logic of the instrumental representation that is the root of the problem, not the computer. The difference is primarily in degree, not kind. However, as Jacques Ellul has stated, at some point great quantitative change must result in qualitative change. (Jacques Ellul, *Perspectives on Our Age*, ed. William H. Vanderburg [Toronto: CBC, 1981; reprint, Concord, ON: House of Anasi Press, 1997], 35–6.) Thus, the computer—as the most powerful tool yet invented for producing these representations, as well as the most aggressively marketed and promoted—undoubtedly poses the greatest threat to the architect's ability to address those aspects of reality that defy mathematical representation. Computerized drawings tend to all look alike, no matter who the draftsperson. This homogenizing tendency is typical of advanced technological instruments, leading Ivan Illich to observe (in *Tools for Conviviality*) that "policemen in patrol cars or accountants at computers look alike the world over, while their poor cousins using nightstick or pen are different from region to region."

389 Cassirer, *Language*, 158.

Author Biography

Daniel Willis is an Associate Professor of Architecture at The Pennsylvania State University, where he teaches courses in architectural design, drawing, and building construction. He is a licensed architect and a member of the American Institute of Architects. He is also currently a principal at LDA, a large multi-disciplinary AE firm based in Pittsburgh. He is a past winner of the Hugh Ferriss Prize for architectural graphics, and his designs or artworks have been published in *Progressive Architecture, Architecture,* and *Landscape Architecture* magazines, and exhibited in such venues as the Art Institute of Chicago and the StoreFront for Art and Architecture, New York. His writings have appeared in such diverse publications as *The Journal of Architectural Education, The Journal of Architecture and Planning Research,* and *Masonry Construction* magazine. After finishing this book, he intends to resume remodeling his house.

	DATE DUE		